Tolley's
Administration of
Small Self-Administered
Pension Schemes

by
John Hayward

Tolley Publishing Company Limited
A UNITED NEWSPAPERS PUBLICATION

Published by
Tolley Publishing Company Ltd
Tolley House, 2 Addiscombe Road
Croydon, Surrey CR9 5AF England
081–686–9141

Printed and bound in Great Britain by
Biddles Ltd, Guildford and King's Lynn

Foreword

The hazards of being a director are legion and growing. Complex new legislative and regulatory requirements are heaped on directors almost daily by Whitehall and Brussels backed up by ever more onerous personal liabilities. In one respect, however, their life has become easier in recent years.

Until the advent of the Small Self-Administered Pension Scheme (SSAS) also known as a Director Plan, most directors of private companies had little choice about how they financed their businesses or their retirement, if they could obtain finance at all. Now these Schemes have been developed to a point where *any* executive director, whether of a one-person company, family company or quoted multinational company, would be foolish and could even be failing in his duty to the company if he has not given serious consideration to having a SSAS, albeit a SSAS will not always be the best answer in the end.

This book, written by John Hayward of EBS (the firm which pioneered the first SSASs in 1973), is a welcome and much needed guide to the subject. It is both a comprehensive manual for the professional adviser and an essential reference book for every director who has a SSAS or who wants to know whether he or she should establish one and, if so, what are all the do's and don'ts. It is also timely because it incorporates the important Inland Revenue regulations which came into effect on 5th August 1991.

The more significant legislative changes from the DSS concern 'self-investment', i.e. where a pension scheme invests in the employing company or in the assets used by the employer. The IOD supported the move to ban significant self-investment by staff pension schemes. Employees should not be coerced into effectively putting their retirement eggs into the same basket as their jobs and trustees of a self-investing scheme who were also directors, employees or shareholders of the company could face awkward conflicts of interest, especially in a takeover situation. The IOD, however, in conjunction with other bodies lobbied hard against 'self-investment' by SSASs being restricted to the same extent. In the end the government was persuaded that the same dangers were not present in self-investment by SSASs and that, on the contrary, the ability to self-invest was essential if SSASs were to continue to play their important (and previously underrated) role in the economy.

SSASs perform the dual role of providing financial security for directors

iii

and their families when they retire or sell their companies and providing a source of finance for the business which among other advantages involves no loss of control. Even in quoted companies where the facility to self-invest may not be needed, the ability to retain control over the investments and manage them directly may enable a higher return to be earned, especially if intermediaries' charges can be avoided. This is very different from the traditional 'top-hat' insured scheme for directors which siphons off the earnings of the business in the form of insurance premiums, which then tend to be invested (or what is left of them after the various charges – hidden or otherwise) in large company shares or government paper.

Self-investment, of course, carries risks. But in the typical SSAS all the beneficiaries are also directors, shareholders and trustees. Not only does this make any conflicts of interests between the scheme members in their various capacities more easily manageable, but it means they are in a position to judge and control the risk exposure – the sort of decision at which directors, of all people, are well practised. Moreover, in a small or medium size private company which is growing, the only alternative may be to make no pension provision which may be riskier still. Confiscatory taxation rates in the past, fiscal privileges for financial institutions and other factors reduced the supply of private risk capital, especially in the hands of family company shareholders. Even now it remains difficult to accumulate significant capital out of after-tax income, and the venture capital industry has only partially filled the gap. Many companies, therefore, need to retain every penny of earnings for expanding the business; but in today's fast moving commercial world it is a brave director who leaves the money in the company trusting that when he retires the company will still exist and the sales value then of his shares will fund a pension commensurate with what is provided for the firm's employees. An SSAS can solve the problem by allowing funds to be extracted at the pre-tax stage from the company and invested in a tax-exempt fund which reinvests a major part of the money back into the business.

I should just like to add a final word about non-executive directors. I am here talking about independent and professional non-executive directors rather than, for example, a former executive director who is now non-executive. The IOD recommends that non-executive directors of a company should not depend on that same company for their retirement security for the very good reason that this could prejudice their independence. They should have independent pension provision through a personal pension scheme or the pension scheme of an employer unconnected with the company concerned and the scheme funds should not be materially invested in the company concerned. A common practice where a person has several non-executive appointments or part-time jobs is to set up a management services company which charges fees to the various clients for the person's services as a non-executive director, consultant etc. This company can then establish a SSAS for the director and there can be other advantages from this arrangement.

Pensions legislation has been in a constant state of flux for some years and there are no doubt further changes to come as a result of the European Court judgments concerning pensions equality between men and women. Let us hope, however, that any further changes will not affect SSASs and that this book will remain the standard work for many years to come.

Peter Morgan
Director General
August 1991　　　　　　　　　　　　　　　　　Institute of Directors

NOTE:

Unless the contrary intention appears words importing the masculine gender include the feminine.

Preface

Whilst writing a series of articles for Pensions World between July 1989 and December 1990 the author became aware of the need for a comprehensive compendium of some sort on small self-administered pension schemes that not only covered those aspects of concern to the Superannuation Funds Office, but also embraced to some extent their establishment, documentation, benefit structure and administration. Part of this book is based on these articles.

This book is essentially about the provision of retirement benefits for the owners/directors of private companies through a type of pension scheme which is very much tailor-made to suit their needs. The small self-administered scheme enables the company directors to be the trustees and therefore control the way the funds are invested and also to be the members and beneficiaries. It is a very tax efficient vehicle despite the restrictions placed on them by the Inland Revenue. The text is as up-to-date as possible (1 August 1991) and includes the latest legislation from the Inland Revenue and proposals from the Department of Social Security which are expected to become law later in 1991.

There are several acknowledgements to be made to those who have helped me in the various stages of the production of this book: Dryden Gilling-Smith for his great encouragement from the inception stage of the book and for the use of facilities at Employee Benefit Services, particularly the word processor; Richard Walker, chief actuary of EBS, for his advice on actuarial matters in Chapter 9; Peter Morgan, Director General of the IOD, for the foreword; Rex de Saram of Tolley's for his invaluable assistance with the text and layout and for contributing Chapter 12 and special thanks to Sharon Greening for her work in typing the manuscript and coping with the innumerable amendments.

Finally, I have to acknowledge with thanks the kind permission of Her Majesty's Stationery Office to reproduce all Crown copyright material, of the Inland Revenue and Superannuation Funds Office to reproduce their documents and forms, the Registrar of Pension Schemes to reproduce Form PR1(90) and the Institute of Actuaries to reproduce the Guidance Note GN9.

JOHN HAYWARD
EBS Management Plc
30 Finsbury Square, London, EC2A 1SB

August 1991

Contents

Contents

Contents

x

Table of Cases

Table of Statutes

Note: **All references in the text to sections and schedules are to ICTA 1988 unless otherwise stated.**

Table of Statutory Instruments

Abbreviations

APC	–	Auditing Practices Committee
APT	–	Association of Pensioneer Trustees
ASB	–	Accounting Standards Board
ASC	–	Accounting Standards Committee (replaced by the ASB)
AVC(s)	–	Additional Voluntary Contribution(s)
CBBR	–	Clearing Banks Base Rate
CGT	–	Capital Gains Tax
CGTA	–	Capital Gains Tax Act 1976
COMP	–	Contacted-out Money Purchase
DSS	–	Department of Social Security
FA	–	Finance Act (followed by the year)
F(No 2)A	–	Finance (No. 2) Act 1987
FIMBRA	–	Financial Intermediaries, Managers and Brokers Regulatory Association
FSA	–	Financial Services Act 1986
FSAVC(s)	–	Free-standing Additional Voluntary Contribution(s)
GN(s)	–	Guidance Note(s) (issued by the Institute of Actuaries, Faculty of Actuaries or the Inland Revenue)
IBA(s)	–	Industrial Buildings Allowance(s)
ICTA	–	Income and Corporation Taxes Act 1970 or 1988
IHT	–	Inheritance Tax
IMRO	–	Investment Management Regulatory Organisation Limited
JOM(s)	–	Joint Office Memorandum (Memoranda) (followed by the number and paragraph)
LIFFE	–	London International Financial Futures Market
LO(s)	–	Life Office(s)
OAC(s)	–	Ordinary Annual Contribution(s)
OPAS	–	Occupational Pensions Advisory Service
OPB	–	Occupational Pensions Board
PN(s)	–	Practice Note(s) (issued by SFO, APC etc. e.g. SFO Memorandum IR12)
PQ	–	Parliamentary Question
RPI	–	Retail Price Index
SERP	–	State Earnings-related Pension
SERPS	–	State Earnings-related Pension Scheme
SFO	–	Superannuation Funds Office
SI	–	Statutory Instrument
SORP	–	Statement of Recommended Practice (issued by the ASC)
SP	–	Statement of Practice (issued by the Inland Revenue)

SSA	–	Social Security Act (followed by the year)
SSAP	–	Statement of Standard Accounting Practice (issued by the ASC)
SSAS(s)	–	Small Self-administered Pension Scheme(s)
SSPA	–	Social Security (Pensions) Act 1975
TMA	–	Taxes Management Act 1970
UK	–	United Kingdom

Table of Joint Office Memoranda

**Note: This Memorandum has been referred to throughout the text as a 'JOM'.
However, it is the SFO's practice now to issue 'Memoranda' and not 'JOMs'
although the consecutive numbering sequence has remained.**

Chapter 1

Introduction

About this book

1.1 This book is about small self-administered pension schemes known almost universally as SSASs. Its prime concern is to examine the tax implications of SSASs which derive from Inland Revenue legislation and guidelines, but it also examines the impact of Social Security legislation on SSASs in Chapter 11 although this examination is somewhat limited.

1.2 Because of the nature of SSASs the Inland Revenue through the Superannuation Funds Office (SFO) places special restrictions on administration, documentation, investments, funding, reporting and winding-up of SSASs and these will be covered in detail in later chapters. However, to appreciate these special restrictions it is necessary to understand the basis of taxation of occupational pension schemes generally as SSASs are subject to the same legislation and guidelines as all other schemes. Thus having explained the legislation which applies to SSASs in Chapter 2, the documentation and benefit structure which applies generally to all schemes is examined in Chapters 3 and 4.

Background

1.3 Until 1973 the directors of private companies could not be members of an occupational pension scheme. This was because of the legislation which then applied to controlling directors (broadly someone controlling more than 5% of the ordinary share capital of a company). They were treated as self-employed for pension purposes and could only provide tax approved pension and death benefits for themselves *via* retirement annuity contracts through *sections 226, 226A, ICTA 1970* (termed 'section 226 policies') which are now embodied in *sections 619–621, Sch 29.*

1.4 Self-administered pension schemes existed at that time, but their members were all at arms-length or, if directors were members, they were likely to be directors of public companies where it is not usual or possible to hold 5% of the equity due to the financial implications of cost.

1.5 *Section 15(a), schedule 22, FA 1973* changed the position of controlling directors radically. This repealed the legislation forbidding controlling directors from being members of tax approved pension schemes and introduced the concept of the 20% director. The definition of a 20% director is contained in Appendix 10. The way was now open for 20% directors to become members of self-administered schemes already in existence, of insured schemes and of new self-administered schemes of which they could become members.

1.6 However, the Inland Revenue was aware that 20% directors could manipulate their pension benefits in certain areas, e.g. level of remuneration and date of retirement, therefore restrictions were introduced into the Inland Revenue's code of practice (PN) to limit the scope for abuse. It is important to note however that no restrictions were placed on scheme investments by the new legislation or PN at that time.

1.7 The Life Offices (LOs) were quick to offer insured schemes to 20% directors, but there were distinct disadvantages to this type of scheme. They lacked flexibility. Although contributions would be high because of high salaries, the expense loadings were also commensurately high. There was no ability to control the investments and large sums of money were lost to the company with no facility to re-invest in itself. With no Inland Revenue restrictions placed on investments, the advantages of a self-administered scheme for 20% directors with themselves as the trustees soon became apparent. The SSASs were born in the mid-1970s and their numbers multiplied very quickly.

1.8 The potential for tax avoidance was exploited, particularly in the area of investments and loan backs to the company and connected parties, often on advantageous terms, and these became prominent features of the early SSAS. The SFO became concerned at the growing number of SSASs and their abuses. This lead directly to the publication of Joint Office Memorandum No 58 (JOM 58) in February 1979, the SFO's statement of practice for SSAS (see Chapter 2).

1.9 The first SSASs were marketed by various insurance agents, pension consultants, actuaries etc. with the LOs noticeable by their absence. When the latter realised in the late 1970s the potential for SSASs they began to enter the market. At first the LOs offered hybrid self-administered schemes i.e. partly self-invested and partly invested in life policies. However, to compete with the growing numbers of SSASs they soon began offering the wholly self-invested scheme while retaining the administration to some extent.

1.10 There are variations of the LOs' SSASs, including what is known as a deferred SSAS, where the scheme is set up as an insured one with the facility to convert later to a partly or wholly self-administered scheme. LOs' SSASs now have a good share of the total SSAS market, but the majority of SSASs are operated by advisers in the main made up of consultants, brokers, actuaries and banks.

The advantages of SSAS

1.11 It is necessary to examine the main financial and commercial advantages of a SSAS in providing retirement benefits for 20% directors and not just the tax advantages. Some of the advantages have been mentioned in paragraphs 1.7 and 1.8 above and deserve looking at in greater depth along with other advantages.

1.12 The facility for the directors of a private company to be the trustees of a pension scheme of which they are the members and to have almost complete control, apart from restrictions imposed by the SFO and the appointment and responsibilities of a pensioneer trustee (see paragraphs 2.24 to 2.32 below), is a very compelling reason for establishing a SSAS. There are clearly areas where the SFO imposes investment restrictions, but these are not unduly onerous. The trustees themselves can decide within limits the various investments they want to make, unlike an insured scheme where the contributions are paid to a LO and the LO decides on the investments to be made.

1.13 It is quite possible for the director-trustees to be the managing trustees responsible for the day-to-day running of the scheme including investment decisions. The pensioneer trustee does not have to be a managing trustee. The sole function of the pensioneer trustee may be that required by the SFO (paragraph 2.25) i.e. the prevention of the scheme's winding-up except in accordance with the rules. Such responsibilities will appeal strongly to directors of private companies who are used to running their own company and who require an element of flexibility. A SSAS may also provide protection to directors in a takeover situation, particularly if the SSAS set up is for the directors of a public company.

1.14 The drawback naturally enough is the additional work involved which would not be present in an insured scheme where the LO is paid to manage everything. The trustees will still need advisers, however, and many SSAS consultants provide a full service from being pensioneer trustee to providing actuarial and investment advice. Companies need to weigh up the costs involved. The total costs of running a SSAS need to be compared with those of an insured scheme. The contributions to an insured scheme will usually include 'hidden' administration expenses, as very often a breakdown of the expenses and the real pension contribution is not known, whereas with a SSAS all the expenses and the contribution will be known. The administration costs of a SSAS plus contributions should be less than premiums paid to a LO thereby making a SSAS more cost effective. The administration expenses are also allowable as deductions for corporation tax purposes.

1.15 A very strong point in favour of SSASs as opposed to insured schemes is the increased opportunity to assist the company itself with its business. The facility to re-invest the contributions paid to the SSAS in loans to the company is widely used and of great benefit to a company's business. Not only will the contributions have obtained relief from corporation tax, but the interest on the loan will also attract relief when the company pays it and the trustees can reclaim any tax deducted from interest payments where interest is paid net of tax. The trustees may also invest in shares of the company subject to certain limits and this can be very useful where shares are being passed on in a family company and there is no immediate purchaser to hand or other members of the family do not have the finance to buy the shares. This is an effective way for the family to retain control. The other most common way of using a SSAS as a vehicle for investing in the company is for the trustees to purchase commercial property and lease it back to the company. This assists in several ways. If the company cannot afford to purchase property, the trustees may well be able to do so. The separate ownership of property by the trustees affords protection to the company should it be taken over or wound up. Furthermore, a leaseback arrangement with the company ensures it has premises from which to operate, the rent it pays the trustees is allowable as a deduction for corporation tax while in the hands of the trustees the rent is tax free. The trustees will also not pay capital gains tax (CGT) on the property when they dispose of it.

Tax advantages

1.16 All approved pension schemes enjoy tax advantages of various kinds. SSASs can, however, be more tax efficient than other pension schemes as explained in paragraph 1.15 above. Nonetheless, it is important to bear in mind that the use of a SSAS as a vehicle to achieve tax avoidance will not satisfy the test of '*bona fide* established for the sole provision of relevant benefits' as there must be no duality of purpose to any approved pension scheme. For instance, the tax reliefs which are incidental to the establishment and administration of a scheme are not perceived as out and out tax avoidance. However, the deliberate use of a scheme, particularly a SSAS where the opportunity exists to a greater extent to maximise the tax opportunities, primarily to achieve tax avoidance will inevitably lead to conflict with the SFO and perhaps loss of the scheme's approval.

1.17 A tax advantage which is however available to a SSAS is in the area of inheritance tax (IHT). By building up assets in their own SSAS directors can usually transfer substantial sums to the next generation free of IHT under the discretionary provisions in the scheme rules (see paragraph 3.28 below).

1.18 Paragraphs 1.19–1.26 below explain the tax reliefs available to SSASs, but it must be remembered that these are generally available to all types of pension schemes, e.g. the treatment of income received by LOs and gains on assets which are all exempt from tax in their exempt pensions business, and therefore there is no perceived advantage to a SSAS here compared with an insured scheme.

1.19 Company contributions are allowable as deductions for corporation tax purposes under *section 592(4)*. Ordinary annual contributions (OAC) are deductible in the company's accounting period in which they are paid. Any other contributions (special contributions) may at the discretion of the Inland Revenue (in effect the SFO) be spread over a number of years under *section 592(6)*.

1.20 The contributions paid to the scheme by the company on behalf of the members are not liable to tax under Schedule E in the hands of the members by virtue of *section 596(1)(a)*.

1.21 Any personal contributions paid by members to a scheme are allowable as an expense for Schedule E purposes in the year in which they are paid under *section 592(7)*. The maximum permitted personal contribution is 15% of gross earnings for a year [*section 592(8)*]. It is interesting to note in passing that in only a small number of SSASs do the members actually make personal contributions.

1.22 The income of the scheme is exempt from income tax at the basic and additional rate under *section 592(2)*. This means that rent and interest received gross by the trustees are not subject to tax and that tax deducted from dividends, interest etc. before payment to the trustees can be reclaimed.

1.23   There is no CGT chargeable on any gains realised on the disposal of an asset by the trustees under *section 149B(1)(g), CGTA 1979* introduced by *paragraph 26, schedule 29.*

1.24   Underwriting commissions received by the trustees are exempt from income tax by virtue of *section 592(3)* to the extent that they are applied for the purposes of the scheme.

1.25   Under *section 56(3)(b)* the trustees are exempt from income tax on profits on gains from transactions in certificates of deposit to the extent that the deposits are again held for the purposes of the scheme.

1.26   Any income or capital gains derived from dealing in financial futures or traded options are exempt from CGT and income tax under *section 149B, CGTA* and *section 659A.*

1.27   There are various tax exemptions which apply to payments made from a SSAS. These will be covered in Chapters 3 and 4 together with the taxation of some payments made.

1.28   Having looked at the advantages of establishing a SSAS, the company with the benefit of its advisers can decide on how the vehicle is to provide the level of benefits within Inland Revenue limits in the most tax efficient way for itself and the directors/members.

SSASs and the future

1.29   The various advantages of SSASs, explained in paragraphs 1.12 to 1.26 above, have been and remain major selling points for this type of pension scheme since their inception. This is despite the development of the SFO's practice in this area since the publication of JOM 58 over twelve years ago, the latest regulations from the Inland Revenue (see paragraph 2.2 below) and the current proposals from the Department of Social Security (DSS), which are covered in Chapter 11, and which will restrict SSASs in some areas when enacted.

1.30   The DSS proposals, and in particular the latest regulations from the Inland Revenue, do, however, contain measures which will restrict the activities of current SSASs and the establishment of new ones and therefore the future increase in the number of SSASs may not be so great as it has been up to the late 1980s. However, as will be seen from later chapters important concessions have been won from both the Inland Revenue and the DSS since their proposals for SSASs were initially published and therefore the future for SSASs is much better than could have been expected. It is a considered view that SSASs still remain the most tax efficient vehicles for providing retirement benefits for the directors of private companies as well as for directors and senior executives of large companies and it is hoped that the contents of the following chapters will convince readers of this view.

Chapter 2

Legislation and Guidelines

Introduction

2.1   The Inland Revenue legislation and guidelines governing SSASs are discussed generally in this chapter and in greater detail in later chapters. The DSS legislation in so far as it affects SSASs is covered in Chapter 11.

2.2   At present SSASs are subject to the following legislation and guidelines:

(*a*)   ICTA 1988 and successive Finance Acts.
(*b*)   Practice Notes (PN) and Joint Office Memorandum (JOM) (Appendices 1 and 5).
(*c*)   Changes in Practice published following the Parliamentary Question (PQ) raised in July 1984 (Appendix 2).
(*d*)   Consultative Document of September 1987 (Appendix 3).
(*e*)   The Retirement Benefit Schemes (Restriction on Discretion to Approve) (Small Self-Administered Schemes) Regulations (SI 1991/ 1614) (Appendix 4)—referred to as 'regulations' throughout this book for convenience.

ICTA 1988, PN and JOM

2.3   *Part XIV, ICTA 1988* has become familiar in the past three years with its consolidation of all the previous statutes relating to pension schemes generally. Of particular relevance is *section 591* which gives the SFO its wide ranging discretionary powers which are perceived to be applied so assiduously to SSASs. Indeed, there must be many of those involved with SSASs who tend to concentrate mainly on JOM 58 and now the regulations as the main statement of practice for SSASs when really the SFO's underlying objections to certain features of a SSAS stem from *section 591* and the application of 'bona fide established . . . sole purpose' test provided in *section 590(2)(a)*, for as a vehicle, SSASs with controlling directors being the members and trustees, present such an infinite variety of opportunities and arrangements for the SFO to challenge on the grounds of duality of purpose.

2.4 The legislation in *ICTA 1988* applies generally to all pension schemes and not just to SSASs. There is not much from which SSASs are exempt in this legislation. Notably SSASs are exempt from the prescribed valuation requirements under the surplus legislation, but approved SSASs are not exempt from the 40% tax charge if a surplus is repaid to the employer. PN also applies generally to all schemes including SSASs, laying down the SFO's guidelines under its discretionary powers, and until the issue of JOM 58 in February 1979, the *FA 1970* and its successors together with PN were all there were to guide the practitioner in administering SSASs from their advent in the mid-1970's. Since *ICTA 1988* there has been the *FA 1989* and the *FA 1991*.

2.5 The principal guidelines for the operation of SSASs were laid down in JOM 58 and these still apply subject to JOM 109 (see Appendix 5) and the regulations. They set out how SSASs should be administered, what practitioner and trustees are expected to do and the boundaries, transgression beyond which may prejudice the approval of the SSAS. However, the SFO has been very careful not to delineate specific 'no-go' areas so far as investments are concerned until more recent times, preferring to keep such guidelines in general terms, but specifically warning about using SSASs as vehicles for tax avoidance without spelling out the precise nature of that avoidance. Thus, there is guidance on the membership, the appointment of a pensioneer trustee, scheme investments with loanbacks to employers provided certain criteria are met, and investment in shares of the employer, non-income producing assets, trading, purchasing of annuities, insurance of death benefits, funding, specific prohibition on loans to members etc. Each of these is a subject by itself and is covered in this and later chapters.

2.6 JOM 58 remained the SFO's principal statement of practice for SSAS for the last twelve years, until the regulations were issued in July 1991 and JOM 109 was published in August 1991. Throughout this period the SFO has continually made it clear that additional conditions may be imposed in a particular case if the facts warrant it and this will apparently continue to apply.

2.7 Some later JOMs do have particular relevance to SSAS—most notably JOM 59 because it covers death benefits payable in respect of controlling directors (see paragraphs 4.57–4.68 below) and JOM 90 and the accompanying application form which requires that all initial actuarial reports or advice must be submitted to the SFO at the time of the application for approval (see paragraph 3.57 below).

2.8 *Legislation and Guidelines*

2.8   It is appropriate to mention two other aspects of the legislation before leaving *ICTA 1988*. The vast majority of SSASs seek the SFO's approval under its discretionary powers contained in *section 591*. Yet *section 590* is available for mandatory approval of SSASs just as it is for other types of schemes. It is hard to imagine such an application being made because of the severe restrictions in *section 590*, but it may be the only avenue available to the controlling directors of an investment or property company and members of their families to whom discretionary approval under *section 591* is not available.

2.9   The other aspect is a more sinister one and it is to be hoped practitioners do not get involved with it too often, namely *section 591B(1)* formerly *section 590(5)* and the SFO's powers to withdraw approval. This particular piece of legislation was clarified in the *F(No 2)A 1987*. Prior to this the SFO had the power to withdraw approval, but a grey area existed as to the actual effective date of withdrawal of approval. *Section 591B(1)* makes it quite clear that if a scheme has indulged in an unacceptable practice, and the scope for SSASs to do this is much greater than for any other type of schemes, approval may be withdrawn from the date when the transgression occurred or 17 March 1987, whichever is the later. Chapter 10 deals with the withdrawal of approval.

Subsequent changes in practice

2.10   As the SFO's experience has grown over the years with the increasing number of SSASs, its discretionary practice has also developed and further guidelines have been promulgated, although not via JOMs. It has been usual for the SFO to inform the various representative bodies concerned, mainly the APT, from time to time of practices it finds unacceptable or to clarify certain areas, particularly investments. By 1984 several changes had been communicated but which were not included in JOMs.

2.11   Following a PQ asked in July 1984, the SFO published to various representative bodies a list of changes in practice that had taken place since February 1979 regarding SSAS (Appendix 2). The list was made freely available to practitioners at the time. The main changes notified were the restrictions on trustees' borrowings to three times the OAC paid, an employer was restricted to one SSAS only for its controlling directors and the value of shares in the employer should be aggregated with loans to the employer for the purposes of the 50% loanback test. It is important to note that these changes were not all effective from July 1984, they applied from the date when the SFO first announced them publicly. For instance the trustees' borrowings limit commenced in January 1983 (see paragraphs 7.37–7.48 below). The regulations confirm that a further SSAS will not be approved by the SFO under its discretionary powers if another SSAS currently exists for the company. JOM 109(8) explains that if a SSAS is being wound-up the SFO will not approve another SSAS for the same employer until the winding-up is complete. Furthermore, if an employer wishing to set up a SSAS is already participating in another employer's SSAS, it will have to withdraw from the latter before its own SSAS can be approved.

2.12   There have been no further major changes in practice by the SFO in relation to SSASs since 1984 until the regulations were promulgated in July 1991, although it may be felt there have been changes in some areas simply because searching enquiries have been fielded on certain fronts. This would appear to be more the result of a sharpening up of the SFO's attitude to some aspects rather than any announced changes. For example, the SFO is perusing with some vigour outstanding triennial actuarial reports on SSASs, noticeably since the surplus legislation was enacted. However, the SFO cannot rely on the surplus legislation to wave the big stick, but can only cite the administration of the scheme as not being in accordance with the approved rules in producing an actuarial report every three years. There are those who feel the proposed terms of the consultative document issued in September 1987 and the subsequent draft regulations, were being operated by the SFO, but there was no statutory basis for this practice until July 1991.

Consultative document

2.13   It was inevitable with the passage of time since JOM 58 was issued and the increase in numbers of SSAS that the Inland Revenue would eventually look at the adequacy of its guidelines on SSASs and the streamlining of procedures. So with the enactment of *paragraph 3(5)* of *Schedule 3, F(No 2)A 1987* (now *section 591(5)(6)*), enabling the Inland Revenue to make regulations to prescribe additional conditions for the approval of pension schemes, the opportunity was taken in September 1987 to publish a draft discussion document outlining the SFO's intentions in the SSAS area. The time passed for practitioners and representative bodies to make their representations and it was nearly three years before the next development took place in July 1990 when draft regulations were published. Further representations were received on the draft regulations and some of these have been incorporated in the regulations laid before Parliament on 15 July 1991 as *SI 1911/1614* and which came into effect on 5 August 1991.

The regulations

2.14   The important point to note about the regulations is that they limit the SFO's discretionary powers in prescribed circumstances. For example, they restrict the power of the trustees to borrow money and sell certain investments. They also require the administrator to provide information and documents to the SFO at the time certain transactions and investments are made. There are a lot of important points stemming from the regulations and accompanying JOM 109 and therefore they are explained in the various chapters where the particular investment or feature of a SSAS is covered.

2.15   It is also important to note the position of JOM 58 following the publication of the regulations. It has not been cancelled. As JOM 109(5) explains where the regulations and JOM 109 overlap JOM 58, the new provisions prevail. Thus some of the guidelines covering the SFO's discretionary practice in relation to SSAS in JOM 58 remain in existence after 5 August 1991 and all the guidelines in JOM 58 continue to apply to SSASs established before that date with some exceptions under the transitional arrangements (see paragraphs 2.16–2.17 below). JOM 109(21) mentions that JOM 58 will be cancelled when the revised PN is published later in 1991 containing a detailed explanation of the effect of the regulations and of the SFO's practice regarding SSAS. So far as this book is concerned in the chapters which cover both the SFO's discretionary practice and the regulations in relation to certain features, in particular in Chapters 5–7 covering investments, the SFO's discretionary practice is explained first and the effect of the regulations afterwards. Thus where the regulations supersede the SFO's discretionary practice the text relating to the discretionary practice should be read accordingly.

Transitional arrangements

2.16   Those SSASs approved by 5 August 1991 which hold assets at 15 July 1991 which are prohibited by the regulations, but permitted under the previous discretionary practice, are provided with an exemption in the regulations. Such assets may be retained after 5 August 1991, but if sold later may not be replaced. They may also be sold to scheme members, despite the ban on such transactions from 5 August 1991 (see paragraph 6.48 below), provided the disposal is at a full open market value.

2.17   SSAS established prior to 5 August 1991, but not approved by the SFO by that date, are permitted under the regulations by virtue of *section 591(A)* introduced by *section 35, FA 1991* to undertake transactions with members or their relatives prior to 5 August 1991. However, where the asset concerned was acquired on or after 15 July 1991, when the regulations were actually made, but before 5 August 1991, the asset cannot subsequently be sold to a member. The asset must have been held prior to 15 July 1991 to enable it to be sold subsequently to a member. In addition for this category of SSASs, an investment that is not consistent with the regulations can only be retained, assuming it satisfies the SFO's guidelines at the time, if it was held before the regulations were made on 15 July 1991. This effectively means a SSAS established on 16 July 1991 cannot make a loan to an employer of more than 25% of the value of the scheme's assets (see paragraph 5.8 below). A summary is provided in Appendix 40 regarding the main changes introduced by the regulations with particular regard to approved and unapproved SSASs which fall within or outside the transitional arrangements.

Definition of 'Small'

2.18 There obviously has to be some cut-off point in the number of members of a self-administered pension scheme below which the SFO's guidelines will apply, and this number is twelve. A SSAS is therefore generally a scheme with less than twelve members. The great majority of SSASs have between one to three members and when the old 20% director, rather than the current controlling director, definition applied it was not possible to have more than five such directors in the scheme. However, there are some SSASs which include arm's length employees in their membership apart from family directors and once the total membership goes above eleven the question arises of whether the JOM 58 and regulation restrictions should apply. JOM 58(3) is quite clear on this. If the scheme is providing maximum benefits for the family directors and derisory benefits for the arm's length employees, then the SFO is likely to take the view that the latter members are included in the scheme solely as makeweights to get round the restrictions imposed by JOM 58 and the regulations. The scheme is still therefore small and the restrictions apply.

2.19 On the other hand a self-administered scheme set up for less than twelve members, who are all at arm's length from each other, from the employer and the trustees, may not necessarily be subject to the restrictions of JOM 58 and the regulations. This could apply for instance to a scheme set up by a large public company for its senior executives who have no sizeable shareholdings in the company and where the trustees are totally independent. In fact the definition of a SSAS in the regulations allows such a self-administered scheme to escape from its provisions. This is because a SSAS is defined as a self-administered scheme with less than twelve members, where at least one of the members is related to another member or to the trustee, or to the partner where the employer is a partnership or, where the employer is a company, the member or person connected with the member has been a controlling director of the company during the previous ten years. On the other hand JOM 109(6) mentions that schemes with twelve or more members, which the SFO has insisted are subject to JOM 58, will not escape the provisions of the regulations. It is always best in these circumstances to approach the SFO for its decision that JOM 58 and the regulations will not apply to such a scheme. The process can lead to argument though with individual examiners whose interpretation of the situation can vary. Therefore the SFO agreed with the APT in 1985 that where this issue became contentious it should be referred to a senior officer in the SFO for his consideration.

2.20 It is possible because of the SFO's wide discretionary powers for that office to require only certain aspects of JOM 58 to be met in relation to a self-administered scheme with less than twelve members. For instance, just the ban on loans to members or on residential property might apply, each case being looked at on its merits.

2.21 Occasionally a self-administered pension scheme's membership falls below twelve, quite fortuitously, perhaps because there are now fewer active members and the rest have retired or withdrawn and taken their retirement benefits. JOM 58(3) is again clear on this matter in that no special action under the memorandum will normally be required if this happens.

2.22 Obviously, conditions for running a self-administered pension scheme outside the confines of JOM 58 with more than eleven members will be less restrictive, yet when contemplating an increase in membership to more than eleven it is necessary to be aware of the additional requirements imposed by the surplus legislation in 1986 regarding actuarial valuations being prepared on the prescribed basis which does not apply to SSASs.

2.23 The definition of a SSAS in the regulations includes a self-administered pension scheme whose assets are invested other than in insurance policies. This therefore includes an insured scheme whose only self-administered asset may be a bank account. However, JOM 109(6) states that in these circumstances scheme monies held in a current account, whether interest bearing or not, with a bank or building society will not be treated as an investment otherwise than in insurance policies if the monies are so held for incidental purposes. Thus by concession the SFO will regard such a scheme as an insured scheme for approval purposes. It will not be a SSAS for the purposes of the regulations so the various restrictions and reporting requirements will not apply. Its documentation may nonetheless permit self-administration and it may include a pensioneer trustee if so desired.

Reference is made in paragraphs 1.9–1.10 above of small schemes administered by LOs which permit self-administration, but where scheme monies are wholly invested in insurance policies from the outset. JOM 109(6) makes it clear that as soon as the trustees of such a scheme invest other than in insurance policies the scheme will immediately become a SSAS and subject to the regulations. If this happens, the SFO must be notified at once and details of the non-insured investments supplied.

The pensioneer trustee

2.24   The SFO was concerned from the start of SSASs in the 1970s that there was considerable potential for the members to walk off with the assets, the members also being trustees of the scheme and directors of the participating company. The SFO therefore insisted on the appointment of an independent trustee to every SSAS who would ensure the scheme was only wound up in strict accordance with its rules upon the unanimous agreement of all the trustees. The SFO rested its argument on the very old case of *Saunders v Vautier [1835–42] All ER 58* (paragraph 2.30 below).

2.25   Thus was created that unique name of 'pensioneer trustee'. It is important to note that whilst the pensioneer trustee is a general trustee of a SSAS he does not have to be a managing trustee. His only function may be solely in relation to agreeing to the winding up whilst the other trustees deal with the day to day running of the scheme, making investments etc. However, in reality most pensioneer trustees find themselves handling the administration side particularly with the SFO and giving advice to the other trustees and companies involved.

2.26   There is provision in the regulations that one of the trustees must be a pensioneer trustee. It is also provided that where the pensioneer trustee no longer qualifies to act as such or ceases to be a trustee of SSAS, the SFO should be notified within 30 days and a successor appointed within 60 days. In addition the SFO must be notified of the successor's appointment within 30 days and a copy of the document removing and appointing the pensioneer trustee sent to the SFO within 30 days.

Qualifications

2.27   JOM 58(4) states it is necessary for the pensioneer trustee 'to be an individual or body widely involved with occupational pension schemes and having dealings with the SFO'. So apart from individuals, both corporate bodies and partnerships can qualify. The acid test is having wide involvement with pension schemes and dealings with the SFO. There are many people who are actively involved with all sorts of pension schemes who do not deal with the SFO and despite their expertise would be turned down. They have also to demonstrate dealings with the SFO over a period of time though not necessarily on SSASs. The application to the SFO for pensioneer trustee status should provide details of the individual's experience with pension schemes generally and of particular schemes where correspondence, discussions or negotiations have taken place with the SFO over a period of several months. If an individual is seeking pensioneer trustee status in his own right, having left a LO or an actuarial firm where he was an employee engaged in dealings with the SFO, then the SFO will not grant pensioneer trustee status until the individual has been involved on his own account with the SFO for several months. This is very much a chicken and egg situation, but it is possible for an individual branching out on his own to become an approved pensioneer trustee within a year providing he becomes involved with the SFO during that period. It does mean, however, that on his own SSAS, he must appoint an approved pensioneer trustee.

2.28   The SFO's qualifications do not apparently imply a test of anyone's professional competence and it stresses this point if for some reason it turns down an application where perhaps there is a lack of dealings with the SFO. If the SFO is satisfied that pensioneer trustee status can be granted it asks the individual to complete an undertaking that he will not consent to the termination of an SSAS of which he is a trustee except in accordance with the approved terms of the winding-up rule, so not only does the pensioneer trustee have to give this undertaking individually, but also each SSAS's rules must contain a provision in relation to the termination of the SSAS that the trustees must act unanimously i.e. *nem con.*

2.29   The SFO sees the pensioneer trustee's role solely to prevent the winding-up of a SSAS except on the terms of the trust. The pensioneer trustee is not a 'watchdog' for the SFO, as JOM 58(4) states, in any area other than the improper termination of the scheme. However, it must be recognised that the appointment of a pensioneer trustee cannot prevent the illegal winding-up of a SSAS by the other trustee(s) and the subsequent misappropriation of the assets. It is nonetheless a sound precaution for the pensioneer trustee to be a co-signatory to the bank account of a SSAS. In reality many pensioneer trustees have become something akin to a 'watchdog' by their very involvement in the administration of SSASs and are well aware that the SFO expects them, if only tacitly, to be well versed in SFO practice and to use their good offices to see that practice is observed. It is interesting to note that the consultative document acknowledged that a pensioneer trustee's main function would continue to be prevention of a premature winding-up. It also realised the service he provides the SFO in discouraging the more unacceptable proposals of employers. However, the proposal to impose the requirement that the pensioneer trustee must notify the SFO of any SSAS transaction which in the pensioneer trustee's opinion is likely to infringe the requirements of approval has been omitted from the regulations.

Saunders v Vautier [1835–42] All ER 58

2.30   The importance of this particular case is because it involved a trust where all the prospective and contingent beneficiaries combined to enforce the winding-up of the trust and the payment of the trust monies to themselves. Its implication for pension schemes is that such an action is directly opposed to the purpose for which they are established and to the spirit behind the legislation. If the SFO were not to interpose an independent trustee in a SSAS, any request from the members of the scheme, who are limited in numbers, to wind it up on the lines of *Saunders v Vautier* could result in the funds being distributed to them contrary to the SFO's requirements. The appointment of a pensioneer trustee is therefore intended to block such a request from the members. It is generally felt nonetheless that the likelihood of a combination of all the beneficiaries to wind-up a scheme is most remote and that the SFO's insistence on the appointment of a pensioneer trustee is not absolutely necessary. However, the presence of an independent trustee does provide a deterrent to the beneficiaries combining to wind-up the scheme. Pensioneer trustees also have a vested interest in preserving the system because it provides them with a discrete area of the pensions scene in which to practise their expertise and they do have a direct avenue to the SFO via the APT on any subject related to SSASs.

2.31   There is a little known important point so far as corporate pensioneer trustees are concerned. If such a company establishes a SSAS for its own directors, then the SFO will insist that an entirely separate pensioneer trustee is appointed. The pensioneer trustee on this SSAS cannot be the practitioners' own pensioneer trustee company or any of the directors even if they are qualified to act as pensioneer trustees in their own right. The restriction is now contained in the regulations.

2.32 *Legislation and Guidelines*

2.32 Pensioneer trustees are practitioners in all fields of pension schemes, though some specialise in SSASs. Others are actuaries, life offices, pension consultants and banks. This could mean that the pensioneer trustee provides some or all of the advice and administration required to operate a SSAS. LOs and pension consultants are likely to provide a full service with actuaries in-house. On some SSASs the actuary is also the pensioneer trustee, but consultants may handle the administration. The current qualifications for a pensioneer trustee restrict the field and although the consultative document recognised this, the Inland Revenue has subsequently decided the qualifications required for pensioneer trusteeship would remain as at present. There can, however, be no substitute for a proven track record in administering pension schemes.

Chapter 3

Documentation

Introduction

3.1   This chapter covers the various documents required for a SSAS, what should appear in that documentation, the procedure for applying to the SFO for tax-exempt approval and reporting requirements.

Establishment of a SSAS

3.2   To obtain tax-exempt approval it is necessary to establish a SSAS under irrevocable trusts. The reason for this is to alienate the pension scheme completely from the company so that on any later change of mind the company cannot reclaim the scheme funds placed in the trust. The trust may be established either by deed or by company resolution. SSASs are invariably established by deed (see paragraphs 3.3–3.7 below), but if a company resolution is used a suggested resolution may be found at Appendix 6. An important initial step in this process is to ensure that the company's memorandum of association contains the power required to establish a pension scheme. If the requisite power is absent, it is preferable to amend the memorandum by special resolution. A suggested clause for insertion in the memorandum to provide this power may be found at Appendix 7.

Interim deed

3.3   The common practice is to establish a SSAS under an interim deed rather than a full definitive deed which can be very lengthy and is not always practicable in perhaps the time available to establish the scheme if a contribution is to be paid before the company's year ends and so qualify for tax relief. The interim deed should declare the trust is irrevocable, set out the main purposes of the scheme and provide the trustees with appropriate powers of investment and administration. The definitive deed (see paragraph 3.12 below) containing the detailed rules and provisions may follow later and it is usual for the interim deed to provide for this to be executed within two years. This period can be extended if necessary.

3.4 The interim deed should include an approved pensioneer trustee among the trustees. If it does not, the SFO will wish to see that a pensioneer trustee has been appointed shortly thereafter (see paragraph 2.26 above).

3.5 It is advisable to include in the interim deed a provision to satisfy the preservation requirements of the Occupational Pensions Board (OPB) (see paragraph 11.2 below). In this respect it will be sufficient to include the wording suggested in JOM 78(234) regarding the operation of the SSASs in conformity with *Schedule 16, SSA 1973*.

3.6 The interim deed does not need to include lengthy rules as to how the scheme should be operated until the definitive deed is executed provided there is an outline prepared by the advisers. The trustees should bear in mind, however, that until the definitive deed, which contains the detailed rules, is executed they may have to approach the SFO beforehand on certain matters in the absence of rules.

3.7 It is very important to ensure that the date the interim deed is executed is either before or the same date that the first contribution is paid to a SSAS. This will ensure that when the scheme eventually obtains formal approval from the SFO relief from corporation tax is given on the initial contribution as the effective date of approval cannot be earlier than the date of execution of the interim deed. If a contribution was paid to the trustees prior to the date of the interim deed it would not qualify for relief under *section 592(4)*, but may possibly be allowed as a deduction for Schedule D purposes by the company's inspector of taxes. Because the tax concessions would not be available there could also be taxation implications for the scheme members in respect of the amount of the contribution paid on their behalf as a result of the application of *section 595(1)(a)* and for the trustees in relation to any income received from investments derived from the contribution in the period prior to the effective date of approval as they may not be able to claim exemption under *section 592(2)* (see paragraph 10.8–10.9 and 10.13 below).

Members' announcement letters

3.8 These are a requirement of the SFO at the stage of applying for approval. They stem from *section 590(2)(b)* which requires that every member must be given written particulars of all essential features of the scheme. The particulars can be given in the form of a short announcement, a letter, a booklet or in a copy of the trust deed and rules. In a SSAS it is usual to provide the particulars in an announcement letter to each member. This is done at the commencement of the scheme and whenever a new member joins the scheme.

3.9 PN 22.10 outlines the main areas which the SFO considers should be covered in an announcement. These are set out as follows:

(*a*)   Main benefits:
  — on normal retirement.
  — on death in service.
  — on death after retirement.
  — on withdrawal from service.
  — on early retirement.
  — on late retirement.
  — any options at retirement (e.g. commutation to provide a lump sum).
(*b*)   Pension increases.
(*c*)   Members' contributions:
  — amount.
  — arrangements for their collection.
  — effect of temporary absence.
(*d*)   Financing details:
  — the basis of the company's contributions.
(*e*)   Legal constitution:
  — documentation.
  — reference to the legislation under which the scheme is or will be approved.
(*f*)   Operational details:
  — the administrator.
  — the trustees.
  — the managing trustees.
(*g*)   Amendment:
  — the powers of amendment and how amendments may be effected.

3.10   Announcement letters quite often describe the basis of a member's interest in the scheme. As a SSAS is a common trust fund it is most important that a member's interest is correctly described and that the description avoids the earmarking of specific assets to a member. A member's interest lies against all the assets of the scheme and not against any specific asset. The assets are therefore usually allocated notionally by the actuary to each member to avoid earmarking apart from any policies in respect of the member or assets specifically representing the investment of a member's personal contributions. The term 'member's credit' or 'contribution credit' is often met with and usually defined in the definitive deed and possibly announcement letter. Wherever it appears, its definition must avoid any suggestion of earmarking.

Actuarial documentation

3.11 It is essential that on the establishment of a SSAS an actuarial report is prepared or actuarial advice is provided on the funding of the scheme as this must be sent with the initial application for approval to the SFO (see paragraph 3.57 below). The form of the report or advice is covered in paragraphs 9.3–9.23 below.

Definitive documentation

3.12 The use of the interim deed procedure allows a scheme to be established quickly and for the lengthier definitive deed containing the detailed provisions and rules of the scheme to be drawn up later very often tailor-made to suit the particular scheme concerned. In fact it is possible to submit draft definitive documentation to the SFO prior to execution of an agreed definitive deed, but this practice is generally not adopted with SSASs because of the widespread use of 'model deeds' (see paragraphs 3.44–3.50 below).

3.13 It is possible to execute definitive documentation *ab initio* without an interim deed. Some practitioners offer this type of documentation particularly where they use agreed model deeds as it can lead to quicker approval of the scheme.

3.14 The definitive deed is usually in two parts. The first part containing the clauses sets out the trustees' powers and discretions and provisions for winding-up the scheme. The second part, often a schedule, contains the rules which cover eligibility, contribution and benefit details, and set out Inland Revenue limits on benefits. There is however no set format as to which provisions should appear in either part.

Contents of definitive deed

3.15 The deed should include all the usual clauses and rules which the SFO expects for a self-administered scheme set up under irrevocable trusts seeking discretionary approval. There are four essential requirements which must appear in the deed so far as the SFO is concerned.

3.16 In the preamble to the deed the SFO will expect to see one of the trustees is an approved pensioneer trustee, otherwise this appointment should appear in the body of the deed for the scheme concerned.

3.17   There must be a rule banning loans to members of a SSAS. JOM 58(9) mentions this restriction is necessary because of the possibility that such loans would in reality become a charge on the retirement benefit. The ban on loans to members includes relatives of members and anyone having a contingent interest under the SSASs. The regulations reinforce this ban. JOM 109(15) stresses that back-to-back loans that involve on-lending to members and which circumvent the ban on a loan to members are also not permissible.

3.18   There must also be a rule providing for actuarial valuations to take place at intervals of no more than three years (JOM 58(9)).

3.19   Somewhere in the deed, either in the provisions as to the powers of the trustees or for winding-up the scheme, there must be a provision that in the event of winding-up the scheme this can only be done in accordance with the rules on the unanimous decision of all the trustees. The pensioneer trustee must agree to the winding-up (see paragraph 2.25 above).

3.20   From 5 August 1991 when the regulations came into effect, the governing documentation has to contain the provisions in the regulations which relate to borrowings, trustee/member transactions, certain investments, loans, the pensioneer trustee and reporting requirements. A period of three years until 5 August 1994 has been allowed to execute the appropriate documentation for those SSASs already approved at 5 August 1991. SSASs not approved at that date must have these provisions in their documentation before approval is granted.

Other requirements

3.21   This is a whole series of provisions and rules which may or may not be included in the definitive deed depending on the circumstances of the scheme. The SFO will not insist on them all, but where they do appear in the deed there are certain requirements to be met because 20% directors are members of the scheme. There are some rules which must be in the deed because the members are 20% directors and limitations apply to their benefits. In addition, because the scheme is self-administered certain other provisions will be expected by the SFO to be written into the deed. It is not proposed to go into too great detail on what should appear in the definitive deed. Readers are referred to the 'Trust deed and rules checklist' published by the National Association of Pension

3.22 *Documentation*

Funds (Notes on Pensions No 16) which provides guidance in drafting a trust deed. Paragraphs 3.22–3.43 below are confined to matters which particularly concern SSASs.

3.22 Somewhere in the opening clauses in the reference in the interim deed to the period of 24 months being allowed for the execution of the definitive deed should be recorded that the provisions of the definitive deed supersede the interim deed. If it was not possible to execute the definitive deed within this 24 month period and the period was extended, then this fact should also be recorded.

3.23 As this is a self-administered scheme the trustees should be given wide powers of investment. There is no need though to include the areas where the SFO makes restrictions except regarding the ban on loans to members (see paragraph 3.17 above) and those investments banned or restricted by the regulations (see paragraph 3.20 above). Two items which can get overlooked in drafting the investment clause are policies and borrowings. Even though the SSAS may be separately administered from a LO it is always advisable to have provision for making investments in insurance policies. As trustees may borrow (see paragraph 7.3 below) it is essential for them to have powers to raise loans and mortgages. A specimen investment clause may be found at Appendix 8.

3.24 It is important to stipulate who should appoint the trustees and who should remove them. This power is usually vested in the principal company. In the event of the company being sold or liquidated this power would reside with the new owners or the liquidator. Therefore before such events occur the trustees and company should consider amending the power to appoint the trustees by conferring that power on the trustees themselves.

3.25 This conveniently leads to the power to amend the definitive deed which should be written into the deed. It is usual for this power to be subject to the agreement of the principal company. A specimen clause containing powers of amendment may be found at Appendix 9. Any deed of amendment should be sent to the SFO after execution for its acceptance.

3.26 It is usual for the rules to include various definitions to avoid repetition. These will often include the definition of 20% directors and of final remuneration which is most relevant to 20% directors. The definition of a 20% director in PN 6.15 and JOM 91(3) may be found at Appendix 10. The definition of final remuneration for 20% directors is set out in PN 6.12(b) and is confined to total remuneration for any period of three or more consecutive years ending in the ten years before normal retirement date. The rules may also allow for each year's remuneration to be increased in line with the Retail Prices Index (RPI) (PN 6.14). Pensions in payment may be increased too in line with the RPI (PN 7.1) providing there is such a provision.

3.27 There is a particular limitation on the pensionable service of 20% directors who remain in service between the ages of 60 and 70. PN 9.9 mentions that if the normal retirement age is between the ages of 60 and 70 and the director's service continues after the specified date, the original age will be disregarded for the purposes of Inland Revenue limits. Those limits will bite as if the normal retirement date were and had always been either the actual date of retirement or the attainment of age 70 whichever happens first. Thus in the rules relating to benefits payable in respect of service after normal retirement date this restriction should be included. These limitations were affected by a change in practice in 1989 (see paragraph 4.56 below).

3.28 JOM 58(21) mentions the SFO's recurring fears of an irregular distribution of death benefits should the principle in *Saunders v Vautier* be applied. To reduce such risks the SFO requires scheme rules to provide that lump sum death in service benefits and lump sum guarantee payments should be distributable at the trustees' discretion among the usual range of individuals and bodies that may be designated for this purpose. The discretionary power afforded to the trustees in this area will of course free the lump sum payments from IHT. However, the general SFO practice precluding a discretionary distribution of a benefit payable on death in service on or after age 75 of a 20% director would still apply. This latter point must be written into the rules of a SSAS as explained in JOM 59.

3.29 It should be noted that there must be a scheme rule providing for full commutation of pension where the member is in exceptional circumstances of serious ill-health for such a benefit to be provided at all (JOM 58(22)). It should be drawn in the terms that apply to all schemes except that in a SSAS the SFO insists that such full commutation is subject to the agreement of the Inland Revenue. JOM 58(22) explains that the reason for this is that in a SSAS an arm's length relationship does not exist and there is no interest of a LO present. In other types of schemes these factors are present and therefore it can be left to the trustees to satisfy themselves regarding the circumstances of the case. In a SSAS the reference to the SFO for approval of full commutation must be accompanied by proper medical evidence. That evidence should show that the member's life expectancy is very short because of a terminal illness. Showing that the member is incapacitated or has a life expectancy reduced to a few years will not be sufficient to secure full commutation.

3.30 *Documentation*

The member's life expectancy must be measured in months rather than years. Full commutation in these circumstances should be dealt with expeditiously including the reference to the SFO and it is reasonable to expect a prompt reply from the SFO.

3.30 It is most advisable to have a rule allowing the trustees to make and receive transfer payments. Its wording should not only allow transfers between occupational pension schemes, but should also allow payments to be made to and received from personal pension schemes. Such a rule is not only important during the continuance of a scheme, but it will also be of importance if the scheme is to be wound-up (see paragraph 3.38 below). Specimen clauses for making and receiving transfers may be found at Appendix 11.

3.31 It is also advisable to have rules allowing other companies to adhere to, and withdraw from, the scheme. This will allow subsidiary and associated companies to participate etc. Such participation is usually effected by a deed of adherence, but it may also be effected in the interim deed or definitive deed. A specimen deed of adherence may be found at Appendix 12.

3.32 Before JOM 58 was published the rules of a SSAS had to provide for a member's pension to be secured immediately it became payable by the purchase of a non-commutable non-assignable annuity from a LO. There were certain exceptions for impaired lives (see paragraph 4.63) and pension increases (see paragraphs 3.34 and 3.35 below). The main reason for this requirement was to prevent scheme members demanding the termination of the scheme in any way they chose, particularly as this situation was more likely to occur where all or most of the members had retired. However, the SFO recognised that such a risk was no more significant during the first five years of retirement than it was during service if the emerging pension was guaranteed for five years and there was a lump sum guarantee payment prospectively distributable to the member's dependants or legal personal representatives in the event of death.

3.33 As a result this rule requirement was changed. JOM 58(17) mentions that the SFO will be satisfied if the rules provide for an annuity to be purchased within 5 years of the member's retirement. It is important to note that the deferment of purchasing the annuity on retirement is written into the rules otherwise it cannot be deferred. The five year period is very useful indeed. It allows members' pensions to be paid from the scheme during that period. They must be paid because they are mandatory following retirement apart from the exception in PN 13.5(v). The trustees need to ensure there is sufficient in the fund to pay the pension at the correct level and they will be required to deduct PAYE. Most importantly it allows the trustees to choose the most propitious time to purchase the annuity, when rates are more favourable, and also time to realise an investment which may take a while to sell as its value may be currently depressed.

3.34 Originally, if the rules of a SSAS provided for pensions increases linked to increases with the RPI, money to finance the increases could be retained in the fund, provided such increases were not at a fixed rate of 3%. The SFO's practice in this area, however, has developed to the extent that pensions increases awarded during the period between retirement and securing the pension should be secured at the time the pension is secured and increases awarded subsequently are secured at the time of the award. This development was published following the PQ of July 1984 (Appendix 2) and the rules should take this into account.

3.35 Also on securing pensions in SSAS, JOM 58(19) mentions that where a contingent widow's or widower's pension is to be provided the rules may allow either for the widow's or widower's pension to be purchased at the same time as the member's pension or its purchase may be deferred until the husband or wife dies. This means that if the member's pension is purchased at the end of the 5 year period allowed, the widow's or widower's pension need not be purchased until the husband's or wife's death. However, if this latter method is adopted then the rules have to provide for the widow's pension to be payable to the woman who is the member's wife at his date of death.

3.36 For SSASs already approved at the time the *F(No 2)A 1987* and *FA 1989* were enacted, the various amendments they contained are covered by the legislative over-ride and do not therefore need to appear in these schemes' rules until such time as major amendments are made in future. However, for all SSASs established prior to this legislation and not yet approved by the SFO, and for all SSASs established afterwards, the provisions of both Finance Acts must be included in the rules. The SFO has made available what are known as packages A and B for use in these circumstances—see the controller's letter of 1 November 1989 at Appendix 13.

3.37 The provisions for winding-up a SSAS, always subject to the agreement of the pensioneer trustee, should cover all the circumstances where this can occur i.e. payments of benefits to the last member, withdrawal of a participating company, sale or liquidation of the principal company. In fact it is an SFO requirement that on the liquidation of the principal company a SSAS should be wound-up (Appendix 2). It may be possible in the circumstances for the SSAS to remain paid up, but that would be subject to the agreement of the SFO and to any conditions it may require.

3.38 The winding-up provisions should cover all the options available to the trustees for meeting the liabilities of the scheme. Members' benefits including those of contingent beneficiaries should be secured if they are already in payment and also if they have reached normal retirement age. They may be provided with early retirement benefits if they have reached age 50. Otherwise the options available are to purchase deferred annuities, or make transfer payments to other occupational schemes or personal pension schemes.

3.39 The priorities as to which members' benefits are to be dealt with first, e.g. pensioners, current members or leavers, may be specified and, in the event of insufficient funds, provision made as to how the funds are to be apportioned between the members. If there are more than sufficient funds, provision to increase benefits to Inland Revenue maxima should be included or use made of a general augmentation provision.

3.40 The expenses of realising assets and of winding-up the scheme may be met from scheme funds if the rules so provide. This can be useful where the company is in liquidation with no funds of its own. There must be a rule providing for any balance of funds to be returned to the company if there is a surplus in the scheme after payment of all benefits and expenses. Such a refund is subject to corporation tax at 40% (see paragraph 9.24 below).

3.41 Sometimes the winding-up of a SSAS can occur before the definitive deed has been executed and the scheme has been approved by the SFO. Obviously formal approval will still be required in these circumstances. The SFO will need to be asked what its requirements are regarding the scheme's documentation for it to be approved. It is possible for power to be reserved in the interim deed for the immediate execution of the definitive deed containing only winding-up provisions. This should be acceptable to the SFO. A specimen clause for inclusion in the interim deed covering this situation may be found at Appendix 14. Alternatively the SFO may accept a short deed or trustees' resolution reciting what has occurred and confirming that since its establishment the SSAS has been administered in accordance with the requirements of the Inland Revenue.

OPB requirements

3.42 The preservation requirements (see paragraph 11.2 below) particularly the entitlement to short service benefit must be included in the definitive deed. Any permitted alternatives to short service benefit either on termination of the member's service or the winding-up of the SSAS must also be included. So the purchase of a 'Section 32' buy-out policy (now *section 591(2)(g)*) needs to be included together with provisions for transfers out and pension increases.

3.43 The rules should comply with the equal access requirements of *section 53, SSPA 1975*. These require membership to be open to both men and women on the same terms as to age and length of service needed to become a member and whether membership is voluntary or compulsory. SSASs usually provide that membership is at the invitation of the company which will satisfy the equal access requirements.

Model deeds

3.44 The practice of agreeing model deeds for SSASs with the SFO has been established since the late 1970s. It is clearly economical for a practitioner with a portfolio of SSASs to have model documentation of some sort so that it may be used on all schemes in almost the same format apart from names, dates etc. This applies to all the different practitioners including LOs and can embrace interim deeds, definitive deeds, deeds of amendment and members' announcement letters. If model documentation is agreed beforehand with the SFO and submitted on particular schemes later it also greatly facilitates the examination procedures in the SFO and can lead to much quicker approval of schemes. To this end the SFO has agreed a model deed procedure whereby practitioners can approach and agree with the standards section of the SFO a model deed to be used on all of the practitioner's SSASs.

3.45 The time taken to agree a model deed with the standards section will very much depend on the contents of the deed and whether or not they can be agreed without further correspondence and negotiation. The definitive deed will require all the usual clauses and rules the SFO expects for a scheme set up under irrevocable trusts seeking discretionary approval. The essential and other main requirements have been covered in paragraphs 3.15–3.43 above and will not be dealt with again.

3.46 Having agreed a model deed with the standards section the practitioner will be given a particular reference to quote when submitting deeds on individual schemes. The procedure on those individual schemes is very simple. The deed is executed with the names and dates inserted for that scheme and a copy sent to the SFO. The practitioner should confirm that the deed submitted agrees in all respects with the model

3.47 *Documentation*

agreed at the standards section reference. If it differs at all, apart from names and dates, then the practitioner should draw the SFO examiner's attention to the differences. These can be mentioned in a covering letter, but it is best to highlight them on the deed itself in red so that the examiner's attention is drawn to them and, if there are not too many changes and they are not lengthy, they are likely to be examined that much sooner. A non-model deed or a copiously amended one is going to take longer to be examined and be accepted.

3.47 A new procedure was adopted by standards section for model deeds from 1 April 1991 which incorporate the *FA 1989* amendments and have been agreed by the standards section. This obviates the need to send executed definitive documentation in model deed form to the SFO on such SSAS. Instead it is mandatory to send a documentation certificate in lieu (see paragraph 3.56 below). JOM 105 describes the procedure. Even where a document in its present form is not suitable for this procedure the standards section will advise how it can be revised to bring it within the procedure. The standards section will confirm that all new model deeds will come within the procedure at the time negotiations on the model are completed. If there are any variations in the model each variation will be treated as a separate agreed model and give a different reference number. Rule amendments intended for use on a large number of SSASs and agreed by the standards section are suitable for this procedure.

3.48 Model deeds need updating from time to time and the standards section will agree amended versions on definitive deeds if approached, for example the substantial amendments necessitated by the *FA 1987* and *FA 1989*. It is probably better to agree a totally new model deed in these instances rather than a model deed of amendment as the former is more likely to be economical. The standards section may indicate that it will only agree a new model deed anyway. The standards section will not agree one-off amendments for use on individual SSASs. Thus the documentation procedure available since 1 April 1991 (see paragraph 3.47 above) is not available for this type of amendment. Advisers need to bear in mind the SFO controller's letter of 1 November 1989 particularly paragraph 8 in this respect (Appendix 13). In addition a package of model rules issued by the SFO JOM 109 incorporates the changes introduced by the regulations standards section shortly after (Appendix 5A).

3.49 Most SSASs use the interim deed procedure and it may be possible to agree with the standards section a model interim deed and members' announcement letters. Some practitioners adopt a definitive deed *ab initio* (see paragraph 3.13 above) with no interim deed at all. Such a deed

30

may still be agreed as a model with the standards section. It is important to understand the distinction between 'model' deeds and 'standard' deeds agreed with the standards section of the SFO. They are not the same. Model deeds are not for instance agreed with LOs and large pensions practitioners for their other schemes. Moreover model deeds are not likely to receive the in depth examination apparently accorded to standard deeds. The documentation procedure available since 1 April 1991 (see paragraph 3.47 above) is not available for interim deeds.

3.50 Finally, it will be found that because model deeds can be agreed in a relatively short period and are used on the vast majority of SSASs, the SFO is most unlikely to adopt the deed of indemnity procedure available to large self-administered schemes where formal approval may be held up for a considerable period pending agreement of a standard deed or a one-off definitive deed.

Application for approval

3.51 The SFO's requirements for the approval of all pension schemes under *Chapter II, Part II, FA 1970* were set out in JOM 90 and various accompanying forms. The procedures took effect from 1 December 1987. The information required to accompany applications for approval were contained in *Schedule 5 paragraph 6, FA 1970* as amended by *Schedule 3 paragraph 11, F(No 2)A 1987*. These requirements are now embodied in *sections 604 and 605(1)(c)* for schemes seeking approval under *Part XIV, ICTA 1988*. JOM 90 contains the SFO guidelines for the procedure to be adopted.

3.52 Applications for approval of SSASs must be made to the SFO in writing using the prescribed form SF176 (Appendix 15) and must be accompanied by certain documents. The timing of the application is also crucial to obtaining the appropriate tax reliefs.

3.53 The SFO operates very strict procedures regarding applications for approval which can be seen from JOM 90(9). This mentions that applications not made on the appropriate form fully and accurately completed and accompanied by the appropriate undertaking and documentation will not be accepted as valid applications for approval. Thus if the form SF176 is left blank in places or entries are made such as 'not known' or 'to follow' the application will be returned. Only a resubmitted complete application will constitute a valid application for approval and the date on which the SFO receives it will constitute the date of application for approval for statutory purposes. Any delay here may therefore affect the eventual effective date of approval and the tax reliefs which flow therefrom.

3.54 The form SF176 requires considerable information which is mainly self-evident and only those parts most relevant to SSASs will be looked at more closely in this book. As one would expect full details of 20% directors are required and other schemes of the employer.

3.55 Section VIII of the form refers to the accompanying documentation. A copy of the executed interim deed is required to be sent and a copy of the definitive deed if it has been executed at this stage. Copies of the members' announcement letters should also be provided (see paragraphs 3.8–3.10 above). If each member's letter is the same the SFO should be able to accept a copy of one letter with an explanation that they are identical for all members.

3.56 If the definitive deed is a model the standards section reference should be clearly quoted (see paragraph 3.46 above) to facilitate examination. If the model deed comes within the documentation certificate procedure outlined in JOM 105(3) then a completed certificate SF5 (Appendix 16) must be sent with the application for approval if the deed has been executed at that stage or the completed certificate should be sent later when the deed is executed. A completed certificate SF6 (Appendix 17) must be sent at the application stage or later as the case may be for model rule amendments agreed with the standards section. Both certificates must be fully completed to show the SFO reference number allocated to the document being used and confirmation is required from the signatory that the document has been used for the specific purpose designated. There is no need under this procedure to send a copy of the definitive deed or deed of amendment itself.

3.57 The requirement to forward a copy of the actuarial report on which the funding of the scheme is based is most important for a SSAS. If the full initial report has not been prepared by the time the application is made for approval then a copy of the actuarial advice provided on the establishment of the scheme must be provided instead. A list of the current investments of a SSAS is also required.

3.58 A composite undertaking should also accompany the application. For SSAS this is the form SF176(U) (Appendix 18) which should be completed by the administrator who thereby undertakes to refer various circumstances to the SFO before taking any action.

Timing of application for approval

3.59 *Section 604(1)* requires an application for approval to be made before the end of the first year of assessment for which approval is required. However, for schemes established shortly before the end of the tax year there may not be sufficient time to obtain and prepare the full information for submission to the SFO by 5 April. A concession is allowed for schemes in these circumstances which extends the period for making application up to six months after the end of the tax year.

3.60 The following table that appears in JOM 90(14) sets out the 'period of grace' allowed for applications for approval to reach the SFO.

Date scheme established	*Date by which application must be received by SFO*
In the 6 months ending 5 October	by the following 5 April
In the month ending 5 November	by the following 5 May
In the month ending 5 December	by the following 5 June
In the month ending 5 January	by the following 5 July
In the month ending 5 February	by the following 5 August
In the month ending 5 March	by the following 5 September
In the month ending 5 April	by the following 5 October

3.61 All schemes therefore have at least six months from inception in which to apply for approval to include the tax year in which the scheme was established. Those schemes set up in the first six months of the tax year in fact have from six to twelve months in which to make application for approval.

3.62 It is important to note that although formal application for approval may be deferred under these time concessions, a scheme's approval under *section 592(1)(a)* cannot pre-date its establishment under irrevocable trusts. Equally it is important to note that a late application for approval will lose the appropriate tax reliefs as the scheme's effective date of approval will be no earlier than the 6 April or the sixth of the month as the case may be following the date the scheme was established. The loss of tax reliefs in these circusmtances is explained in paragraph 3.7 above although it may be possible to have the company's contribution paid before the effective date of approval allowed as a deduction for Schedule D purposes.

Provisional reliefs

3.63 The time taken to obtain formal approval from the SFO for a SSAS can vary considerably. It will depend to some extent on the execution of a definitive deed and the satisfactory outcome of the SFO's enquiries into investments and other features of the SSASs. Provisional tax relief will be given meanwhile on members' personal contributions provided the SFO is satisfied that all the essential features of the scheme have been communicated in writing to every member. The company cannot obtain relief meanwhile however on contributions paid, but the company's inspector of taxes may hold over the tax in respect of the contributions until such time as the scheme is formally approved. The trustees cannot obtain repayment of tax deducted from income received. They are unlikely to be assessed, however, on income received without deduction of tax.

3.64 As trustees are not able to reclaim tax until approval is granted a SSAS is at a disadvantage compared with an insured scheme where a LO is allowed to invest premiums received in its tax-exempt pension funds and obtain relief on a provisional basis. The trustees may therefore not feel it worthwhile investing in equities to start with, but to invest where interest is paid gross. Bank deposits can be arranged to pay interest gross as they are not 'relevant deposits' for the purposes of *section 479*. Similarly building society accounts can be held by the trustees and interest paid gross under the arrangements set out in *section 476(7)*.

3.65 Formal notification of approval is sent by the SFO to the applicant. At the same time the SFO sends instructions to the appropriate tax districts to put the tax reliefs into effect. This will result in reliefs being granted retrospectively to the effective date of approval and the trustees may also expect to receive a repayment supplement representing interest on tax repaid to them.

Reporting requirements

3.66 There are various reporting requirements imposed upon the administrator of a pension scheme. Those relating to SSASs are covered in the remainder of this chapter. The requirements for an administrator are laid down in *section 590(2)(c)*. The administrator must be resident in the UK. Usually the trustees as a body are defined as the administrator in the trust deed.

3.67 The administrator is responsible for making applications for approval (see paragraphs 3.50–3.62 above) and for complying with the Inland Revenue undertaking (see paragraph 3.58 above).

3.68 Under *section 605(1)(a)(b)* the administrator is required to provide information on contributions paid to a scheme and payments made under a scheme within 30 days of a notice from the SFO. Failure to do so may give rise to penalties under *section 98(1), TMA 1970*.

3.69 *Section 605(1)(c)* requires the administrator to provide the most recent scheme accounts and such other information and particulars including actuarial reports within 30 days of a notice from the SFO. This is a catch-all provision as the SFO has power thereunder to request the production of anything it considers relevant. Failure to provide the information may also give rise to penalties.

3.70 It is noticeable that the SFO has been using the provisions in *section 605(1)(a)(b)(c)* increasingly in the last year or so, although the sanction threatened is apparently loss of the scheme's approval rather than penalties. In support of this line the SFO usually states that it cannot be sure in the absence of the required details that a SSAS is being administered in a manner compatible with Inland Revenue approval. Property and loan details are often subject to such notices as are actuarial valuations. The latter are required triennially under the rules of a SSAS and the use of the provisions of *section 605(1)(c)* to obtain them is clearly related to the SFO's practice in this area described in paragraphs 9.27–9.29 below.

3.71 The administrator is liable to deduct and account for tax in relation to various payments made from a SSAS e.g. pensions, refund of members' contributions, commutation of pension in circumstances of serious ill-health. This entails making annual returns of tax due. Claims for repayment of tax may be submitted at the same time. The inspector of taxes may require copies of the scheme's accounts in connection with a repayment claim. Scheme accounts are sometimes requested by the SFO. They are in fact a requirement of the approval process under *section 605(1)(c)*. In addition scheme accounts are also a statutory requirement under the disclosure provisions of the *SSA 1985* (see paragraph 11.9 below). The production of scheme accounts is the responsibility of the administrator.

3.72 Under the regulations further reporting requirements are imposed on the administrator. Within 90 days of certain prescribed transactions by the trustees, the administrator must furnish the SFO with details of acquisitions of land, loans to the company and connected companies, unquoted shares, borrowings, and purchases of property from, and sales of property to, the company and connected companies and leases thereto. These reporting requirements are covered in the paragraphs relating to the investment or feature concerned.

3.73 *Documentation*

This is intended to provide the SFO with a more up to date picture of the assets of a SSAS and to prevent trustees from concealing dubious features for considerable periods of time.

3.73 These reporting requirements should result in a decrease in action by the SFO under *section 605(1)(a)(b)(c)* although the interaction between the deadlines in *section 605* and the regulations may take some time to become clear. Problems can be foreseen for advisers in obtaining the information to be reported to the SFO in 90 days. Experience shows that some legal documentation particularly involving the Land Registry can take longer than three months to be produced. The SFO has granted a concession regarding the production of leases (see paragraph 6.50 below), but it remains to be seen if this concession is sufficient.

Chapter 4

Benefit Structure

Introduction

4.1   As mentioned in paragraph 2.8 above the vast majority of SSASs apply for discretionary approval under *section 591* from the SFO. This is because under *section 591* the SFO can exercise its discretion to approve higher levels and types of benefits than those that are provided under *section 590* where approval is mandatory and because some benefits cannot be provided under *section 590*. The full benefit limitations are set out in PN and various JOMs. This chapter will highlight the main benefits and their limitations and explain them further subject to what has already been stated in Chapter 3 on the rule requirements applicable to them.

4.2   The maximum benefits that may be paid will always depend upon the rules and it cannot be stressed enough how important it is when drafting the definitive deed and the rules thereunder to allow for the maximum level of benefits in all circumstances. Amendments can always be made later to extend the benefits to the SFO permissible limits, but these take time and may, in the meantime, delay the payment of a benefit unless the augmentation provisions are wide enough to allow it.

4.3   It should also be borne in mind that SSASs are usually money purchase schemes sometimes referred to as defined contribution schemes as opposed to final salary schemes although they may well provide benefits based on final salary. Money purchase schemes mean that the level of benefits to emerge will depend on the level of contributions paid by the company and the member and the amount of growth of those contributions once invested.

From April 1988 it was compulsory for all occupational pension schemes (including SSASs) to permit members to make additional voluntary contributions (AVCs) up to 15% of gross earnings in any year. From April 1987 the amount and timing of the AVCs can be varied in accordance with the employees' wishes. From 26 October 1987 AVCs can be made outside the pension scheme and such payments are called Free-standing AVCs (FSAVCs).

4.4 *Benefit Structure*

However, controlling directors cannot be members of a FSAVC scheme. If a member of such a scheme becomes a controlling director, he must stop his contributions and his options with regard to the acquired benefits are to:

(a)   take an additional pension,

(b)   take a section 32 buyout policy, or

(c)   allow a transfer payment to the SSAS once he becomes a member.

Commuted lump sums are not available in respect of AVCs or FSAVCs made after 7 April 1987 and it is only possible for these benefits to be taken as an income pension.

4.4   In a final salary scheme sometimes referred to as a defined benefit scheme the level of benefits to be provided are based on the length of service, the definition of final remuneration and the fraction of final remuneration to which a member is entitled. The fraction may be based solely on length of service with the principal employer or together with service from associated employers or may include previous service with another employer from whose scheme a transfer payment has been received. Additionally the uplifted scales for pension and lump sums in PN 6.18 and PN 8.6 respectively may be used for this purpose.

4.5   There are several reasons why a money purchase basis is preferred for SSASs. The main reasons though are those of cost. The financial commitment of the company to fund a final salary scheme can be financially burdensome. In addition salary increases entail increased contributions to meet the final salary commitment. Any underfunding at the time a member retires would have to be met by payment of a special contribution which in turn may require to be spread as a deduction for corporation tax purposes [*section 592(6)*].

4.6   A money purchase scheme is however still subject to Inland Revenue limits on the level of benefits it may provide. Thus a SSAS is usually funded on a money purchase basis with a target of maximum Inland Revenue limits. The member's credit or contribution credit in these cases representing the member's interest in the scheme from which benefits will be paid is limited to no more than the Inland Revenue maximum.

4.7   The maximum benefits for which it is possible to fund depend upon the actuarial assumptions which are made in determining the level of contributions to be paid to the scheme (see paragraphs 9.7 and 9.8 below) and the maximum benefits which the Inland Revenue will allow.

Paragraphs 4.8 *et seq* below look at those maximum benefits and other features on which they are based.

Normal retirement date

4.8   As the majority of members of a SSAS are 20% directors their normal retirement date has to be set at a minimum age of 60 for both men and women (PN 6.4A). The concession for women to retire prior to age 60 does not apply to 20% directors. The upper age limit of 70 for both sexes also does not apply to 20% directors who may continue in service beyond 70. It should also be noted that the lower retiring ages available in some employments do not apply to 20% directors as they will still be able to carry out their 'directing' of the company after the activity for which an early retirement age is acceptable has ceased.

Pensions

4.9   For any member of a SSAS prior to 17 March 1987 it is possible to receive the maximum pension of 2/3rds of final remuneration after ten years service has been completed. This is because the normal accrual rate of 1/60th of final remuneration for each year of pensionable service may be accelerated in accordance with the table in PN 6.18. Otherwise 40 years service would be needed to provide the maximum permitted pension of 2/3rds of final remuneration. The following permissible scale appears in PN 6.18.

No of years of pensionable service completed before normal retirement age	Maximum permissible pension as a fraction of final remuneration
1–5	1/60th for each year
6	8/60ths
7	16/60ths
8	24/60ths
9	32/60ths
10	40/60ths

4.10   For any members joining a SSAS after that date or for members of a SSAS established after that date, *schedule 23 paragraph 2(2)* changed the position. Pensions for these members accrue by 1/30th of final remuneration for each year of pensionable service. This means 20 years service need to be completed before the maximum permitted pension of 2/3rds of final remuneration may be paid. Despite the longer period of service now required to receive the maximum pension, the new accrual rate gives a better pension for those who have completed up to five years service e.g. for those who have five years service their entitlement is 1/6th as opposed to 1/12th of final salary.

Cash lump sums

4.11 It is permissible for all members of a SSAS to receive a tax-free lump sum by commuting part or all of a pension not exceeding 3/80ths of final remuneration for each year of service up to a maximum of 40 years. This is an attractive benefit for a higher rate taxpayer. As for pensions, there is a permitted higher rate of accrual so that after 20 years service the maximum lump sum of 1½ times final remuneration may be paid. The accrual table which may be found in PN 8.6 is reproduced below.

Number of years completed to normal retirement age	80ths of final remuneration
1–8	3 for each year
9	30
10	36
11	42
12	48
13	54
14	63
15	72
16	81
17	90
18	99
19	108
20 or more	120

4.12 The *F(No 2)A 1987* did not change the minimum period of service required to obtain the maximum cash lump sum, but it did introduce some restrictions now incorporated in *schedule 23 paragraph 3*. Previously it was possible for the accrual rates in PN 8.6 to be used to augment the commutable element with no corresponding augmentation to the pension benefit. From 17 March 1987 if the pension is not calculated by reference to accelerated accrual, then accelerated accrual cannot be applied to the calculation of the lump sum. This restriction is aimed at preventing excessive tax free lump sums at the expense of pensions.

4.13 Additionally, if a member has the benefit of the accelerated accrual scale of 1/30th for each year of service, then the proportionate accelerated accrual scale for lump sums may be used. On the other hand if the member has a pension based on an accelerated accrual scale of less than 1/30th for each year of service, an appropriate proportionate amount may be taken in lump sum form.

4.14 In commuting a pension to provide a lump sum commutation rates are necessary to determine the cash value provided by each £1 of pension given up. The rates differ for men and women because of their differing life expectancies and they also differ according to the date of retirement. The commutation factors agreed by the SFO and set out in PN 8.17 are as follows:

	Age	Factor
Men	60	10.2
	65	9.0
	70	7.8
Women	55	12.2
	60	11.0
	65	9.8

It is possible to agree enhanced commutation factors with the SFO where pensions are being provided that increase by more than 2% p.a.

4.15 The inter-action of pensions and lump sums is an important aspect of the decision to be made on retirement. It may be that the member's credit is no more than can provide a lump sum. Or the member's credit may be less than the sum needed to provide maximum benefits. A balance may therefore have to be struck between taking the maximum cash and a smaller pension or no lump sum and the maximum pension. The member has to decide if the residual pension which will be taxed under PAYE will be sufficient. Whilst the cash lump sum is tax free, once invested the income it generates will become taxable. However if it is invested to purchase a further annuity to supplement the residual pension there could still be a financial advantage as the capital element of the annuity would be tax-free and only the interest element taxable.

Transitional arrangements

4.16 Paragraphs 4.10, 4.12 and 4.13 above described some of the restrictions brought about by the *F(No 2)A 1987*. For those who were members of schemes prior to 17 March 1987 some measure of protection was needed so that they would not be disadvantaged in certain circumstances e.g. a move on promotion from the company's scheme of which they were members prior to 17 March 1987 to another scheme of the company after that date. A list of the instances in JOM 87(12) where the restrictions will not apply may be found in Appendix 19.

Final remuneration

4.17 It can be seen from paragraphs 4.9 to 4.13 above how important the member's final remuneration is in the calculation of the benefits payable on retirement. This is also true of benefits payable in other circumstances as will be explained later. The definition of final remuneration of a 20% director in paragraph 3.26 above is rather basic and its application needs further explanation at this stage as does clarification of what actually constitutes final remuneration.

4.18 Once a 20% director enters the 13 year period prior to normal retirement age the level of remuneration should be closely watched. There will need to be a consecutive three year period somewhere in these 13 years that will provide the final remuneration figures on which benefits will be based. The last three years in this period may not provide the best figures if the company is unable to sustain a director's remuneration at previous levels. Fortunately dynamisation helps in this situation as earlier years' remuneration may be increased in line with the RPI. However, where a director's remuneration fluctuates from one year to another finding three consecutive years that produce the best results can create problems.

4.19 The following example illustrates how complicated it can be to arrive at the best period of three years. Here it is assumed the 20% director retired aged 60 on 31 December 1990.

Example

Year ended	Basic remuneration	Fluctuating remuneration	Total	Increased by RPI	Three year average
31.12.78	£23,000	nil	£23,000	£57,720	
31.12.79	£25,000	£600	£25,600	£54,799	
31.12.80	£23,000	£600	£23,600	£43,882	£52,134
31.12.81	£32,500	nil	£32,500	£53,934	£50,872
31.12.82	£30,000	£500	£30,500	£48,018	£48,611
31.12.83	£35,000	£500	£35,500	£53,069	£51,674
31.12.84	£30,000	£1,000	£31,000	£44,313	£48,467
31.12.85	£40,000	£1,500	£41,500	£56,128	£51,170
31.12.86	£45,000	£2,000	£47,000	£61,286	£53,909
31.12.87	£25,000	nil	£25,000	£31,438	£49,617

Year ended	Basic remuneration	Fluctuating remuneration	Total	Increased by RPI	Three year average
31.12.88	£45,000	£1,500	£46,500	£54,763	£49,162
31.12.89	£50,000	nil	£50,000	£54,672	£46,958
31.12.90	£50,000	£1,000	£51,000	£51,000	£53,478

It can be seen that the three years ended 31 December 1986 gives the highest average final remuneration (£53,909) for any three consecutive years ending in the ten year period prior to retirement. The next best average is for the three years ended 31 December 1990 (£53,478).

4.20 It is always best to smooth out the troughs and peaks of remuneration if at all possible as one really good year on its own may not come into the reckoning if remuneration on either side of it is substantially less. Another point to watch is where no remuneration is paid. This should not be allowed to happen for too long because, although the director's service may still be pensionable, nil remuneration in any of the last three consecutive years will reduce the final benefits.

4.21 The date the particular years end that is used for calculating final remuneration is flexible providing it falls in the ten years prior to the retirement date. It may be convenient to use company years, tax years, the three years ending on retirement or any other convenient date.

4.22 The remuneration itself which makes up the final remuneration is generally any earnings paid by the company which are subject to tax under Schedule E. There are some restrictions and exceptions as will be explained later. It is therefore most important that in framing the definition of pensionable earnings in the rules everything that is permissible to be included must be brought within the definition. Thus not only basic salary should be pensionable, but so should bonuses, fees, commission, benefits-in-kind etc. 20% directors are most likely to be in receipt of taxable benefits-in-kind and other remuneration which may fluctuate from year to year, and will be averaged over the best three consecutive years anyway. For non-20% director members these so called fluctuating emoluments' cannot be taken for one year only unlike basic remuneration, but must be averaged over three consecutive years.

4.23 Because directors of private companies are able to control the remuneration paid to them, the three year averaging was imposed in the 1970s to limit their ability to increase their remuneration just before they retired. Further restrictions were imposed by the *F(No 2)A 1987* (now *schedule 23 paragraph 5(3)*). These restrictions ensure that not only are controlling directors at the time of their retirement restricted to the three year averaging, but they also will be subject to this if they held that position at any time in the last ten years.

This prevents a director relinquishing control just before he retires and using the best year in the last five for final remuneration purposes. The same restriction as to final remuneration also applies to any other employees whose remuneration since 6 April 1987 exceeds £100,000 p.a.

4.24 For members who joined a scheme after 17 March 1987 their final remuneration used to determine the cash lump sum must not exceed £100,000 under *schedule 23 paragraph 6(2)*. This means that the maximum cash lump sum payable to such members on retirement after completing the minimum 20 years service is £150,000. The final remuneration figure of £100,000 is capable of being increased from time to time in an order made by the Treasury [*section 590(3)*].

4.25 *Section 612(1)* debars the inclusion of certain forms of remuneration from the calculation of final remuneration for all employees for 1987/88 *et seq*. These forms of remuneration include any sums chargeable to tax under *section 148* (popularly known as 'golden hand-shakes') and share options. Remuneration paid in the form of unit trusts and taxed under Schedule E may still be included in final remuneration, but it will probably be a fluctuating emolument.

4.26 Payments made under *section 148* are usually for termination of employment of office and compensatory by nature. The first £30,000 of such payments is normally tax-free and the excess subject to tax under Schedule E. It is the excess element which cannot form part of the final remuneration even though it is subject to Schedule E tax.

4.27 PN 6.12A excludes from final remuneration any sums chargeable to tax under Schedule E that arise from the acquisition or disposal of shares or from a right to acquire shares except where the shares or rights giving rise on or after 17 March 1987 to liability under Schedule E were acquired before that date. It is unlikely that this will have any effect on SSASs established by private unquoted companies as they probably do not have share option or incentive schemes. However, some SSAS are established for the senior directors of large public companies and this restriction may have considerable impact.

Section 37, Finance Act 1989 and final remuneration

4.28 Until 5 April 1989 all emoluments assessable to income tax under Schedule E were either assessable on a receipts or earnings basis. Broadly this meant that emoluments were assessable in the year in which they were paid or made available unless the taxpayer elected to have them assessed for the year in which they were actually earned. Thus a bonus, fees or commission received on 1 December 1988 in respect of a company's year ended 30 March 1988 would have been assessable under Schedule E for the tax year 1987/88 if an election to be assessed on an earnings basis had been made. The earnings basis once adopted could not be changed from year to year.

4.29 In calculating final remuneration for pensions purposes it did not matter whether a receipts or earnings basis had been adopted for Schedule E purposes as the amounts used for basic earnings and fluctuating emoluments followed the amounts assessed or assessable to Schedule E.

4.30 From 6 April 1989 the Schedule E position has been changed by *sections 202A and 202B* inserted by *section 37, FA 1989*. With effect from 6 April 1989 the earnings basis of assessment has been abolished. From that date all emoluments are assessable to Schedule E on a receipts basis regardless of the year in which they were earned. The effect of this change does, however, mean that a bonus etc. paid or voted on or after 6 April 1989 in respect of a company's year ended prior to that date will be assessable to Schedule E both under the old earnings basis for the year in which it was earned and under the new receipts basis for the year in which it is paid or voted.

4.31 Fortunately, to avoid this double assessment there are relieving provisions in *section 38, FA 1989*. These provide for a taxpayer to elect to remove emoluments assessed on an earnings basis prior to 6 April 1989 from any Schedule E assessment and for them to be assessable solely on the receipts basis. The election had to be made to the Inland Revenue before 6 April 1991 and only applies to emoluments paid or voted on or after 6 April 1989 and before 6 April 1991 in respect of a company's year ended prior to 6 April 1989.

4.32 If an election was made regarding any emoluments paid or made available between 6 April 1989 and 5 April 1991 which would have been assessable to Schedule E under the old earnings basis for 1988/89 or earlier years, and the final remuneration on which pension scheme benefits are based includes remuneration for 1988/89 or earlier years, then the retirement benefits would be reduced as the emoluments concerned cannot be included in remuneration for 1988/89 or earlier years.

4.33 *Benefit Structure*

4.33 This is best illustrated by the following.

Example

A 20% director retired on 31 March 1991, the best three year's earnings being as follows (leaving aside any uprating for RPI):

Year end	Salary	Bonus
31 March 1987	£30,000	£3,000
31 March 1988	£35,000	£4,000
31 March 1989	£40,000	£5,000

The bonuses were always paid after the year ended in which they were earned, the bonus of £5,000 being paid on 30 September 1989. If the director was assessed to Schedule E on an earnings basis and did not make an election under *section 38, FA 1989* for the bonus of £5,000 paid on 30 September 1989 to be assessed on a receipts basis, final remuneration would be:

Salary	Bonus
£30,000	£3,000
£35,000	£4,000
£40,000	£5,000
£105,000 +	£12,000 = £117,000 ÷ 3 = £39,000

Tax would be paid under Schedule E twice on the bonus of £5,000; once in 1988/89 on the earnings basis and again in 1989/90 on the receipts basis.

4.34 If the same director had elected under *section 38, FA 1989* for the bonus to be assessed on a receipts basis, final remuneration would be:

Salary	Bonus
£30,000	£3,000
£35,000	£4,000
£40,000	Nil
£105,000 +	£7,000 = £112,000 ÷ 3 = £37,333

Tax would only be paid once under Schedule E on the bonus of £5,000 in 1989/90.

4.35 It can be seen that even if a 20% director is not retiring for, say, another ten years, the effect of making an election before 6 April 1991 reduces final remuneration and consequently retirement benefits if remuneration assessable to Schedule E for 1988/89 or earlier years is included in the three year average. The same situation would apply to someone who is not a 20% director where the best year's earnings in the last five years are used. In the latter instance it could affect the calculation of the average of fluctuating emoluments.

The earnings cap

4.36 *FA 1989* also introduced other far-reaching effects on pension schemes. It brought in legislation which, like the 1987 legislation, overrides the rules for schemes approved by 27 July 1989 limiting pensionable earnings to £60,000 p.a (see paragraphs 4.37 to 4.39 below), limiting the maximum approvable accelerated accrual of lump sums (see paragraph 4.40 below) and simplifying the calculation of maximum benefits on early/late retirement or leaving service (see paragraphs 4.45, 4.49 and 4.54 below).

4.37 *Section 590C* was introduced by *schedule 6 paragraph 4, FA 1989* and restricts pensionable earnings for the years 1988/89 *et seq* used in the calculation of maximum benefits based on final remuneration to £60,000 p.a. The restriction applies to the aggregate of benefits from all approved schemes in respect of all service with the company or associated companies. Concurrent service is not counted twice, so it is not possible to obtain benefits based on remuneration of £60,000 from each of a series of associated companies.

Allowance is made in the legislation to increase the figure of £60,000 annually in line with the RPI. The limit from 6 April 1991 has been increased to £71,400 by Treasury Order.

4.38 The 'earnings cap' as it is known applies to all schemes established on or after 14 March 1989. It does not apply to members of schemes who joined before 1 June 1989 where the schemes was already in existence before 14 March 1989. Remuneration above the 'earnings cap' may now be pensioned through an unapproved pension scheme without prejudicing the approval of a scheme already approved or one seeking approval.

4.39 *Sections 590, 590A, 590B* as amended by *schedule 6 paragraphs 3(3)4, FA 1989* contain rather complicated legislation defining associated employments and connected schemes to prevent the capping restrictions being circumvented. Broadly where a holding company/subsidiary company relationship exists or another company acquires the whole of the previous participating company, the member's remuneration will not be subject to the cap on any future re-structuring of the company and its pension scheme. Service pre- and post-14 March 1989 will remain continuous and therefore aggregable. However, where these relationships do not exist, particularly where another company participates in a scheme after 14 March 1989 and is only an associate of the other company and they both remunerate the member, pensionable service cannot be counted as continuous and aggregated for benefit calculation purposes.

4.40   *Schedule 6 paragraph 23, FA 1989* limits the maximum approvable accelerated accrual of lump sums for all members of schemes established after 14 March 1989. It does not apply to members of schemes who joined before 1 June 1989 where the scheme was already in existence prior to 14 March 1989. It will be recalled from paragraph 4.11 above that the maximum lump sum is 3/80ths of final remuneration for each year of service. The new alternative limit is 2.25 times the initial amount of pension payable before commutation or allocation in favour of dependants. A member may be paid the greater of this later alternative or the earlier one. A member who joined the scheme after 17 March 1987 and before 1 June 1989 and who is subject to the old limits may elect to be subject to the new maxima, but this would entail being subject to the earnings cap also.

Concurrent and part-time employment

4.41   Concurrent service is mentioned in paragraph 4.37 above. This and part-time service often apply to 20% directors who may be directors also of associated companies within the same SSAS or totally unassociated companies in other schemes or which do not participate in other schemes at all. Problems can arise where, although the periods of service are concurrent, the time spent in each employment and remuneration received fluctuates considerably or one employment ceases and another commences outside the scheme. No remuneration may also be paid at certain times from any of the concurrent employments. This can cause difficulties in arriving at an accurate number of years full-time service on which benefits are to be based. Where all the concurrent employments run together in the same scheme there should be no difficulty, but in other circumstances the guidance in PN 6.10 is rather unhelpful. It simply states that where there are other concurrent employments special consideration will need to be given. Full-time service of more than 10 or 20 years to obtain maximum pension or lump sum benefits may need to be substantiated to the SFO where concurrent or part-time employments are involved.

4.42 Benefits may be provided for part-time employees by reference to years of part-time service and remuneration therefrom as explained in PN 6.10. The administrator is obliged to notify the SFO under the terms of the undertaking (Appendix 18) where there has been a change from part-time to full-time service or *vice-versa* if the part-time service is to be converted to its full-time equivalent in calculating benefits. JOM 100(70) mentions an instance where the SFO was not prepared to approve a method, where following full-time service, part-time service and remuneration up to retirement were converted to their full-time equivalents and aggregated. It is now prepared to consider such proposals except where the remuneration relates to a director (JOM 100(71)).

Early retirement

4.43 Early retirement benefits may be taken at any time within ten years of a member's normal retirement age. This effectively means that benefits may be taken at any time after age 50 if the member retires. A female 20% director cannot retire early after age 45 as her minimum normal retirement age is 60 (see paragraph 4.8 above). This can be an attractive proposition for a 20% director particularly if the company is being sold. The benefits are, however, scaled down as would be expected in comparison with those payable at normal retirement age. The scheme cannot be funded on the basis of the benefits payable at any age between 50–60 even if it was always the intention of the director to retire early. It must be funded on the basis of benefits payable on retirement at normal retirement age.

4.44 The maximum benefit payable in pension on early retirement is set out in PN 10.3 with the formula for calculating and is reproduced below.

The maximum immediate pension (including the annuity equivalent of any lump sum) is either 1/60th of final remuneration for each year of actual service with a maximum of 40, or if this is more favourable, the amount calculated by the formula:

$$\frac{N}{NS} \times P \text{ where:}$$

N is the number of actual years of service with a maximum of 40

NS is the number of years of potential service to normal retirement date and may be limited to 40

P is the maximum pension approvable had the employee served until normal retirement date.

4.45 *Benefit Structure*

Any restriction for retained benefits must be made in arriving at P before multiplying by the fraction N/NS.

4.45 The maximum benefit payable on early retirement in lump sum form is either 3/80ths of final remuneration for each year of actual service with a maximum of 40, or if this is more favourable, the amount calculated by the formula:

$\dfrac{N}{NS} \times LS$ where:

N is the number of years of actual service with a maximum of 40

NS is the number of years of potential service to normal retirement date and may be limited to 40.

LS is the maximum lump sum receivable had the employee served until normal retirement date.

Any restriction for retained benefits must be made in arriving at LS before multiplying by the fraction N/NS.

For members who joined on or after 17 March 1987 the formula N/NS × LS may only be used if the total benefits have been calculated on a similar basis.

4.46 The restrictions on remuneration used to calculate pension and lump sum benefits introduced by the *F(No 2)A 1987* and incorporated in *schedule 23 paragraphs 2(2), 3, 5(3), 6(2)* (see paragraphs 4.9, 4.12, 4.13, 4.23 and 4.24 above) and by *schedule 6 paragraph 4, FA 1989* (see paragraphs 4.28–4.31, 4.36–4.40 above) should be taken into account where appropriate.

4.47 An alternative basis for calculating benefits on early retirement was introduced in 1989 (JOM 99(24) and JOM 100(52)). This allows the accrual rate of 1/30th of remuneration for each year of service to be used instead of 1/60th up to a maximum of 20/30ths and subject to it not exceeding 2/3rds of final remuneration when aggregated with any retained benefits. This basis does not apply to members who withdraw voluntarily from scheme membership but continue in service with the company. The scheme must also continue to be funded on the basis of benefits payable on retirement at normal retirement age (see paragraph 4.43 above).

4.48 In paragraph 4.18 above the importance was stressed of ensuring a period of three consecutive years remuneration in the last thirteen years was maintained at the highest level possible to achieve maximum benefits. It may be that the best three years of a director's remuneration were before age 50 and helped by dynamisation these may influence the decision to retire early. The band of highest earnings could be lost at normal retirement age and any increase in benefits they generate on early retirement may compensate for the proportionate reduction then suffered due to the scaling down of early retirement benefits.

Leaving service

4.49   If a member of a SSAS leaves employment before normal retirement age several options are available regarding the member's accrued benefits. If the member is over 50 years old then early retirement benefits may be paid. Benefits may be left in the scheme and taken at normal retirement age. A deferred annuity may be purchased or a transfer made to the member's new occupational scheme or to a personal pension scheme. It should be noted that there are limitations on transfer payments for controlling directors and individuals whose remuneration exceeds £60,000 p.a. who are members of personal pension schemes (JOM 100(84)). Transfer payments made from a SSAS to a personal pension scheme may not therefore be the full amount of the member's accumulated interest in the SSAS. This is to prevent a transfer being used to maximise the advantage of the tax-free lump sum in a personal pension scheme. Thus a transfer payment must not exceed the amount calculated by reference to regulation 6(3) of the Personal Pension Schemes (Transfer Payments) Regulations 1988 (SI 1988/1014).

4.50   The maximum benefits payable on leaving service in respect of pensions and lump sums are set out in PN 13.2 and 13.8. The calculations are similarly based to those used for early retirement benefits. However, if the member's actual service is less than 10 or 20 years for pension purposes and 20 years for lump sum purposes, the benefits payable should not exceed the maximum approvable at normal retirement age for the same service in accordance with the accrual tables in PN 6.18 and 8.6 respectively (see paragraphs 4.9 and 4.11 above).

4.51   The alternative basis for calculating benefits on early retirement described in paragraph 4.47 above is also available for deferred benefits on leaving service.

Late retirement

4.52   It was possible where a member retired after normal retirement age to receive a pension and a lump sum in exchange for a pension in excess of the normal maximum of 2/3rds final remuneration for a pension and 1½ times final remuneration for a lump sum. The increased limits are set out in PN 9.2 and 9.5 respectively and both depend on actual service exceeding 40 years. For pension purposes each year in excess of 40 falling after normal retirement date could earn a further sixtieth of final remuneration up to a maximum of 45/60ths of final remuneration at the actual date of retirement. If total service exceeded 40 years, the lump sum could be increased in respect of each year in excess of 40 falling after normal retirement date by 3/80ths of final remuneration at the actual date of retirement, but the maximum number of years that could count is 45 and the maximum sum therefore 135/80ths

4.53 Benefits could have or may still be taken at normal retirement age in both pension and lump sum form and these may have to be taken into account in calculating the benefits on final retirement. If a lump sum is taken at normal retirement age, however, then on final retirement no further commutation is permitted. This is because lump sums cannot be paid in instalments.

4.54 Clearly 20% directors were in a position to manipulate their normal retiring age and actual retirement and take advantage of the increased benefits described in paragraph 4.52 above. So any 20% director retiring between age 60 and 70 after the stated normal retirement age was treated for maximum benefit purposes as if actual retiring age were in fact the normal retiring age. (See paragraph 3.27 above regarding the rule requirements for this restriction). For example, where a 20% director with a normal retirement age of 60 actually retired at age 65 with 43 years of service with the company up to the actual retirement date the maximum benefits of 2/3rds final remuneration for a pension and 1½ times final remuneration for a lump sum only could be taken. If the same 20% director had only completed 28 years service on retirement age 65 the five years service beyond age 65 would still be permissible and is not restricted. On the other hand if the same 20% director actually retired at age 72 having completed 52 years service by that time, then the twelve years service from age 60 would be restricted and the maximum pension and lump sum benefits could be paid together with additional pension and lump sum benefits as described in paragraph 4.52 above in respect of two years service after age 70.

4.55 All members with normal retirement ages of 75 or above must take all benefits at normal retirement age rather than at actual retirement age if later.

4.56 As a result of the introduction in 1989 of the alternative basis for calculating benefits on early retirement (see paragraph 4.47 above) it was no longer appropriate to allow the increases above the maxima on late retirement described in paragraph 4.52 above. Increases in late retirement are now limited to 1/30th of final remuneration for each year of service to bring benefits up to 2/3rds of final remuneration or by reference to final remuneration at actual retirement where that is higher than at normal retirement age.

Death benefits

4.57 On a member's death in service before reaching normal retirement age a lump sum may be paid of up to four times final remuneration. As it is assumed a member's death in these circumstances could not have been foreseen the definition of final remuneration is not so restricted as for benefits payable on retirement. This is particularly useful in the case of 20% directors.

4.58 Final remuneration can be defined here as:

(a) the annual basic salary immediately before death; or

(b) basic salary in (a) plus the average fluctuating emoluments during the three years up to the date of death; or

(c) total earnings fixed and fluctuating, paid during any period of twelve months falling within three years prior to death.

4.59 The lump sum is payable free from IHT provided the scheme rules are worded so that the exercise of discretion in paying the lump sum is vested in the trustees to pay the benefits among a wide class of beneficiaries (see paragraph 3.28). Provision should be made for members to complete an expression of wish regarding to whom the lump sum benefit should be paid in the event of their death. An example of an expression of wish may be found at Appendix 20.

4.60 In addition to a lump sum benefit spouse's and dependant's pensions may be provided subject to a total of 2/3rds of the member's final remuneration. The maximum pension for any one person however is limited to 4/9ths of final remuneration which would usually be payable to the surviving spouse. Dependants means any persons who were financially dependent on the deceased at the date of death. Children are considered to be financially dependent if under age 18 or in full time educational or vocational training. It is possible for a woman living with the deceased at the time of death who was not a lawful wife to receive a dependant's pension instead of a spouse's pension.

Insurance of death benefits

4.61   In a large self-administered scheme because of the wide spread of membership and size of the fund it is possible to pay out benefits from the fund should a death in service occur. However, in a SSAS with one or two members and especially in its early years, such cover does not fully exist in the fund to pay out benefits in the event of an unexpected death. So the SFO has allowed for insurance cover to be provided for this eventuality. Term assurance is usually used for this purpose.

4.62   JOM 58(21) states that all death-in-service benefits should be insured from the outset to the extent that they exceed the value from year to year of the member's interest in the scheme based on his accrued pension and other benefits. There are two points to note from this. The first point is that such insurance is not compulsory and if insurance cover is required it is not a rule requirement. It is important to understand that if insurance cover is not provided then the amount of any death-in-service benefits will be limited to the member's interest in the scheme provided that does not exceed the Inland Revenue maxima. The second point to bear in mind is that the insurance cover provided should not, when added to the member's interest in the scheme, exceed the Inland Revenue maxima. It follows from this that if maximum death-in-service benefits are to be provided, the level of insured cover should decrease over the years as further contributions are paid and the value of the member's interest increases, even after allowing for increases in remuneration.

4.63   There will be instances where it is not possible to obtain insurance cover of this nature i.e. the member has an impaired life and is uninsurable or the premiums quoted are prohibitive. If such a member died in service the death-in-service benefits would be limited to the member's interest in the fund, but it may be possible to approach the SFO after the death to ascertain if it would allow a special contribution to be paid to the scheme to fund for the balance of death-in-service benefits up to the maximum permitted.

Death benefits in retirement

4.64   If a member's pension has been secured following retirement a lump sum may be payable under a guarantee attaching to the pension. The SFO allows a guaranteed pension to be paid for up to ten years after retirement. If the guarantee is limited to five years from retirement a lump sum will become payable on the member's death within that five years equal to the balance of pension due at the end of the five-year period.

4.65 The lump sum is also payable free of IHT (see paragraph 4.59 above) provided the trustees have discretion as to its disposal.

4.66 Following the death of a member a dependant's pension may be provided to the spouse. They may already have been secured at the time the member's pension was purchased and will come into payment automatically or they can be secured following the member's death or increased to the maximum allowable. The limits as set out in PN 12.2 allow pensions to be provided up to 2/3rds of the maximum pension approvable for the deceased member before any lump sum commutation at retirement and as if the deceased had no retained benefits from earlier occupations. The maximum pension so calculated may also be increased in line with the RPI from the date on which the deceased's own pension became payable.

4.67 If a leaver dies before normal retirement age having deferred benefits in the scheme, a cash lump sum and spouse's and dependant's pensions may be paid. PN 13.9 explains any lump sum benefit payable will be governed by the practice relating to death-in-service benefits in PN 11.3 and 11.4 and based on final remuneration at the date of leaving. PN 13.9 also explains spouse's and dependant's pensions may be provided as explained in PN 11.6 and 11.7 except they are to be calculated by reference to the deceased member's maximum approvable deferred pension.

4.68 Where a member dies in service after normal retirement age, PN 11.11 allows maximum benefits to be provided on the basis that either

(a) the member had died in service, or

(b) the member had died in retirement having retired the day before the date of death.

Ill-health

4.69 If a member's retirement is caused by incapacity benefits may be paid immediately whatever the age. Higher pension and lump sum benefits are allowable than on early retirement as the benefits may be based on the fraction of final remuneration the member could have received had service continued until normal retirement age. Incapacity is defined in PN 11.6 as physical or mental deterioration bad enough to prevent members from following their normal employment or seriously impairing their earnings capacity.

4.70 Where a member is in exceptional circumstances of serious ill-health, full commutation of the member's pension is permissible. The rule wording and SFO requirements are explained in paragraph 3.29 above. A lump sum paid in these circumstances is subject to a tax charge under *section 599(1)* on the excess of lump sum payable less the maximum lump sum which would otherwise have been payable on grounds of incapacity. Thus, if the full commutation produces a lump sum of £300,000 and the maximum lump sum permitted on grounds of incapacity was £200,000, tax would be payable on the excess of £100,000 at 10% and accounted for by the administrator to the Inland Revenue.

Increases in pensions

4.71 Following retirement a member of a SSAS may receive the pension payable direct from the fund for a period of up to five years. At some time during this period the pension should be secured from a LO (see paragraph 3.33 above). The trustees may increase the pension during this period up to the level of the RPI and when the pension is secured the level of pension then in payment must be secured. It is possible if the SSAS continues to exist for further increases to be secured later still subject to the level of the RPI.

4.72 If the SSAS has not been funded to a level sufficient to provide the member with the maximum pension allowable and it is desired when the pension is purchased to make some provision for future increases, a decision will be needed at the time of retirement to pitch the level of the pension that can be maintained. It may have to be set at a lower level to secure future increases which can be costly.

4.73 Pensions are liable to income tax under Schedule E and therefore whilst the pension is paid from the scheme's resources the trustees should operate PAYE on the pension being paid and account to the Inland Revenue for the tax deducted.

4.74 This chapter has covered the main benefits and limitations thereto that apply to SSAS. The actuary will take into account the benefits that are to be provided and have been communicated to the members in their announcement letters in preparing the initial and subsequent actuarial reports on the scheme and in recommending the funding rates for the scheme. The main actuarial considerations are explained in Chapter 9.

Chapter 5

Investments

General

5.1   JOM 58(9) makes it clear that it is not necessary to include in the trust deed any special restrictions on the investment powers of the trustees apart from banning loans to members of a SSAS (see paragraph 3.17 above). JOM 58(13) goes on to say that it is not for the Inland Revenue to interfere in the way trustees invest scheme funds unless tax avoidance, member use of benefits or liquidity is involved. This means the trust deed is usually drawn up giving the trustees wide powers of investment.

5.2   It also means that apart from specific areas of investment to which the SFO's guidelines apply, the trustees may put their funds into a very wide range of investments. Specific types of investments such as loans and property, to which the SFO's guidelines apply, which are major subjects in themselves, are covered in detail in Chapters 5 and 6 respectively. Unquoted shares and other investments to which the SFO's guidelines also apply are covered in Chapter 7. Investments such as equities, gilts, deposit accounts, building society accounts, insurance policies, unit trusts, managed funds etc. do not give rise to problems with the SFO. If trustees are investing in these, they need only have regard to the SFO's liquidity requirements i.e. are the investments easily realisable to purchase annuities when the latter are due?

Loans to employers

5.3   The ability of the trustees to invest for themselves is one of the major selling points of SSASs. One of the great attractions of SSASs is the facility to lend money back to the employer, so much so that it is a common feature of SSASs. So what are the SFO's guidelines on such loans and what can and cannot be done?

5.4   JOM 58(11 and 12) set the parameters and the SFO's policy since then has been fleshed out from time to time at meetings with the APT.

5.5 *Investments*

Broadly, loans may be made from a SSAS to an employer on commercially reasonable terms provided they do not amount to more than half the value of the assets of the scheme, that they are not too frequent and that the scheme's future liquidity requirements are able to be met.

Which employer?

5.5 Over the years the employer receiving the loan has come to mean in the eyes of the SFO not just the principal company. The SFO's definition of employer for the purposes of loans includes any company, whether it participates in the SSAS or not, which is associated in any way with the principal company either as a subsidiary or holding company or through common directorships or shareholdings. This connection may be extended further to any other company connected with the trustees or members. This definition is incorporated in the regulations.

5.6 It follows that the trustees may lend to totally unassociated companies. Whilst this would be a perfectly legitimate investment for the trustees and the JOM 58 guidelines and regulations would not in its terms apply, the SFO in some instances still looks at such loans quite critically and they may need to be defended as *bona fide* investments. Indeed JOM 109(15) makes it clear that the SFO will enquire about loans to unconnected companies or individuals particularly to establish whether arrangements have been made to circumvent the ban on loans to scheme members or to exceed the limit on loans to companies by means of reciprocal loans to the members or companies by the unconnected companies or individuals.

The amount

5.7 This is quite straightforward. No more than 50% of the value of the scheme's assets may be lent at any one time once the SSAS is two years old. For this purpose the amount of the loan plus the value of any shares in the employer must be aggregated and no more than 50% in total can be lent to or be invested in the employer. The point about the aggregation of shareholdings arose shortly after JOM 58 was published and was confirmed as an earlier change in the SFO's practice following the PQ relating to SSASs raised in July 1984. This is confirmed in the regulations.

5.8 It is possible for the trustees to make more than one loan to an employer or to make loans to more than one associated employer at the same time provided that they do not amount in aggregate to more than half of the value of the assets. The value of the assets may include transfer payments received and policies assigned to the scheme, although the consultative document proposed to exclude these in future when loans are made in the first two years of a scheme. The regulations confirm that SSASs established from 5 August 1991 cannot make loans exceeding 25% of the value of the assets in their first two years including any shares in the employer and that the value of the assets for this purpose is that derived from employer and member contributions only i.e. transfer payments are excluded.

5.9   Most employers find it extremely useful and financially efficient when setting up a SSAS to obtain a loan from the trustees. They can after all make a payment of an initial contribution of say £100,000 and obtain corporation tax relief on it and on the same day get back £50,000 as a loan for genuine business purposes and obtain further tax relief on the interest paid on the loan. The proposed 25% restriction may not be so popular, but the full 50% can be borrowed after two years. It has, however, to be accepted that the *bona fide* establishment of a SSAS has to be demonstrated to the SFO, as opposed to the employer's intention being to obtain a 50% loan back from a large transfer value received and small contribution and at the same time incidentally established a pension scheme.

5.10   There are two other points to be aware of regarding the value of loans. The first being that the value of the assets may go down either fortuitously or by design and as a result the value of the loan may exceed half of the value of the fund. The trustees clearly have no direct control over the value of the assets if they fall as a result of stock market fluctuations. In these circumstances the SFO should take a lenient view and not require a reduction in the loan to bring it within its guidelines as a result of the fall in value. The case should certainly be made that the situation has only come about through circumstances outside the direct control of the trustees and probably ameliorated within a relatively short time. The second point is not likely to find favour with the SFO. If one member has left taking a transfer value or another has retired and taken retirement benefits, both of them being from that part of the fund invested other than in a loan to an employer, then if because of the reduced value of the assets, the loan now exceeds the 50% limit, the trustees will have no option but to reduce the loan.

Frequency

5.11   JOM 58(11) mentions that employer's contributions should not be lent back with such frequency as to suggest that a SSAS which is being presented as funded is in reality an unfunded or partly unfunded scheme. This does not mean that the trustees may not go on lending to the employer on a regular basis each year, making a repeat loan for the same amount every time a contribution is paid, although care is needed here because JOM 109(14)(iii) contains a warning that funds should not lodge with the employer for longer than is necessary. What the SFO is looking to stop is a succession of loans made at the full 50% value of the assets.

5.12 The following simple illustration of loans made on the same day as each contribution should help to clarify matters.

			Example A		Example B	
Date of Contribution	Amount of Contribution	Value of Fund	Loan to Employer	Repaid	Loan to Employer	Repaid
1.1.87	£20,000	£20,000	£10,000	31.12.87	£10,000	31.12.87
1.1.88	£20,000	£45,000	£10,000	31.12.88	£22,000	31.12.88
1.1.89	£20,000	£70,000	£10,000	31.12.89	£35,000	31.12.89
1.1.90	£20,000	£100,000	£10,000	31.12.90	£50,000	31.12.90

In Example A there should be no objection by the SFO to the series of loans provided they meet all the usual criteria. However, in Example B 50% of the fund is being lent every year and the SFO would maintain the SSAS is partly unfunded and such loans should cease. It is also likely to lay down the condition that no future loans can be made unless the SFO is approached first with proposals for another loan. It is not likely that an objection would be made by the SFO in Example B until at least three loans at 50% had been made as there would be no pattern of regularity established until that time.

Purpose

5.13 There is no other area of loans to employers which lead to more contention with the SFO than their purpose. JOM 58(11) does not spell out what is an acceptable purpose other than loans must be 'commercially reasonable'. However it was established early on that loans must be for proper business purposes i.e. the money must be used by the company for the furtherance of its trade. In fact the regulations use the phrase 'utilised for the purposes of the employer's business' and JOM 109(14)(V) makes the general point that loans should not be made unless the trustees would be prepared to lend the same amount on the same terms to an unconnected party of comparable standing. Utilisation of a loan on purchasing fixed assets, stock, buildings, on developing land by a building company are all acceptable purposes. The SFO has made it plain that using a loan to purchase luxury items, e.g. yachts, or assets which a scheme member may use, e.g. residential property, or to lend on to scheme members or to purchase assets which if owned by the trustees themselves would be unacceptable is not acceptable. JOM 109 states that loans should not be used for purely speculative purposes such as the purchase of shares or other investments, although a holding company may use a loan to make or manage investments on its trading subsidiaries where it owns 51% or more of the shares. There is a very wide area of acceptable and unacceptable purposes despite the regulations and the JOMs and in the middle is a grey area too.

5.14   One would think cars would be acceptable, but if they involve private use at all the loan is likely to be objected to by the SFO. Commercial vehicles would be all right. Re-scheduling the company's finances often means taking out a loan to rationalise or re-organise the company's existing financial commitments. The SFO is likely to ask what those existing commitments were and, if they included a loan whose purpose is unacceptable, then the further loan would be unacceptable too.

5.15   It is no good recording the purpose of the loan in the loan document as 'business purposes', 'operating capital', 'cash flow' or informing the SFO that it is for such general purposes. The SFO wishes to know the precise purpose of the loan or on what it was specifically expended. The SFO is aware that companies have cash flow problems which are either seasonal because of the nature of their trade or perennial, but it is most likely to look at the cash flow problem critically perhaps after consulting the company's tax district. It is no good maintaining the company has a cash flow problem if its accounts show otherwise or if the loan was made in January to a retailing company whose main profits are derived from the Christmas trade! A succession of loans for cash flow purposes is also likely to meet with resistance from the SFO on the lines that the company should by now have sorted out its cash flow problems and not be relying on its pension scheme to keep bailing it out. If the company is short of funds from which to pay its directors, then a loan from the trustees to enable them to pay the directors will not be acceptable.

5.16   If the trustees make a loan whose purpose the SFO finds unacceptable, then it is most likely to have to be repaid if the scheme's continued approval is not to be prejudiced or if approval is to be granted.

5.17   It is always open to the SFO to check later with the inspector of taxes how the loan was actually expended. If the inspector of taxes is aware of how the loan was spent and the SFO finds out that it is different to what it has been told, then the trustees would be in trouble unless there is a very good reason for spending the loan differently. If for some reason a company changes its mind how it uses the loan, then it is best to inform the SFO in time.

Rate of interest

5.18   JOM 58 does not mention the rate of interest the SFO expects to be paid on loans to employers. JOM 58(11) says these loans must be 'on commercially reasonable terms'. To be commercial, the SFO has said that the rate of interest must be at least 3% above the Clearing Bank Base Rate (CBBR) at the time the loan was made. This is widely known as CBBR + 3% and has been in operation since 1980. The rate was confirmed in July 1984 following the PQ raised about the SFO's changes in practice on SSASs. The regulations refer to a commercial rate of interest applying, but do not specify the rate. However, JOM 109 confirms that CBBR + 3% is the acceptable rate.

5.19   The rate of interest can be expressed as a straight percentage or as the lending rate of a particular lender, but it should be ensured that whatever this rate is, it is equivalent to or greater than CBBR + 3%.

5.20   It is possible for loans to be made to employers at less than CBBR + 3%, but the SFO will require evidence that such a rate, for example CBBR + 2% would be generally available to the employer for the same purpose from other lending sources. The trustees will need to produce something in writing from a bank or other lending source to this effect.

5.21   It is almost self-evident that loans cannot be made interest-free to employers, but there are good reasons for the SFO finding this unacceptable. Firstly, the employer would be enjoying a commercial advantage which could not be obtained elsewhere. Secondly, the trustees would not be acting in the best interest of the beneficiaries in not securing a reasonable rate of return on their investment. JOM 109(14)(V) emphasises the point that interest on loans must be charged and paid.

5.22   If the SFO finds the rate of interest on a loan below its guidelines it will almost certainly seek an amendment to the rate of interest to increase it to an acceptable level. If the loan has been made interest-free the SFO's line is likely to be harsher and could involve refusal to approve the scheme or even withdrawal of approval.

Deduction of tax

5.23   When the employer pays interest on the loan to the trustees it would normally deduct tax and account for it to the Inland Revenue [*section 348*]. The trustees being exempt from tax may then claim repayment of the tax suffered if the SSAS has been approved. However, if the loan is for less than a year the interest may be paid gross by the employer. This saves the trustees the trouble of reclaiming tax and it is also very useful to them when tax cannot be reclaimed until approval has been granted if loans are made in the meantime. The interest on loans of one year or more in duration must, however, be paid under deduction of tax.

5.24   The advantages of loans of less than one year have to be carefully considered, however, because there is legislation in force to frustrate the advantage of a series of loans being made with interest paid gross for periods of less than one year. This is a matter mainly for inspectors of taxes, but it should not be overlooked that the scheme's approval may be prejudiced if a series of short loans can be shown to be a device to get round the deduction of tax from interest using the pension scheme as a vehicle to achieve it. It would have to be shown that the series of short loans do not amount to an overall contract for a long period for lending to the employer. Renewals of the same loan after 364 days or less therefore need to be considered with care, particularly in the light of JOM 109(14)(iii). The JOM explains that it is not acceptable to make a series of 364 day loans just to enable interest thereon to be paid gross when in reality there is no intention of repaying the loan for a number of years.

Liquidity

5.25   As with any other type of investment the trustees need to take their imminent cash needs into account when making a loan. JOM 58(12) mentions that the making of a loan should not be inconsistent with the need to purchase annuities. The trustees are limited to lending no more than 50% of the fund to an employer, so in setting the date for repayment of the loans they need to look at when the SSAS will need to pay any benefits and whether those benefits can be paid from the remainder of the fund if the loan continues beyond then. If there is only one member in the scheme or the other assets are fixed and not readily realisable for cash, the SFO generally expects the loan to end about a year before retirement benefits are due to be paid. This would allow a reasonable period for any action to be taken to recover the loan should there be any default.

5.26 This leads to the conclusion that open ended loans to employers, for example repayable on demand, are unlikely to find favour with the SFO. There is not only the possibility that they may never be repaid, but the SFO is likely to seek a definite repayment date sometime before retirement benefits are due to be paid. It would be difficult to argue for the acceptability of a loan without a repayment date and such a condition may have to be accepted for a loan already made in order to preserve the scheme's approval or to ensure that approval is granted. The regulations not only state that loans must be for a fixed period but also that the amount lent will become immediately repayable if it is required to pay benefits which have become due.

5.27 Loans can be made for short periods of a few months or for much longer. There is no specific limit, only the liquidity consideration will eventually limit the length of a loan and funds should not lodge with the employer for a longer period than is necessary (see paragraph 5.11 above). Therefore they can be for several years. A longer loan may well be useful to an employer to enable the repayments to be spread over the whole period or, if it is more convenient, to repay the whole loan at the end of the period. The employer's cash flow circumstances will clearly dictate when and how the repayments are made.

Security and default

5.28 The SFO currently has no requirement as to security. This is a matter for the trustees of the SSAS.

5.29 The minimum rate of interest CBBR + 3% applies to both secured and unsecured loans. The SFO has never sought a differing rate of interest on either type of loan and this is confirmed in JOM 109(14)(IV). However, if the trustees make a secured loan to the employer at less than CBBR + 3%, then the evidence from a bank required by the SFO (see paragraph 5.20 above) should make it clear that the bank's terms are based on a similar secured loan being made to the employer.

5.30 It has become increasingly apparent of late that the SFO has tightened its attitude to loans made to employers in financial difficulties particularly where later the employer goes into liquidation or receivership and there is no prospect of the repayment of the loan. Such loans may eventually be written off, but the question arises as to whether the loan should have been made by the trustees in the first place? Indeed, JOM 109(14)(V) contains a warning that loans made solely to keep an ailing business afloat or to employers who are technically insolvent could lead to the scheme being considered by the SFO as not being properly administered and in such situations the scheme could lose its approved status. Was it a prudent investment on their part bearing in mind that as trustees of a SSAS, they would have been only too aware of the company's financial position? This raises the question of their fiduciary capacity to act in the best interest of the members of the scheme which is a point made in JOM 109(14)(V). There may well be instances where a loan had been made to the company which later faced liquidation. To reduce its debts and obtain bank borrowings the company wanted the trustees to write-off the loan before repayment was due as there was no prospect of its repayment, but the SFO would take the view that the fact that the SSAS had been prepared to lend money to help prop up an ailing company was an aspect of the SSAS administration it regarded as prejudicial to continuing approval. The SFO could further insist that should the loan be written-off, the release of the debt would be a payment to the employer liable to tax under *section 601(1)(2)*. This is a tricky area for advisers who may not be aware of the financial position of the company at the time even if they are kept informed by the other trustees regarding scheme investments.

5.31　The majority of loans to employers are unsecured and it is not uncommon for the employer to get into difficulties in meeting the repayments. One way round this is to renew the loan for a further period, but the trustees have to watch that they are acting in the best interests of the members and that benefit payments are not imminent. There is nothing in principle to prevent loans being renewed, but the SFO will need some convincing where the employer is in financial difficulties. A renewal will be acceptable to the SFO after the interest due on the original loan has been repaid, but as stated in JOM 109(14)(VI) the SFO will not agree to a loan being rolled over more than twice in the future. Some unsecured loans do in fact have guarantors, so if the repayment cannot be met the trustees should ask for the guarantee to be honoured. But what if the employer cannot pay back the loan? Supposing it goes into liquidation. Very often the loan has to be written-off by the trustees and the member's benefits are consequently reduced. However, the SFO may take a tough line particularly where the money was lent in the full knowledge that the employer was in financial trouble. It will probably want to know what action has been taken by the trustees with the liquidator or receiver to recover the capital outstanding and interest accrued thereon. Even if the employer has not gone into liquidation, the SFO will insist on the trustees taking appropriate steps to recover the capital and interest. It is not only possible for the SFO to take action under *section 601(1)(2)* as already mentioned. The SFO may insist on the debt being deducted from the lump sum benefit payable to all members. This area is fraught with problems for trustees and solutions acceptable to the SFO may not necessarily be the same for each SSAS.

Documentation

5.32 The SFO expects all loans to employers to be documented, but there is no set format. In fact the regulations lay down that they must be documented and also prescribe what conditions must be included (see paragraph 5.33 below). Many practitioners nonetheless have their own standard form for loans incorporating the basic details required by the SFO. The SFO will find the circumstances unacceptable if there is no loan document at all and that in turn will cause approval problems. A simple trustees' resolution will suffice provided it shows the date of the loan, the amount, the borrower, the rate of interest and the date of repayment. The purpose of the loan need not be recorded in the resolution or loan document provided the SFO is informed of the purpose when the documentation is sent. Renewals should be documented in similar fashion. A specimen loan document may be found at Appendix 21.

5.33 The regulations in prescribing the conditions to be included in the loan document make it clear that these must also include provisions for earlier repayment of the loan if the conditions are breached, the borrower ceases business or becomes insolvent and to enable benefits which have become due to be paid. The regulations provide detailed definitions of the circumstances in which the borrower is deemed to have become insolvent. These circumstances include where the borrower has been adjudged bankrupt, or has died and the estate is being administered in accordance with an order under *section 421, IA 1986*, or, where the borrower is a company, a winding-up order or administration order has been made a voluntary winding-up resolution has been passed or a receiver appointed. Because of the differences in the legal systems of Northern Ireland and Scotland compared with England and Wales, the regulations provide separate definitions for insolvency in Northern Ireland and Scotland as appropriate.

5.34 Unless the SFO has specifically asked to be informed of all loans on a SSAS, the loan documentation for loans made up to 5 August 1991 need only be presented to the SFO when investment details generally are supplied. This is usually at the time of the triennial actuarial valuation or when the SFO asks for investment details, often at the commencement of a scheme before it is approved. Thus if a loan is one of the investments detailed in the actuarial valuation, the loan documentation will be requested by the SFO. There is a stock form SF192 which the SFO asks to be completed with details of each loan (Appendix 22) and sent with the loan document. The various details requested on this form have been covered in this chapter. It is quite possible if short-term loans are made and repaid between actuarial valuation for them to escape the SFO's notice. This will however change in future. The regulations require that loans to employers made after 5 August 1991 should be reported to the SFO at the time they are made. There is a prescribed form for this purpose SF7013 (Appendix 23) and the completed form and a copy of the loan agreement should be sent to the SFO within 90 days of the loan being made under the reporting requirements (see paragraph 3.72 below).

Chapter 6

Investment in property and land

Introduction

6.1   The facility for trustees to invest in property and land, very often purchased from and leased back to the employer, is another major selling point and common feature of SSASs. Property and land are not, however, without problems so far as the SFO is concerned and investments therein can lead to considerable contention with that office. For simplicity reasons in this chapter reference will be made in the main to property and only land is mentioned where the considerations are quite different.

6.2   The SFO's guidelines on property investments are set out in JOM 58(13) in very broad terms. These guidelines were further delineated in the early 1980s at meetings with the APT and re-iterated as the SFO's policy following the PQ on SSASs raised in July 1984. The regulations and JOM 109 set out the rules and guidelines from 5 August 1991. With regard to JOM 58(13), there is no hard and fast 'no go' area laid down regarding property. The trustees may invest in land or buildings both freehold and leasehold, as they see fit provided tax avoidance is not the objective or the scheme's cash needs are not affected if annuities have to be purchased. The question of the use by members of such investments is hardly alluded to in JOM 58, but it soon became clear that the SFO was opposed to SSASs owning residential and holiday accommodation because of its potential use by members. There are numerous aspects of property regarding its acquisition, nature, use etc, which will be dealt with in turn.

SFO's basic requirements for all types of property and land

6.3   There is no requirement at present to notify the SFO of the acquisition of property before 5 August 1991. When the SFO learns of a property acquired prior to 5 August either by production of a list of investments or disclosure via an actuarial valuation, it will continue to ask for some basic information, e.g. date of purchase, the name and address of the vendor, the price, the name and address of the tenant or occupant, and for a valuation of the property and the rent payable. This is usually to be provided along with other details on the stock form SF191 (Appendix 21). For transactions from 5 August 1991 see paragraphs 6.48–6.50 below.

6.4   The date of purchase is required to ascertain whether the trustees had sufficient assets in the fund at that time to enable them to make the purchase. It may also be required to establish if the property was acquired before or after the scheme was set up and sometimes evidence of purchase may be required in the form of the transfer document or conveyance itself.

6.5   The name and address of the vendor is all important in establishing whether the property was purchased at arm's length. An acquisition from someone or an organisation not at arm's length is going to be looked at by the SFO more closely to establish that an open market value was actually paid. This is where the question of the valuation becomes relevant. If a property is purchased from a totally independent third party or at an auction then a valuation is not required by the SFO. The price paid, in these circumstances, is clearly its open market value. However, if the vendor and the trustees are connected in any way at all, an independent professional valuation will be required by the SFO to substantiate the price paid as being the open market value. The connection for these purposes is very wide as any vendor will be connected if he/she/it is also a trustee, scheme member or director or shareholder of the employer.

6.6   If the vendor is a company, then it is connected if it participates in the scheme or is part of the same group of companies to which the employer belongs or its shareholders/directors are trustees or scheme members.

Valuations

6.7   The reason for establishing the open market value of a property is basically to demonstrate that tax avoidance, e.g. specially CGT, is not involved. The temptation to a connected vendor may be to sell to the trustees at an undervalue and thus avoid CGT on the disposal. The SFO would see this as using the SSAS to achieve tax avoidance and obviously such a transaction would put the scheme's approval in jeopardy. An independent professional valuation is therefore necessary and its absence would only alert the SFO's suspicions that an undervalue has been paid. Even where valuations have been produced, it is well known that the SFO has recourse to the district valuer to check the value.

6.8   Investment in property and land

It may be possible for the trustees to pay the difference in value to the vendor if the district valuer maintains the open market value is more, but this will very much depend on the circumstances of the case and on major negotiations with the SFO.

6.8   Similar problems may be experienced where an overvalue has been paid. Here the SFO is likely to maintain there has been a leakage of scheme funds by the trustees to a connected party. This may be a very prejudicial transaction if the vendor happens to be a scheme member. Furthermore, by paying over the odds the trustees could hardly have acted in the best interests of the beneficiaries. The trustees may be able to get their money back, but would the SFO see this act by itself as a cleaning up of the scheme? Each case is likely to be contentious and treated on its merits by the SFO.

6.9   It is important that the valuation supports the price paid by the trustees at the time of the acquisition. Thus, although the valuation may be carried out sometime after the acquisition, either because the trustees omitted to do so at the time or because the SFO has insisted on having a valuation, the valuation must state that at the date of purchase in the valuer's view it was worth the price paid for it. The SFO is not likely to accept a belated valuation with a value as at the belated date and it is likely to make enquiries of the district valuer if the independent value differs from the price paid. Sometimes, trustees obtain valuations in advance of the acquisition and for various reasons the purchase is delayed. The longer the gap between the valuation and the date of purchase the more likely the open market value may have changed and such a situation is likely to precipitate questions from the SFO.

The terms of occupancy

6.10   There are several reasons for the SFO wanting to know who is occupying or will occupy the property and the rent payable. It needs to be demonstrated that the occupier or tenant is someone other than a scheme member or a relative of a scheme member. If a scheme member or relative is occupying the property and even paying rent the scheme would not be solely providing relevant benefits and its approval would be prejudiced. Having established the occupier or tenant is not a member or relative, then the SFO is interested in establishing the length of the lease and what rent is payable by the occupant whether it is an independent third party or a connected person. The rent payable in both circumstances should be commercial, but the SFO accepts that where the occupant is totally at arm's length the terms of any lease/rental arrangement between the trustees and the occupant are bound to be commercial and on open market terms. In such situations the SFO does not usually ask for a copy of the lease and for an independent valuation of the rent. However, where property is occupied by the participating company, as leasebacks is a specially attractive feature of SSAS, as well as by any other company connected with the trustees or the participating company, the SFO looks more closely to establish that a commercial rent is being paid just the same as it looks at the acquisition from someone not at arm's length. In such cases the SFO will ask for an independent valuation of the rent that is also required. It may, however, be possible where the company has taken over the lease from a previous arm's length-tenant at the same rent to avoid a valuation of the rent, as the rent being paid in this situation can be shown to be commercial. In addition the SFO may ask for a copy of the lease possibly to check that the rent payable thereunder is at least that substantiated by the independent valuation. The SFO is also likely to check the length of the lease, any premiums paid for it (which again would have to be supported by an independent valuation if the parties are not at arm's length) and the date from which the rent commences. The latter point is quite important as the SFO will wish to ascertain, where a property was occupied some time ago but where the lease is currently dated, that arrears of rent are accounted for to the trustees and that any valuation of the rent applies at the date the rent commenced to be payable.

6.11 Problems are going to arise with the SFO if no formal lease/tenancy agreement exists or the rent being paid in the SFO's view is less than a commercial one particularly where the parties are not at arm's length. It is always best to get these arrangements formalised at the time to avoid problems with the SFO and they must be formalised to comply with the regulations for reporting property transactions that take place after 5 August 1991. There will, however, be circumstances where this cannot be done, for instance where the trustees have purchased property which they wish to renovate or refurbish before letting, but the SFO may still be looking to see if the trustees are getting a reasonable return on their investment as of course they should, in their fiduciary capacity, act in the best interests of the scheme members. A low return in terms of rent payable may mean the rent is less than commercial or even if it can be justified, the SFO may suspect that the situation is contrived. If in the SFO's view the rent is less than the commercial rent, it may make the point that the company, if it is the tenant, is enjoying a commercial advantage. Such an argument could be difficult to counter and it may be best to agree to a higher rent to preserve or obtain the scheme's approval. If no rent is being paid it may be possible to pay any arrears due at a commercial rate, but each case is likely to be looked at on its merits and there is no easy answer in this area apart from the need to avoid the problems in the first place.

6.12 *Investment in property and land*

Liquidity

6.12 Another reason for the SFO wanting to know the name of the occupant of property is the question of liquidity. It was mentioned earlier that the scheme's cash needs should not be prejudiced by an investment in property if annuities have to be purchased. JOM 58(13) states that 'investments in land and buildings may be a good long-term investment . . . where the members are many years from retirement, but questions would need to be asked if the property appeared to be an important part of the employer's own commercial premises and thus potentially difficult to realise'. Thus the SFO may see problems where the major asset of a SSAS is a property leased to the company or the property is jointly owned.

6.13 There is no basic objection to the trustees investing 100% of the fund in property and that property being leased back to the participating company, provided the lease is on commercial terms. However, the trustees need to take into account the date when they will be required to realise their assets to provide retirement benefits for the members. If a member, or perhaps the sole member, is due to retire in two to three years time, the trustees must have cash available at that time at least to provide any cash lump sum and to pay a pension, and also to provide the cash to purchase an annuity to secure the pension, although the latter can be deferred for up to five years. It is unlikely that in such a time span there will be sufficient cash resources to do this, so the trustees are faced with the problem of realising their major asset which may take time and if occupied by the company as its main trading base could create further problems. The SFO will enquire into such situations and it needs to be assured that there will be sufficient cash in the fund at the appropriate time to provide benefits. It may be that the members do not actually propose to retire on reaching their normal retirement ages as controlling directors often continue in service after that age. However, the SFO is still likely in these circumstances to regard the appropriate time to provide benefits as being the normal retirement age because cash may still be needed from that date onwards to pay benefits.

6.14 Over the years the SFO has applied a general rule of thumb of five years i.e. if scheme members are due to retire within five years of a property purchase the SFO may find the purchase unacceptable if there are no other assets or other assets are not likely to be sufficient in quantity to meet the needs of an imminent retirement. It is therefore always best to acquire property many years before retirement and to ensure that when benefits become due there are sufficient easily realisable assets in the scheme or that there will be no protracted problems with realising the property itself.

6.15   Joint ownership of property by trustees may give rise to liquidity problems. There should be no basic objections from the SFO to the trustees owning property jointly, either with the participating company or a third party providing the SFO's usual requirements are met. However, joint ownership with the members or partnerships of which the members are partners is not acceptable. It may be that the trustees do not have sufficient funds at present to purchase the whole, so they purchase a half now and the remaining half later or effect the acquisition in a series of tranches. However, where the trustees' interest is a joint one at the time when they come to realise the property, problems may arise. It could be that delay will occur in selling because it is more difficult to sell property in joint ownership. In addition the price the trustees get for the property could be less than the proportionate value of the whole property. The reduced price will reflect the difficulties of joint ownership. These are aspects the trustees will need to take into account and may have to defend if the SFO questions the acceptability of jointly owned property.

6.16   Another aspect which touches on liquidity is whether scheme property is subject to a mortgage or legal charge. Clearly, if the trustees have borrowed money and secured it on the property by a mortgage or legal charge, they need to make arrangements to pay off the borrowings to release the property from the mortgage or legal charge before they sell it. This is not to say that they cannot sell a property subject to a mortgage or legal charge, but where they do problems may arise with the sale and it may certainly affect the price.

Commercial property

6.17   Under this heading is included all commercial premises such as offices, shops and land and industrial premises such as factories, warehouses etc. but does not include agricultural property and land, forestry and woodlands which will be covered separately.

6.18   This type of property is by far the most common and is a popular investment of SSASs particularly as it allows participating companies to rent scheme property, albeit on a commercial basis, and to obtain tax relief on payments of rent and allows the trustees to receive the rent tax free. Providing all the transactions relating to the property are undertaken on an arm's length basis and there is no residential accommodation involved there should be no problems with the SFO.

6.19 *Investment in property and land*

6.19 There are matters, however, which can arise over the change of use of the property which can create problems with the SFO and which the trustees therefore need to consider carefully. If a property being purchased has some residential element currently unoccupied and which is being changed to office or some other commercial use, then it should be acceptable to the SFO as there is no likelihood of it being used by a scheme member or as residential accommodation in future. The costs of refurbishment would be borne by the trustees from the assets of the scheme. The trustees may also see a particular investment in property or land currently unoccupied as a good one for the scheme especially if they can obtain planning permission for change of use or development as this could increase the value of their investment considerably. Having obtained planning permission the trustees could refurbish the property or develop the land from scheme funds, but there are several aspects they need to bear in mind if difficulties with the SFO are to be avoided. Straight refurbishment should be acceptable if the nature of the property remains commercial. Development of the trustees' land to build (say) a factory or warehouse which is leased to a third party or the company (on a commercial basis) should also be acceptable apart from industrial units qualifying for industrial buildings allowance (see paragraphs 6.39–6.42 below), but the questions of who pays for the development and whether the development is residential may attract the SFO's attention. If the principal company or an associate is a building company and it develops the land or it borrows from the trustees to finance the development costs difficulties can arise. The SFO may find these aspects unacceptable particularly if they are not done at arm's length and it may deem the company and/or the trustees are enjoying a commercial advantage. To avoid any problem in this area it is best to clear the arrangement with the SFO in advance. This is also the case where land is to be developed by building residential property even if the property is to be sold later on the open market and there is no question of the scheme members or their relatives having the use of such property. Indeed, repeated transactions of this nature, or frequent purchases and sales of property by the trustees may attract the attention of the inspector of taxes and whilst not prejudicing the scheme's approval may involve the trustees in trading (which is dealt with in Chapter 8) and may result in having to pay tax on such activities.

6.20 Finally, the increase in value of property and land brought about by obtaining planning permission and development can lead to serious overfunding problems. This will not necessarily entail the application of the surplus legislation to a SSAS, but if the scheme is approved and the actuary recommends a refund to the employer then the 40% tax charge would apply to any refund.

Residential property

6.21 For convenience, holiday accommodation is included in this paragraph because the SFO's requirements are similar for both types of property. Right from the issue of JOM 58 the SFO has made it clear that residential property and holiday accommodation are unacceptable investments for SSASs. The reason for this is that such property could be used by the members or their relatives and therefore the scheme would not be solely providing relevant benefits. It matters not that the residential accommodation may be let to a member at a fully commercial rent or to a totally independent third party and is never likely to be occupied by a scheme member. The point the SFO makes is that the potential exists for abuse and very often in correspondence on a particular scheme it mentions it does not have the resources to police this area. This policy has been adhered to quite rigidly by the SFO. It was re-iterated in reply to the PQ in July 1984 and the consultative document in 1987 made it clear the ban would appear eventually in the regulations and this has now happened.

6.22 It is probably worthwhile repeating what was published following the PQ in July 1984 (Appendix 2).

'The purchase of residential property for leasing to a director/ shareholder or to the employer will not normally be regarded as consistent with scheme approval because of the likelihood of beneficial use by or for the benefit of members.

The investment of scheme monies in the purchase of holiday cottages and the like is normally regarded as inconsistent with approval.'

6.23 It can be seen that leasing residential accommodation to the company will not escape the prohibition. Thus if the company wishes to make available a flat in London for the directors to use on business trips to the capital and the flat is leased by the trustees, the flat is an unacceptable investment. The same applies to a flat overseas even if the company requires its directors to undertake frequent foreign trips for business reasons and they use a flat owned by the trustees.

6.24 It may be possible for the trustees to give the SFO a written undertaking that accommodation acquired before 5 August 1991 will never be made available to scheme members or their relatives, although this is likely to be met with resistance by the SFO. However, if the property concerned is (say) terraced property in a poor condition or in a run-down area and occupied by third parties on fixed tenancies it is hardly likely that a director or his family would consider using the property.

6.25   Ground rents receivable from long leasehold premises occupied by third parties also should be acceptable investments prior to 5 August 1991.

6.26   What aspects would the SFO look for regarding residential/holiday accommodation? Obviously the location, any valuation, plan and lease is going to be looked at. Residential accommodation at the seaside or well-known inland holiday areas or in large cities will be unacceptable. There are other features of holiday accommodation too that may attract the SFO's attention. Short lettings are prevalent in the holiday trade although they could equally be features of student occupation. The valuation and any accompanying plan often describe the property in detail and even if part of the property contains residential accommodation the SFO's interest will be aroused.

Residential accommodation

6.27   The circumstances in which the SFO would allow residential accommodation to be an investment of a SSAS appear to be only where that accommodation is never going to be used by the members or their relatives. Thus a caretaker's flat or a flat above a shop are usually acceptable. The caretaker's flat would need to be an integral part of the whole commercial premises and the employee concerned would be required to live there to carry out the duties of the job. A good example is a builder's yard with accommodation for a caretaker or night watchman where the yard is leased to the principal company. The trustees may invest in a retail shop which is tenanted by a third party. The third party also rents the residential accommodation above the shop which is indivisible from the shop. Provided both rentals are on a commercial basis this should be acceptable to the SFO.

6.28   The regulations actually proscribe residential accommodation, and by analogy holiday accommodation also. There are exceptions for the caretaker's or night-watchman's accommodation and for a flat above a shop which are both integral and occupied by the same arm's length tenant. There is also an exception for residential property held indirectly by the trustees as investment units in a unit trust scheme provided the trustees of the unit trust scheme hold such property subject to the trusts of the SSAS.

6.29 Finally, as regards residential accommodation, there are taxation implications for the members quite apart from the implications to the scheme's tax exempt status should the SFO find such accommodation to be an asset of a SSAS. Tax liability under Schedule E may arise on a member in respect of the residential accommodation occupied by the member. The sale of the property to preserve the scheme's tax exempt status will not obviate any previous Schedule E liability.

Agricultural property and land

6.30 The considerations regarding property generally already covered earlier in this chapter apply equally to agricultural property and land, but there are other aspects, particularly as regards agricultural land problems that can arise with the SFO. The acquisition by the trustees of agricultural property and land and its leaseback to a third party or to the principal company at a commercial rent is usually acceptable to the SFO. However, leasing back the property and/or land, even at a fully commercial rent, to a partnership of which a member is a partner or to a member's unincorporated business is not acceptable. The reason for this is the same as for the SFO's objection to residential accommodation as the sole provision of relevant benefits test is not met because the scheme is providing a benefit to the member other than a retirement benefit. There may not be a property involved, but the member has the use of land. Another contentious area may be where the farmhouse is part of the scheme assets or the member's residence is adjacent to the agricultural land. The SFO may pick this up from any valuation or location map supplied on the acquisition and commence to ask various questions. If the trustees have purchased the farmhouse then it will be unacceptable if occupied by a member or relative. The farmhouse needs to be occupied by a third party on an arm's length tenancy to be acceptable. It is not unusual for the land to be leased back to the principal company and for the member to occupy the adjacent farmhouse either owned by the member or the company. This ought to be perfectly acceptable, but the SFO may take the view that the member in one way or another has the use of the scheme asset, perhaps as an amenity. It is not unknown for agricultural land to consist of rough grazing, coppices etc. which could be used by a member to keep horses or on which to entertain friends to a rough shoot. Amenity rights are covered in more detail in paragraphs 6.31 and 6.32 below, but suffice it to say there is a need to be aware that the acquisition of agricultural land is not always straightforward and personal use by members in all its varieties needs constantly to be borne in mind to avoid the pitfalls.

Forestry and woodlands

6.31 Once again investment in these areas is usually acceptable, although it is possible in certain circumstances for the trustees to be considered as trading. The aspects of this type of investment which will attract the attention of the SFO are any amenity rights which attach to the land e.g. hunting, shooting and fishing. Rivers, lakes and bothies are bound to show up on location maps submitted to the SFO either with valuations or leases. The SFO will wish to establish if any hunting, shooting or fishing rights exist, who has them and what the trustees receive for them. The point to bear in mind is that these rights must not be held by a member or a relative even if a fully commercial price is paid for them. The SFO will, as mentioned before, take the view that the member is enjoying the use of scheme assets which is inconsistent with approval.

6.32 It is as well to remember with regard to amenity rights that other types of property and land may attract such rights or they may provide recreational or leisure facilities. For instance, a commercial property with a river frontage may have mooring facilities. It will need to be demonstrated to the SFO that there is no use by a member of the scheme assets in this connection or at least that use by a member is incidental with that of the public at large and that the member pays for any such use on the same basis as the public.

Property abroad

6.33 In view of the SFO's attitude to residential and holiday accommodation, any type of residential property abroad will not be an acceptable investment of a SSAS. Villas on the Mediterranean are clearly unacceptable and so too will be a flat abroad, as mentioned in paragraph 6.13 above, leased to the company and used by the company director on business trips abroad. But what about commercial and industrial property abroad? These ought to be acceptable to the SFO, but practitioners may need to justify them in the first place. However, after 1992 there should be no objection to investment in commercial and industrial property at least in the European Community.

Clearance in advance

6.34 It has always been possible to approach the SFO in advance of a particular investment being made to ascertain if it would be acceptable. Such an approach regarding property can be very useful where there are doubts about certain aspects and in the event it can save much time

78

and cost later if the investment has to be disposed of on the instruction of the SFO because it is unacceptable. There are drawbacks however in making this approach which are mainly time constraints. A quick answer to a proposal on the phone is unlikely unless the circumstances are clearcut. It is much more likely that such an approach will meet with a request for the proposal to be put in writing with the result that a delay will occur in getting a reply because of the SFO's work load. Experience has shown that it takes about two months to obtain a written reply to a property proposal and that may be too long if an offer must be made quickly for a good property investment. However, if there are doubts about a particular investment the only sure way of avoiding problems, particularly in obtaining approval for a SSAS, is to seek the SFO's clearance in advance. Detailed information should be given as failure to do so will probably lead to a request for further details before a decision can be given causing additional delays.

Sales

6.35 The trustees of a SSAS are usually empowered to buy and sell property and during the course of a scheme's existence they may do this on a number of occasions. They will need to watch that the frequency of property transactions or the development of land in their ownership does not lead to these transactions being treated as trading by the Inland Revenue (Chapter 8). Whilst such a situation would not necessarily lead to the loss of the scheme's tax exempt status, nonetheless it could mean that property transactions within the scheme are taxable which is a distinct loss of the tax advantage an approved scheme enjoys. It is not possible to have hard and fast rules on the circumstances that will attract the Inland Revenue's attention and lead to a taxable trading situation. The Inland Revenue will not pronounce on a situation in advance, but only after it has happened. It is therefore best to be aware that frequent purchases and sales of property at a profit could cause problems in this area. Furthermore, whilst it is laudable for the trustees to acquire derelict land, spend time and money obtaining planning permission to develop it, then carry out the development and sell it at a substantial profit, they should avoid the possibility that they may be trading and at the same time allay any suspicion on the part of the SFO that there is no duality of purpose in their motives for the development.

6.36 Another aspect of sales of property relevant to its development is where a sale at a substantial profit can lead to a surplus within the scheme. The surplus may also be fortuitous in that the value of land may have risen considerably during the period of its ownership, perhaps because of the removal of a planning blight in the area. At the next triennial valuation when the actuary considers the land's current value, even if it is not to be sold, he may consider that such an increase may well have outstripped the previous assumptions for increases in the value of the scheme's assets. The trustees will need to be guided by actuarial advice in these circumstances, but it must be borne in mind that if any surplus is to be repaid to the employer it will be subject to the 40% tax charge if the SSAS is approved or the SFO will insist on approving the scheme before a refund is made.

6.37 The details of the sale of a property are not likely to attract the attention of the SFO if the sale is to an unconnected third party. However, if the sale is to a scheme member, relative of a member or the company then because the transaction would not be at arm's length the SFO will usually ask for certain details, though not as many as on the acquisition. For the position regarding sales of property to members from 5 August 1991, paragraph 6.48 below should be referred to.

6.38 The SFO will want to know the date of sale, the sale price, the name of the purchaser and have a copy of an independent professional valuation of the asset to support the sale price. This is obviously to establish that the price being paid to the trustees is the open market value and to guard against a member perhaps acquiring the property at less than its true value. On the other hand if the property is sold at a price in excess of its open market value it would not only have avoided CGT on the disposal by the trustees, but established a higher acquisition value for the purchaser. Both instances could lead to problems with the SFO and prejudice the scheme's approval, although it ought to be possible to remedy the situation by the purchaser paying the trustees or the trustees repaying the purchaser the difference between the open market value and the purchase price.

Industrial buildings allowances

6.39 The investment in industrial property and units can be particularly tax efficient because of the industrial buildings allowances (IBAs) that are available to the owner of the freehold of such property. IBAs have been phased out in recent years, but they are still available in development zones, so whilst the opportunities to invest in this area have diminished there are nonetheless still substantial tax savings available. However, before describing the arrangements that would involve the trustees of

SSASs it is well known that the SFO is aware of the tax avoidance device underlying the arrangements and this can create serious problems.

6.40 There have been several articles in accountancy magazines over the years describing how the involvement of a SSAS can achieve large tax savings using IBAs. This is how it works. The company purchases an industrial building or a site on which it constructs an industrial building. The company could claim tax relief in respect of the IBAs available up to 100%. The trustees purchase the leasehold interest in the building from the company. The company would not then suffer a clawback of the tax relief it has obtained. This effectively avoids a corporation tax balancing charge. There are variations on this which still achieve the same results. Instead of the company, the owners of the freehold could be the directors or scheme members. The industrial building is then let on a long lease to the trustees with a further sub-letting running almost concurrently to the company. If a claim for IBAs were then made by the freeholder no corporation tax balancing charge would arise.

6.41 In the normal commercial world such an arrangement without using a pension scheme as the intermediary would be generally acceptable to the Inland Revenue. But problems arise with the SFO if a pension scheme is involved in the scheme. The nub of the issue is that the scheme is being used as a vehicle to achieve the tax avoidance. The SFO would therefore find the arrangements objectionable and not consistent with approval under *section 590(2)(a)*, as the pension scheme could not be said to be *bona fide* established for the sole provision of relevant benefits. Thus the arrangements would not only fail to pass the '*bona fide* established' test, but would also fall foul of the guidelines in JOM 58(13 and 14) regarding tax avoidance. Any SSAS with such a feature would almost certainly fail to obtain approval or, if it was already approved, have its approval withdrawn from the date the claim for IBAs was made providing it was not made before 17 March 1987 [*section 591B(1)*]. If the claim for IBAs was made before 17 March 1987 and the trustees acquired their interest before then, approval could not be withdrawn before 17 March 1987.

6.42 It may be possible to negotiate a way out of the problem with the SFO in conjunction with the local inspector of taxes. Possibilities are for the IBA claim to be withdrawn, for the company or member to pay the tax on the balancing charge which has been avoided or for the trustees to sell their leasehold interest at an open market value. This is however a rather complicated subject and close liaison with clients' tax advisers is needed if a satisfactory result is to be achieved.

'Contrived' situations

6.43 This heading covers a wide variety of situations which can occur with property and which to the SFO appear to be contrived and which suggest to the SFO that the scheme has a duality of purpose. By way of illustration suppose a SSAS is established by deed on Day 1 with an ordinary contribution of £100,000 and a special contribution of £100,000. Also on Day 1 the trustees lend back £100,000 to the company to develop land and with the remaining £100,000 they purchase a piece of land to be leased to the company and which it will develop with the loan. Even if all the necessary back-up information was supplied to the SFO at the outset, e.g. actuarial report, loan document, property and rent valuations, one would expect the SFO to have doubts about the overall position, particularly the intention behind the establishment of the scheme, and some pretty searching questions could be expected. For instance, how did a piece of land come to be worth exactly £100,000 to fit in with the contribution and loanback position? Furthermore, the purpose of the loan is going to cause problems with the SFO. This shows that in setting up a SSAS the need to avoid the suspicion that the whole thing has been contrived to achieve something other than a *bona fide* pension scheme. Long and convoluted investment arrangements involving property are bound to attract the SFO's attention and it must always be borne in mind that it does have the last word under its discretionary powers. In the end no amount of reasoning with the SFO may prevent a refusal to approve a scheme unless a particular investment is got rid of.

6.44 Another example is a scheme which has been established for some years and the last actuarial valuation was done almost three years ago. It recommended annual contributions of £50,000 p.a. The trustees wish to buy a commercial property for £500,000 and do not want to use their other assets to finance the purchase. Therefore they borrow £180,000, the company pays an annual contribution of £70,000 to the scheme, and the trustees buy a half share of the property for £250,000. There is nothing wrong with this superficially, but can the contribution of £70,000 be justified and is a half share of the property actually worth £250,000? It all looks very simple, but is there something contrived about it? Would the SFO see a duality of purpose behind the arrangements?

6.45 The trouble with many situations is that argument develops with the SFO well after the event because until 5 August 1991 there were no formal reporting arrangements regarding investments and the triennial actuarial valuation may be the starting point for a purchase some three years ago. There is a paramount need for care and to demonstrate that the prime motive for any arrangement is the provision of retirement benefits.

Remedies

6.46 There are some situations where it should be possible to come to an agreement with the SFO over a property and avoid prejudicing the scheme's approval. Difficulties in this area are, however, more likely to arise where the scheme has already been approved rather than where it is still to be approved. Advisers should also bear in mind the date when the property was acquired and what if anything the SFO had said about it on previous occasions. For instance, was the 'offending' property owned by the trustees prior to the issue of JOM 58? The case can then clearly be made that at the time the investment was made it did not offend the SFO's guidelines and should therefore remain an asset of the scheme. Similarly, if a property was included in a previous actuarial report sent to the SFO and accepted by that office either in writing or tacitly where no comment was made, then a case can be made for its retention.

6.47 Other situations may necessitate disposing of a lease to a third party instead of a member, but with residential or holiday accommodation it is almost certainly going to mean its disposal to maintain the scheme's approval. Fortunately the SFO is not so harsh as to insist on an immediate sale in every case. There will be difficulties in selling certain types of property and property in certain areas, and the trustees should be able to secure a reasonable time in which to sell them to get a decent price. It would be as well from the outset to agree the timescale with the SFO.

The position from 5 August 1991

6.48 The regulations not only ban the purchase of residential property (see paragraphs 6.21 and 6.28 above), but also ban purchases from and sales to scheme members or their relatives, including partnerships of which the members are partners, of all other types of property (*SI 1991/ 1614, reg 8(1)*) except for property already owned at 5 August 1991. The reason for this is that such transactions may be undertaken at artificial prices or involve leakage of scheme funds to members. It also brings SSASs into line with self-administered personal pension schemes. The ban on purchases from members includes property owned by the member in the previous three years and sold prior to the acquisition by the trustees. Similarly the ban extends three years beyond the sale by the trustees during which period the property must not subsequently be sold to a scheme member (*SI 1991/1614, reg 8(3)(a)(b)*).

6.49 Purchases from, or sales to, the company of property continue to be allowed providing the trustees obtain an independent professional valuation and the purchase or sale price accords with the valuation. These were the requirements of the SFO anyway under its discretionary practice prior to 5 August 1991.

6.50 The form SF7012 (Appendix 25) has to be completed under the 90 day reporting requirements (see paragraph 3.72 above) in respect of any acquisition or disposal of land and any lease from, or to, the company or associated company. The information to be supplied on the form SF7012 is basically the same as on the form SF191 (see paragraph 6.3 above). If the transaction, purchase or sale, is between connected persons a copy of an independent valuation must be supplied with the completed form. If the property is let to a connected person, e.g. the company, an independent valuation of the rental value is also required by the SFO together with a copy of the lease. As the legal process of completing leases may take some time a concession beyond the 90 day period may be allowed for production of a copy of the lease.

6.51 Finally, it is not possible to cover every conceivable form of property investment in this chapter. Of necessity only the main ones have been referred to. Those areas not covered will be few and far between and of a very specialised nature and would have to be tackled on a one-off basis with the SFO if they give rise to problems.

Chapter 7

Unquoted Shares and other Investments

Introduction

7.1 This chapter covers the various aspects which concern the SFO with ownership of shares in the employing company and in unconnected unquoted companies. It also covers non-income producing assets, commodities, futures, options and trustees' borrowings.

Shares in the employing company

Guidelines

7.2 These were set out in JOM 58(14) and need updating for legislation purposes. Thus, if the acquisition of shares or debentures in the employer, whether by subscription, bonus issue or by purchase from existing shareholders involves tax avoidance or is part and parcel of a transaction to which *section 703* may apply then the SSAS will not be approved or it may lose its tax exempt status. In addition, if IHT (formerly Capital Transfer Tax) avoidance is involved the same fate may befall the SSAS. Subsequent SFO pronouncements in this area have been via the APT, on individual schemes or following the PQ raised in July 1984. The regulations and JOM 109 contain the latest rules and guidelines. All these aspects will be covered in turn, but it is sufficient to be said at the moment that there are several hurdles to overcome before shares in the employer company can become acceptable investments of a SSAS.

Section 703 (formerly section 460, ICTA 1970)

7.3 *Part XVII, ICTA 1988*, which includes *section 703 et seq*, is concerned with countering tax avoidance. It is not intended to explain its scope. Trustees should discuss this with their professional advisers. How the subject concerns the SFO is, however, covered in detail. Any purchase of preference or ordinary shares by the trustees which would or has fallen foul of this legislation will not be an acceptable investment of a SSAS. To avoid withdrawal of approval or a refusal to approve it may be possible to seek the sale of the shares, but this will depend on the circumstances of the case and it may be difficult to find a buyer because of the restrictions on the sale of shares in unquoted companies.

7.4 There is an arrangement whereby such share transactions, either proposed or actual disposals, can be cleared with the Inland Revenue. This is very useful because it can cover transactions at the proposal stage relatively quickly and avoid later problems with the SFO if the acquisition by the trustees has gone ahead. If full details of the transaction are given to the Inland Revenue, technical division, for clearance under *section 707*, then the technical division is obliged to pronounce on the transaction within 30 days. The technical division will notify that it is satisfied that *section 703* does not apply or that it is not satisfied that *section 703* does not apply. It is important to note that only the Inland Revenue, the technical division, gives a clearance under *section 707*. Neither the SFO nor local inspectors of taxes can do so and approaches to them will only result in applicants being advised to make their application to the technical division.

7.5 When the SFO becomes aware of a holding of unquoted shares or it is asked if such a holding will be acceptable, it will ask if a *section 707* clearance has been obtained. If a clearance has been obtained, then this particular hurdle has been overcome subject to any IHT implications or other objections the SFO may have. If on the other hand a clearance has been refused then the shareholding will not be acceptable to the SFO even if it satisfies the SFO on the IHT requirements of the SFO, unless it can be shown that the tax advantage has been counteracted under *section 703(3)*. It is sound advice therefore to obtain a clearance beforehand under *section 707*, otherwise the SFO is likely to investigate the transaction itself.

7.6 Fortunately not all transactions in unquoted shares are within the scope of *section 703*. For example, it does not apply where the company concerned is not connected in any way with the trustees or the directors/ members of the SSAS, the vending shareholder is at arm's length, or the shares are an initial allotment at par. This is however a grey area and trustees should consult their tax advisers as to whether or not a clearance should be sought. The technical division is not generally known to be forthcoming about the types of transactions that do not require a clearance and on top of that SFO examiners may differ widely in their interpretation of what constitutes a connected company. It is therefore safest to assume that the shareholding in question will be looked at in detail by the SFO if the company is the principal company or a participating company or even, if it is neither of these but its directors or shareholders are connected in any way with the trustees or members of the SSAS.

Inheritance tax

7.7   JOM 58(14) simply states in relation to shareholdings in companies the possibility of IHT avoidance may be grounds for withholding a scheme's tax approval. It follows that the SFO looks at this aspect regarding all transactions in the shares of unquoted companies, not just in those connected or associated with the principal employer. The reasons for this are not hard to find. There is a very restricted market for transactions in such shares, transactions are usually between parties not at arm's length and the price paid for them may not necessarily be their open market value.

7.8   The SFO has access to the shares valuation division of the IHT office, which values shares in unquoted companies, to check the price paid. This is why it usually asks for full details of the share transaction, even if it is only at the proposal stage. The details requested on the stock form SF193 (Appendix 26) are the date of purchase, type and number of shares concerned, purchase price, name of the vendor and the relationship if any of the vendor to the trustees/directors, total issued share capital, vendor's beneficial interest prior to sale, trustees' reasons for acquiring the shares, details of any *section 707* clearance, total amount invested in loans to and shares in the company, a reasoned valuation for the share price, the company's latest accounts and details of any associated agreements with any scheme member or connected person. Transactions from 5 August 1991 are dealt with in paragraph 7.16 below.

7.9   If the SFO, after consulting the shares valuation division, is satisfied that the price paid for the shares is an open market one then the shareholding should be an acceptable investment of the SSAS having already got over the *section 703* hurdle (subject to later comments). The trouble for trustees and their advisers begins if the shares are purchased by the trustees at an over or under-value. For instance, if a shareholding is purchased by the trustees at £1 per share and the shares valuation division is of the view that they are worth £2 per share in the open market, then IHT and/or CGT may be involved in the acquisition at a lower value by the trustees. Or the trustees may be acquiring or have acquired a shareholding at more than its open market value in the opinion of the shares valuation division. In this instance the SFO could maintain that by purchasing the shares for more than they are worth, particularly if the vendor is a scheme member, there has been a leakage of scheme funds to the member which is unacceptable. Both instances will give rise to withholding approval or possibly withdrawing approval. It may be possible to negotiate with the SFO for the trustees to pay the difference in value to the vendor or for the vendor to refund the difference in value to the trustees to make the investment acceptable to the SFO. It will very much depend upon the circumstances of the case whether the SFO will adopt this route. It may simply demand that the shares be sold to preserve the scheme's approval or to obtain its approval. It is therefore doubly important to ensure the purchase price placed on the shares in an unquoted company represents their open market value.

Other factors

7.10 There are two very basic considerations to take into account however before making any approach to either the SFO or the technical division as there will be no point going through the *section 703* and IHT hurdles if the SFO cannot be satisfied on these points. They concern the value and size of the holding. The value of the holding itself or when taken together with any loans to the employer, should not be more than 50% of the value of the assets of the scheme. JOM 58 is not clear on this point and the SFO's practice in this area developed in 1980 and 1981 after JOM 58 was promulgated. Advisers became aware of the practice either from individual SSASs or from discussions between the APT and the SFO. Eventually, the SFO's practice on the point was published in 1984 following a PQ. Thus if a loan to the employer currently exists, then the size of the shareholding being purchased may need trimming to fit within the overall 50% limit.

7.11 The actual size of the holding being acquired in terms of the issued share capital in any unquoted company, whether connected or not, should be a minority holding to satisfy the SFO. If a majority holding is being acquired the SFO is unlikely to find this acceptable as the trustees would be in a position to control the company and manipulate its profits and dividends. The SFO would maintain in these circumstances that the scheme was being used as a vehicle to achieve a tax advantage and the scheme's approval would be prejudiced. Such a claim would be very difficult to counter and only a very good case would satisfy the SFO. Reduction of the holding to a minority one or its complete disposal may be the only way to preserve the scheme's approval. However, it should be possible to make a good case if the SFO was aware of the transaction previously and accepted it as satisfactory or acquiesced in the situation without commenting at all for a considerable time.

Sales

7.12 The sale of shares in unquoted companies will be of interest to the SFO because they are unlikely to be made at arm's length. Transactions in such holdings are not only restricted because of the nature of unquoted companies, but also because of the SFO's restrictions applicable from 5 August 1991. The prospective purchasers are probably going to be connected parties, e.g. the members, their relatives or the company, who may only purchase shareholdings acquired prior to 5 August 1991, unless the unquoted company is entirely unconnected in the first place. Once again the SFO will usually ask for certain details of the sale though not as many as on the acquisition.

7.13 *Section 703* may or may not be relevant as the case may be, so the trustees would need to discuss this aspect with their professional advisers. The SFO will probably want to know the date of sale, the sale price, the name of the purchaser and have a reasoned valuation of the sale price. The object is clearly to establish that the price being paid is the open market value of the shares and to ensure the purchaser is not acquiring the shares at less than their proper value.

7.14 Obviously IHT and CGT considerations come into this and the SFO may have recourse to shares valuation division to check the value attributed to the sale price. Problems can arise if an under or over-value has been paid for the shares. However, it may be possible as mentioned in paragraph 7.9 above to negotiate with the SFO for the purchaser to pay the difference in value to the trustees or for the trustees to refund the difference in value to the purchaser to preserve the continued approval of the SSAS.

The future

7.15 Advisers are aware from individual cases in the last two years or so that the SFO has been paying particular attention to the size of holdings in unquoted companies. Considerable pressure was being applied to reduce holdings to around 25–30% of the issued share capital. Following representations to the SFO that it appeared to have changed its practice in this area without any widespread publicity through the APT etc., the SFO stated it was undertaking a review of the acquisition of shares in employing or associated companies by SSASs. Meanwhile, each case was being treated on its merits, but the APT would be informed once the review has been completed. A recent development in this area was the publication of the draft regulations in July 1990. These stated that shareholdings in private companies would be limited to those carrying no more than 30% of the voting power or that would entitle the trustees to more than 30% of any dividends declared. These restrictions are included in the regulations and JOM 109(12) mentions that any attempt to circumvent the 30% limit by means of dividend waivers will prejudice the approval of the scheme. The point to note is that any private company's shares will be included, not just the employing company or its subsidiaries/associates. The reasons for this proposed limitation stem from SSASs being used to give directors effective control of companies at no cost to themselves and thereafter to strip companies of profit. It is always best, where any doubts exist as to whether a shareholding will be an acceptable investment, to approach the SFO before the investment has actually been made. After all, it can be extremely difficult and embarrassing to unscramble such a transaction once it has gone ahead and then falls foul of *section 703*, the SFO or IHT.

7.16   The form SF7014 (Appendix 27) has to completed by the administrator under the 90 day reporting requirements (see paragraph 3.72 above) in respect of any acquisition or disposal of shares in the company, associated company or unlisted company. The information to be supplied on the form SF7014 is similar to that on the form SF193 (see paragraph 7.8 above). If the purchase or sale of shares is between connected persons and was effected privately, i.e. not through a recognised stock exchange, the form should be accompanied by calculations used in valuing the shares, a copy of any professional valuation or advice, copies of the most recent scheme accounts and the company's accounts for the last three years, together with details of any associated agreement with anyone connected with the scheme to purchase or sell the shares in the company.

7.17   Another aspect of the regulations (*SI 1991/1614, reg 8(1)*) which will clearly affect the number of SSASs holding shares in the company is the ban on transactions between trustees and scheme members and their relatives (see paragraph 6.48 above) for holdings acquired after 5 August 1991. Holdings in the company will be particularly affected by this proposal as the vendors or purchasers are a restricted group and will almost certainly include the members and their relatives. The scope for a SSAS to own shares in the company in future has been severely limited and for those acquiring such shares, after 5 August 1991, the only future purchaser may be the company itself.

7.18   Finally, it is clear that the Department of Social Security's proposals to limit self-investment to 5% of scheme assets is going to cause further problems for those SSASs outside the concessions announced before Christmas 1989 and May 1991 which hold shares in the company. These proposed restrictions and concessions are covered in Chapter 11.

Non-income producing assets

7.19 The following paragraphs cover those investments which do not specifically produce income in the hands of the trustees, but which are made because of the capital appreciation they produce. They also cover the problems arising therefrom which concern the SFO.

Guidelines

7.20 These are to be found in JOM 58(15), the regulations and JOM 109(10). Advisers may be aware from their own experience with the SFO of that office's attitude towards specific investments of this type and what the SFO will and will not allow in this area for investments acquired prior to 5 August 1991. Until publication of JOM 109 (see paragraphs 7.30 and 7.31 below) there was no list of acceptable and unacceptable non-income producing assets.

7.21 JOM 58(15) says the SFO is unlikely to approve a SSAS which invests a significant amount of its funds in works of art or other valuable chattels or non-income producing assets which could be made available for the personal use of scheme members and lead to transactions between trustees and members being otherwise than on a purely commercial basis. So not only is the size of such investments likely to cause problems, but use of the assets by members certainly will. The sole purpose test in *section 590(2)(a)* is most apposite here regarding the provision of 'relevant benefits'. The SFO may not appear to be so concerned with the possibility of tax avoidance with non-income producing assets, although this aspect should never be disregarded, but rather with their use by scheme members. It is their potential use which needs to be considered not just their actual use, as the SFO's objections are frequently based on the argument that even if the member does not currently use the asset, the potential exists for the member to do so in future and it does not have the resources to police such use.

Types of assets

7.22 There appear to be two general categories of non-income producing assets as far as the SFO is concerned. These are 'pride in possession' assets, which appear to be barred (the consultative document actually said in no case will such pride in possession assets be approved), and 'others' in the absence of any definition, which are apparently acceptable if acquired before 5 August 1991. However, the acceptability and unacceptability cannot be taken for granted as will be gathered from later comments. It is possible to form a list of assets in both categories, but it would not be exhaustive and there may be other assets omitted. Generally, pride in possession assets such as fine wines, vintage and veteran cars, yachts, stamps, jewellery, stallions etc. are unacceptable. Paintings, antiques, porcelain, in fact all sorts of *objets d'art*, foreign currency and industrial diamonds are acceptable subject to certain limitations which are mentioned later.

7.23 It can be seen from the first group of assets that the potential exists for them to be used by scheme members. Even where a vintage car or yacht is leased on a commercial basis to an independent third party the asset is still likely to be unacceptable to the SFO. The second group of assets is somewhat different. There is no possibility of industrial diamonds being used personally by a scheme member and foreign currency similarly, although someone could 'borrow' the latter for a foreign trip! All works of art can however create problems. If they are kept, for instance, in the company's boardroom or at the member's residence then the member would be enjoying their use and the SSAS would be providing a non-relevant benefit. Paintings, antiques and their like should therefore be kept either in a public gallery where they are available for everybody to enjoy or stored in a bank vault.

'Significant amounts'

7.24 It was mentioned earlier that the SFO's guidelines limit acceptable non-income producing assets to a 'significant amount' of the scheme funds. A significant amount was never quantified after JOM 58 was published until the emergence of the consultative document. Until then it was known through individual SSASs or SFO meetings with the APT that a 'significant amount' was taken to be about 5% of the value of the fund. This was confirmed in the consultative document. So works of art, foreign currency, industrial diamonds etc. should be limited prior to 5 August 1991 to 5% of the value of the fund to be acceptable. This means a SSAS is hardly likely to own a Picasso unless its assets exceed £20 million!

Problems

7.25 Non-income producing assets are often by their very nature highly speculative and constitute very much a grey area because they appear to be looked at individually by the SFO. In some SSASs such an asset may have been found unacceptable whereas in another it is acceptable. Fine wines seem to come into this category. It cannot therefore be said that any such investments are 100% acceptable to the SFO apart from industrial diamonds and foreign currency. It is nearly always prudent to clear this type of investment in advance with the SFO to avoid any later problems, even though the process may take a while.

7.26   It is quite possible that the trustees propose to purchase a non-income producing asset from the members or their company or to sell it to one of these parties. JOM 58(15) warns that such transactions unless conducted on a proper commercial basis may prejudice the scheme's approval. So, just as for property transactions between the trustees and connected persons, so in these cases the same procedure of obtaining independent professional valuations of purchase or sale prices is a necessity. The SFO will need to see that an open market price has been paid in this situation, just as it does for property transactions that are not wholly at arm's length and for the same reasons that were explained on property investment in paragraph 6.7 above. A stock form SF194 (Appendix 23) is used by the SFO to request details of non-income producing assets. The details requested are covered in this chapter. Transactions in this type of investment from 5 August 1991 are dealt with in paragraph 7.30–7.33 (below).

7.27   The most common difficulties to arise with this type of asset with the SFO, leaving aside an outright refusal to accept the investment, are in the areas of member use, potential member use or where the asset is nonetheless acceptable, but worth more than 5% of the value of the fund. It should be possible to overcome the claim of potential member use by the trustees ensuring the asset is locked away in a bank vault or placed on view to the public at a gallery. There is no harm in quoting previous cases where this has been accepted by the SFO in defence of the position, although it may be met with the counter-argument that all cases are looked at individually on their merits. The acceptance by the SFO would have to have been since JOM 58 was published. If the SFO insists that the level of the investment must be reduced to make it acceptable, then there is probably no alternative other than to reduce the investment if that is possible to around 5% of the value of the assets otherwise the investment should not be made or it should be sold.

7.28   It may be that in objecting to a particular investment of this type the SFO is doing so for the first time albeit somewhat belatedly. There would be good grounds for its retention as mentioned previously if it can be shown that the investment was acquired pre-JOM 58, or even if acquired later that the SFO has been aware of it and either accepted or acquiesced in its ownership by the trustees due to the absence of comments in the past by the SFO.

Schedule E tax

7.29 The second part of JOM 58(15) contains a nasty sting in the tail. It mentions the possibility of Schedule E liability arising if a non-income producing asset is placed at the disposal of a member, or a member's family or household under *section 156(5)(6)* (derived from *section 63(4)(5) FA 1976*). In essence this could mean income tax being charged on the member on 20% of the market value of the asset. The fact that a member may be assessed to tax on such a benefit will not make the investment itself acceptable to the SFO. Its ownership by the trustees would still prejudice the scheme's approval even if the Schedule E tax was paid if for instance a painting owned by the trustees remained on the wall of a member's living room. The Schedule E liability in these circumstances is a matter for the member's local inspector of taxes to determine and not the SFO, so practitioners should not be surprised if the SFO makes no mention of the Schedule E liability whilst objecting to member use of the investment. It is as well therefore to be aware of this and to warn scheme members of the taxation consequences as well as of the implications for the investment concerned.

The position from 5 August 1991

7.30 With the coming into force of the regulations on 5 August 1991 the position of non-income producing assets has changed considerably since the consultative document was published. Personal chattels other than choses in action are banned. JOM 109(10) provides a list of assets which are personal chattels that are not choses in action and therefore are prohibited from 5 August 1991. These include antiques, works of art, rare books and stamps, furniture, fine wines, vintage cars, yachts, jewellery, gem stones, gold bullion, oriental rugs and Krugerrands.

7.31 JOM 109(10) also describes a chose in action as something which is not corporeal, tangible, moveable or visible and of which someone has not the present enjoyment, but merely a right to recover it. It provides a list of choses in action which includes company shares, copyrights, factoring, financial futures, traded options, commodity futures, and deposit accounts, that are permitted investments. Some of these are looked at in more detail in paragraphs 7.34–7.36 below and in Chapter 8 which covers trading as they may be taxable in the hands of trustees.

7.32   The lists in JOM 109(10) are not exhaustive. Foreign currency deposit accounts for instance are apparently choses in action and therefore still permissible. However, trustees should seek professional advice if they are uncertain as to whether a particular investment is a chose in action before making an investment. The regulations do not mention the 5% limit at all (see paragraph 7.24 above) and neither does JOM 109. This will need to be clarified.

7.33   Whilst there is now much less scope for investment in this area, nonetheless there is a form SF7016 (Appendix 29) which must be completed by the administrator under the 90 day reporting requirements (see paragraph 3.72 above) in respect of any acquisitions or disposals of this type of investment. The details required are a description of the asset, date of purchase or sale, purchase or sale price, name of the vendor or purchaser and whether connected to the trustees, employer or members and details of any leasing of the investment. If the purchaser or vendor is connected a copy of an independent valuation must also be provided. If the investment is to be leased or was leased to a connected person copies of the lease and of an independent valuation of the rental must be provided as well.

Commodities, futures and options

7.34   Until 1984 if the trustees held this type of investment it could have resulted in them being assessable to tax on trading profits. However, with the enactment of *section 659* (derived from *section 45, FA 1984*) gains realised from dealing in financial futures or traded options by approved pension schemes were exempted from tax. Then in 1990 *section 659A* derived from *section 81(2)(4), FA 1990* replaced *section 659* and exempted from tax all trading income from futures and options owned by pension schemes. JOM 58(16) should be read in the light of these changes, so apparently commodities held by SSASs remain taxable although very few invest in this area.

7.35   JOM 58(16) goes on to mention that if the trustees invest in plant or machinery for hiring out they may become assessable to tax on trading profits. This may involve leasing of some sort and if used as a tax avoidance device in conjunction with a SSAS it is likely to prejudice the scheme's approval. The well known case of *Wisdom v Chamberlain 45 TC 92* is quoted where the Inland Revenue maintained that dealing in platinum bars was taxable. The trustees of a SSAS are unlikely to invest in this kind of medium or gold or silver because of their volatility, but if they do they need to be aware that they may be deemed to be trading and thereby lose tax exemptions on this activity. Even if they escape this penalty they are still likely to be subject to an overall investment in this area of 5% of the scheme's funds as mentioned in paragraph 7.24 above.

7.36 It is quite significant to note that JOM 58(16) states the SFO is not competent to give any information as to whether the income from specified activities will be regarded as trading income or not. This is an area in which the inspector of taxes will pronounce, not the SFO, and only after the transaction has been carried out. The inspector of taxes will not normally comment on a transaction's taxability in advance. Thus, as mentioned in paragraph 6.35 above on property, it is best to be aware of the possibility of trading by the trustees in this area and to seek professional advice before proceeding with an investment of this type. Trading by trustees is covered in more detail in Chapter 8.

Borrowings

7.37 The final paragraphs of this chapter deal with a common feature of SSASs which is a liability of the trustees rather than an asset.

7.38 Until January 1983 there were no specific guidelines laid down by the SFO regarding the amount the trustees of a SSAS could borrow. The situation on each scheme was considered on its merits. The SFO then pronounced through the APT its revised practice in this area. This was to set a ceiling on trustees' borrowings of three times the ordinary annual contribution (OAC) paid to the scheme. The significance of 'three times' is wholly arbitrary and the SFO made it clear that it would consider larger borrowings providing the circumstances were satisfactorily explained. The guidelines were again mentioned in 1984 following the PQ about changes in the SFO's practice since JOM 58 was published. The SFO stated that each case would be considered on its own merits, but excessive borrowing by trustees might give rise to doubts as to the 'sole purpose' of the arrangements and lead to difficulty over approval. It added that any significant proposed borrowing should be cleared in advance.

7.39 The important point to note is that the three times OAC guideline is missing and, whilst it is understood that it still applies, cases can be made to the SFO for 'significant' borrowings, i.e. above the three times OAC, to be arranged. It will need a good case though to justify such a level of borrowings, for example it would probably be no use stressing the good potential of the investment to be made with the finance raised by the trustees, rather the emphasis should be on the lack of any need for some years yet to realise scheme assets to provide benefits.

7.40 It is important to understand what the SFO means by OAC in the context of borrowings. Firstly, it is the employer's contribution that determines the level of borrowing. Any member's personal contributions should not be taken into account at all for this purpose. If more than one employer participates in the scheme, then their total contributions can be counted. Secondly, the contributions must be that paid to the scheme at the time the borrowings are arranged. This can cause problems if the borrowings are arranged well into the scheme year and the last contribution was paid at the end of the previous scheme year. Here the borrowings should be based on the last contribution or the trustees could wait a while until the current year's contribution is paid and then take the finance on board based on the latest contribution. Thirdly, and this is the area which probably leads to most problems with the SFO, the contribution on which the borrowing is calculated must be the regular ordinary annual contribution. This is easy enough if contributions are being paid in full in line with the actuary's recommendations, whether they are at a flat rate or a percentage of salaries. However, if contributions have been paid at less than the rate recommended then the regular ordinary annual contribution will need to be established to calculate the ceiling for borrowings and that could be difficult. The position becomes worse if, say, no contribution was paid in the year prior to the borrowings, because then a contribution must be paid to justify any borrowings at all. Finally, special contributions and transfer values received cannot be taken into account as part of this exercise. Where a regular pattern of ordinary annual contributions has not been established, the SFO may already have deemed some contributions as special and this too will affect the ceiling on borrowings.

7.41 Trustees' borrowings may be secured or unsecured. They must however be on commercial terms and for the purposes of the scheme. In other words if they are used to finance an investment, that investment must be one which is acceptable to the SFO. The trustees may borrow in the short term to finance the payment of benefits. Very often they may use an overdraft facility for this while assets are being realised. So it is possible for the trustees to take on a mortgage or a legal charge, or a straight bank loan or overdraft, or borrow from another third party or even a connected party. In the last case mentioned, it is most important to ensure the terms of the loan are at a commercial rate, especially the rate of interest, otherwise the scheme's approval may be prejudiced.

7.42 The trustees may only mortgage or charge trust property in respect of their own borrowings. They must on no account charge scheme assets in respect of a loan taken out by a third party e.g. a member of the scheme. Charging scheme assets in this way would prejudice the scheme's approval as the scheme would not be *bona fide* established for the sole provision of relevant benefits. Thus a pension mortgage granted by a third party to a scheme member must in no way be linked directly to the assets of the scheme.

7.43   If the trustees acquire a property already subject to a mortgage, then in taking on board the mortgage the trustees still need to have regard to their borrowings ceiling of three times the OAC. If the trustees take on further borrowings any previous borrowings not then repaid have to be aggregated for the purposes of the three times the OAC ceiling.

7.44   The consultative document promised that the regulations would actually incorporate the limit on borrowings of three times the amount of the employer's ordinary annual contribution to the scheme. In the event the regulations themselves are somewhat different having been amended following consultation between the Inland Revenue and representative bodies. The regulations allow the trustees to borrow up to three times the OAC paid to the scheme plus 45% of the value of the scheme's assets after 5 August 1991. The OAC includes both the employer's and the member's contributions, but does not include members' additional voluntary contributions. The limit on borrowings applies at the time they are undertaken by the trustees.

7.45   For the purpose of calculating the ceiling on borrowings, the regulations define the employer's OAC and provide for it to be restricted. Thus the employer's OAC is the average of the contributions paid in the three years ended at the end of the previous accounting period of the SSAS or the amount of the annual contributions within the period of the three years prior to the date of the borrowings recommended in writing by the scheme actuary whichever is the lesser. Whilst this formula could include special contributions it is obviously aimed at schemes where the company's contributions fluctuate substantially. For SSASs that have been established for less than three years at the time borrowings are undertaken a two year average of company contributions is to be taken or just one year if the scheme was established less than a year previously. The borrowings ceiling from 5 August 1991 is much more generous than previously and should be of considerable assistance to mature SSASs or where the company is experiencing difficulties in maintaining contribution at the recommended level.

The following examples should help clarify the amount the trustees may borrow.

Example A

At 10 August 1991 the trustees wish to borrow £500,000 to acquire a commercial property. The value of the schemes at that date was £800,000.

Scheme year ended	Contribution paid by employer	Annual contribution recommended by actuary
31 March 1989	£100,000	£100,000
31 March 1990	£ 75,000	£100,000
31 March 1991	£125,000	£125,000
	£300,000	

Total employer's contribution divided by three equals £100,000, which is the same or less than the annual contribution recommended by the actuary in the last three years.

Borrowings ceiling is therefore:

3 × £100,000	=	£300,000
plus 45% of £800,000	=	£360,000
		£660,000

Example B

At 10 August 1991 the trustees wish to borrow £150,000 to acquire commercial property. The value of the scheme's investments at that date is £175,000.

Scheme year ended	Contribution paid by employer	Contribution paid by member	Annual contribution recommended by actuary
31 March 1989	£20,000	£1,000	£50,000
31 March 1990	Nil	Nil	£50,000
31 March 1991	£25,000	£500	£50,000

Total employer's and employee's contributions divided by three equals £15,500 which is less than the annual contribution recommended by the actuary in the last three years.

Borrowings ceiling is therefore:

3 × £15,500	=	£46,500
plus 45% of £175,000	=	£78,750
		£125,250

In Example A the trustees may borrow the full £500,000 they require, but in Example B they are restricted to £125,250 instead of £150,000. In both examples, however, the trustees are able to borrow substantially more than they were able under the SFO's guidelines prior to 5 August 1991.

7.46 JOM 109(9) mentions that any borrowings should be used for the purpose of the SSAS. If the borrowings are in turn lent to the employer or an associated company the trustees need to ensure they receive a higher rate of interest on the lendings than they have to pay on the borrowings.

7.47 Borrowings like other features of SSASs are to be reported to the SFO under the regulations whether they are used to finance investments or expenses. Temporary borrowings not exceeding six months and which do not exceed the lesser of 10% of the market value of the fund or £50,000 and the borrowing is repaid at or before the due date do not have to be reported. Thus if borrowing is rolled over into a further term it has to be reported. Problems are likely to arise with trustees' overdrafts as it will probably not be known in advance when the overdraft facility will end.

7.48 The form SF7015 (Appendix 30) is to be used by the administrator under the reporting requirements (see paragraph 3.72 above) to report trustees' borrowings within 90 days of their commencement. The form incorporates the date of borrowing, the amount, rate of interest, purpose, repayment date, name and address of the lender, value of the fund at the time, the amounts of the employer's contributions in the last three years or lesser period from commencement and the total amount of employee contributions. It is clear the SFO will pay some attention to these details, not just to check the amount borrowed is within the permitted ceiling. For instance if the lender is a connected person a copy of the loan agreement has to be sent to the SFO with form SF7015. Whilst there can be no objection to the employer or a scheme member making a loan to the trustees, clearly the SFO will be concerned to establish that the loan is on fully commercial terms. In addition the purpose of a loan may come in for close scrutiny by the SFO. For example, if the trustees borrow to finance the payment of retirement benefits to a member, this would only be acceptable in certain circumstances as retirement dates are generally well known to the trustees in advance and steps should have been taken to realise assets in good time to pay benefits. However, if a property is proving difficult to sell or an unexpected early retirement occurs such borrowings may be acceptable to the SFO.

Chapter 8

Trading

Introduction

8.1 Reference has been made earlier in various paragraphs dealing with the investments of a SSAS of the possibility of the trustees being considered as trading by the Inland Revenue. These circumstances are looked at in greater detail in this chapter together with other situations where the trustees could be considered as trading.

8.2 It should be borne in mind that the scope for trading is rather limited in a SSAS particularly when compared with a large self-administered scheme, but trustees and their tax advisers need to be alert nonetheless to the problems such activities can create with the Inland Revenue and not just with the SFO. Another important point to bear in mind is that even if it is conceded that the trustees have been trading, this will not necessarily result in the loss of tax approval or a refusal to approve a SSAS. The trustees would as a result only have to pay tax on the transaction concerned. It is only where the trading activity has deliberately involved a SSAS in order to achieve tax avoidance that its approval may be prejudiced e.g. bond washing or dividend stripping (see paragraph 8.8 below).

JOM 58

8.3 JOM 58(16) refers to trading in specific areas, such as commodities and leasing of plant and machinery (see paragraphs 7.34 and 7.35 above). It only covers trading generally to the extent that if the trustees receive profits from 'an adventure in the nature of trade' they may be assessable to tax. As mentioned in paragraph 7.36 above the SFO will not give a ruling as to whether a specific activity is liable to tax. That is a matter for the inspector of taxes to decide and he will not give an opinion on the activity until it has taken place. It is therefore appropriate to look at the criteria on which a decision would be made by the inspector of taxes that trading has taken place and then to look at various investment and transaction areas where it is likely that the Inland Revenue will consider whether or not trustees are trading.

The badges of trade

8.4 The question of whether a transaction has given rise to a profit and is to be treated as a trading transaction has been considered before the various appellate bodies. A series of six tests is listed in the final report of the 1954 Royal Commission (Command 9474 paragraph 116) as constituting the relevant considerations in deciding if a transaction involved trading. These are known as the badges of trade, not one of which or all of which are necessarily conclusive that the activity amounted to trading. They are, however, very useful pointers.

The subject of the transaction

8.5 The subject matter of the transaction must be something capable of being traded in. Thus where an asset does not produce income or cannot be enjoyed personally it is unlikely to be an investment. This test is particularly relevant to works of art. A non-income producing asset such as this is not an investment, but this would depend on the use to which it was put whilst owned, for instance it could have been leased at a commercial rent so as to generate income.

8.6 Securities usually produce income and consequently do not give rise to such a problem. However, securities are not always held as an investment and there are cases where it has been established that in certain situations they can be the subject matter of trading. Commodities are normally the subject of trading (see paragraphs 7.34 above and 8.27 below) and only exceptionally may be the subject of investment.

The length of the period of ownership

8.7 Length of ownership may be conclusive in establishing trading, but if an asset is sold shortly after acquisition it is more likely to be considered a trading transaction rather than an investment. It would be necessary to demonstrate that the circumstances changed materially between the purchase and sale of an asset which was held for a short period to avoid the transaction being treated as trading.

8.8 This is the area where bond washing and dividend stripping are prone to be attacked. These activities involve the transfer and re-transfer of securities on dates spanning an interest or dividend payment either to avoid tax by selling or to benefit from a tax exemption in receiving it. The use of an approved pension scheme to receive a dividend would free it from tax, but if there is tax avoidance present the likelihood is that the scheme's approval would be prejudiced. However, any action regarding the scheme's approval by the SFO would need to be considered in the light of any action taken by the inspector of taxes under *sections 732, 734, 735*. Counter-action under *section 732* would entail a substantial proportion of the tax credit attaching to a dividend not being recoverable by a scheme. If a SSAS is involved in such counter-action it should be argued that this cancels the tax advantage and therefore the scheme's approval would not have been prejudiced.

The frequency or number of similar transactions

8.9   It is unlikely that a single transaction would be taxed as trading. However, where the same type of transaction is repeated frequently then the volume of transactions involved may be sufficient to establish trading. As mentioned in paragraphs 6.19 and 6.35 above frequent purchases and sales of property by a SSAS may attract the attention of the inspector of taxes who may consider such activities to be trading.

Supplementary work on, or in connection with, the property realised

8.10   This of course is relevant to sales of land, particularly its development by the trustees (see paragraph 6.35 above). The inspector of taxes will be looking to see if the land was purchased and resold as it stood or whether work was done on it to facilitate a resale. If it was worked or developed before sale this could suggest an intention to sell by way of trading. It is most important that the trustees seek their tax advisers' advice on these aspects before development is undertaken to ensure an SSAS is not taxed on the 'profit' realised.

The circumstances that were responsible for the realisation

8.11   There may be a very good reason for the sale of an investment shortly after its acquisition. For instance, there could have been a sudden change in market conditions or a situation may have arisen which called for ready money. This should effectively scotch any idea that the original purchase was prompted by a plan to deal. If the trustees minute the reason for the sale at the time it occurred, this should give weight to the non-trading case.

8.12   Another counter-argument the trustees could employ where the investment has fallen in value due to a fall in the market is that the investment is no longer prudent and to retain it would have meant that the trustees were not acting in the best interests of the members i.e. the trustees would have been in breach of trust if they did not sell.

Motive

8.13 The intention of the trustees is a most important factor in determining whether transactions may be regarded as trading. The intention extends to the trustees' tax advisers who may have given advice on the purchase and/or sale of an investment. Whilst it would assist any case to record that the trustees were purchasing on investment grounds care should be taken not to provide evidence of the motive in reselling.

8.14 The badges of trade are very general tests so it may be relevant for the trustees' tax advisers to consider what the courts have decided in cases where it has been argued that a taxpayer was trading. There are, however, no leading cases where the Inland Revenue has argued that the trustees of a pension scheme were trading. The leading cases all concern taxpayers who made losses on the sale of securities and therefore claimed the losses against other taxable income on the grounds they were trading losses. If a pension scheme were held to be trading the trustees' profit would be taxable, but if they made a net trading loss it would go unrelieved as there would be no other income against which to set the loss. It can therefore be gathered how important it is to the Inland Revenue not to concede that a taxpayer buying and selling securities was trading otherwise it would have to deal with a flood of claims at a time of falling markets.

8.15 For the record the leading cases are *Salt v Chamberlain, Lewis Emanuel & Son Ltd v White and Cooper v C and J Clark Ltd*. It is not proposed in this book to go into great detail of these cases. The table of cases at the front of this book provides the appropriate references for those wishing to consider their contents in greater depth. Two of the cases involve companies engaged in buying and selling shares as an ancillary activity to their main business which is unlikely to be the basis for finding a pension scheme to be trading. The primary activity of a pension scheme is not to trade and therefore different considerations ought to apply. This should give rise to a presumption against trading so far as a pension scheme is concerned (see also paragraph 8.17 below).

Forms of trading

8.16 Having looked at the criteria on which the inspector of taxes may base a decision that the trustees are engaged in trading, it is appropriate now to look at specific areas where trading may or indeed does occur. It should also be mentioned that in 1987 and 1988 there were indications that the Inland Revenue was focusing its attention on the investment practices of some large self-administered schemes with a view to determining whether these schemes may have been trading. There have subsequently been some direct pronouncements by the Inland Revenue which are as relevant to SSASs as they are to large schemes and are therefore mentioned in the paragraphs covering the form of trading concerned.

Trading in shares

8.17 It would be very difficult for the Inland Revenue to argue that shares were sold as part of an organised arrangement to make a profit. The frequent buying and selling of shares or short-term transactions therein are much more likely to be dictated by stock market conditions. Such transactions would also have to be looked at in conjunction with the trustees' other activities as a whole. The question that also has to be asked in connection with a SSAS, is would the Inland Revenue consider it a worthwhile target in this area? It seems highly unlikely that the purchase and sale of securities would be shown to be trading in cases where a scheme has been run solely in accordance with normal investment criteria. It is much more likely that any action by the Inland Revenue would only be concentrated in areas of tax avoidance such as bond washing or dividend stripping (see paragraph 8.8 above).

Stock lending

8.18 Income from stock lending is taxable by virtue of *section 727(1)*. Stock lending is the transfer of the title to securities of a market maker who is short of stock due for delivery, together with the right to acquire the same amount of securities within a specific period. The lender obtains security in cash or treasury bills and is remunerated by a fee. It is this fee which is taxable in the hands of the trustees because the fees arc not income from investments held for the purposes of the scheme.

Commissions

8.19 Underwriting commissions are exempt from tax under *section 592(3)* (see paragraph 1.24 above) if they are applied for the purposes of the scheme. There is however some degree of doubt as to whether fee income from underwriting new issues of stocks and securities constitutes trading income. This ought not to concern SSASs, but only large self-administered schemes. The Inland Revenue's argument would appear to be that such income is not applied for the purposes of the scheme and indeed it would be difficult to show that such activity was directly linked to investment purposes.

8.20 Schemes do receive other commission income which does not fall within the exemption contained in *section 592(3)*. For instance, the trustees may insure buildings in their ownership from damage and may as a result obtain commission. Such commission could not be said to arise from investments or deposits held for the purposes of the scheme. They are derived from an insurance contract rather than the property itself and are therefore taxable under Schedule D Case VI.

Options, financial futures and forward contracts

8.21 An option is a right to buy or sell something without any obligation to take it up whereas a forward contract is a firm agreement to buy or sell something in the future. A future is a standardised forward contract traded on an exchange.

8.22 During the 1980s there was considerable uncertainty regarding the taxation of options, futures and forward contracts despite legislation purporting to deal with them. In 1984 pension schemes were exempted from tax on gains arising from transactions in traded options and financial futures (see paragraph 7.30 above). Previous legislation actually defined a traded option as 'an option which is for the time being quoted on a recognised stock exchange or on the London International Financial Futures Exchange' (LIFFE). In addition *section 72, FA 1985* defined a financial future as one which is 'for the time being dealt in on a recognised futures exchange'.

8.23 There was some doubt whether gains from financial futures were exempt from tax in the hands of pension scheme trustees. Indeed this uncertainty of tax treatment was shared by other exempt bodies such as investment and unit trusts, charities etc. Following consultation between the Inland Revenue, LIFFE and other interested bodies the Inland Revenue issued a statement of practice (SP4/88) on 22 July 1988 regarding 'The Tax Treatment of Transactions in Financial Futures and Options' (Appendix 31).

8.24 SP4/88 makes it clear that profits and losses arising from investing in financial futures and options are exempt from CGT subject to the reason for and frequency of such investments. Point 5 of SP4/88 is repeated here because of its importance.

'If a transaction in financial futures or options is clearly related to an underlying asset or transaction, then the tax treatment of the futures or options contract will follow that of the underlying asset or transaction. In general, the Inland Revenue take the view that this relationship exists where a futures or options contract is entered into in order to hedge an underlying transaction, asset or portfolio by reducing the risk relating to it; and the intention of the taxpayer in entering into the transaction is of considerable importance. Where the underlying transaction is itself treated as giving rise to a capital gain or loss, the related futures or options contract will also be treated as a capital matter and not as trading'.

8.25 It can be gathered from SP4/88 that transactions will not be treated as trading if they are infrequent or used to hedge investments. Hedging in this context would reduce the risk of an underlying investment. The variations in price of the futures and options must correspond with the difference in value of the underlying transaction. Such transactions are not liable to CGT. SP4/88 is also helpful in that it provides examples of when an investment may produce a capital gain or loss.

8.26 In 1990 all trading income of pension schemes from futures and options was exempted from tax by virtue of *section 659A* introduced by *section 81(2)(4), FA 1990* (see paragraph 7.34 above) so the position now is very favourable to approved schemes.

Commodities

8.27 These are mentioned in JOM 58(16) with a warning that income therefrom may be taxable in the hands of the trustees. If the trustees derive profits from purchase and sales of commodities, e.g. metals or foodstuffs, there is not much doubt that they will be taxed (see paragraphs 7.34 and 8.3 above).

Other forms of trading

8.28 If the trustees invest in a business venture of any kind, they need to be aware of the taxation implications. They may invest in part or the whole of a business and if they do the profits received will be taxable. If they invest in a successful commercial venture they also need to be aware of the problems that may arise regarding the scheme's funding if the investment generates substantial income which may not only fund the scheme without the need for company contributions, but leads to overfunding and resultant actuarial difficulties with regards to surplus repayments. A too successful investment of this nature may well prejudice

8.29 *Trading*

the scheme's approval if the provisions of *section 590(2)(d)* are not met i.e. the employer must be a contributor to the scheme.

8.29 It may be possible to confine all taxable or trading activities of a scheme in a company totally owned by the scheme itself. This may well be a practical proposition for a large self-administered scheme, but it has clear tax implications for SSASs. Paragraph 7.11 above mentions that a majority holding by a SSAS in a company would not be acceptable to the SFO. The trustees would be able to control the company, including its profits and dividends and not just use it for trading activities.

Chapter 9

Funding and Actuarial Matters

Introduction

9.1   It is an SFO requirement for both large and small self-administered schemes that actuarial reports are provided on the establishment of the scheme and submitted to the SFO together with the application for approval (PN 22.17 and see paragraph 3.56 above). If a full actuarial report was not prepared at the time the scheme was established, then the SFO will expect to receive it later, but meanwhile the informal actuarial advice given on the establishment of the scheme must be provided at the time of application for approval (JOM 90 and Section VIII of Appendix 15). The reason for this is that the SFO wishes to see that the scheme is established properly based on actuarial recommendations for its future funding. The absence of any actuarial advice will mean that the application for approval will not be accepted (see paragraphs 3.53, 3.57 above).

9.2   The company will need to commission an initial report from a qualified actuary that sets out the likely cost of establishing the SSAS and recommends the initial contribution rate. In some cases this service may be provided by an in-house actuary. In other cases an actuary may be independently commissioned and may also be the pensioneer trustee. Subsequently triennial valuations will be needed showing what has happened to the scheme since the last valuation and the actuary's recommendations for future contributions. Mention was made at paragraph 2.23 above of small schemes administered by LOs where the documentation permits self-administration but where the scheme monies are wholly invested in insurance policies. The SFO has given a dispensation to such schemes from submitting full scale actuarial valuations provided their only investments are insurance policies taken out with one LO and on the understanding that a short report was provided every three years relating to the remuneration and contribution details of the members in the preceding three years. Confirmation is also required that the scheme remains fully insured with one LO. JOM 109(6) states that such reports and confirmations are no longer required in these cases.

Both the Institute of Actuaries and Faculty of Actuaries have guidelines for their members setting out how actuarial reports should be generally prepared (Appendix 32). Paragraphs 9.3 to 9.23 below explain the aspects the SFO will expect to see in initial and subsequent actuarial reports.

Basic details

9.3   In a large scheme the initial actuarial report usually groups the membership into different classes by age, remuneration etc. and makes an allowance for early leavers. In a SSAS because of the small number of members and their position in the company it is not viable to make an allowance for early leavers, but the SFO will expect to see full details of each individual member. These will include to start with such basic details as the name of the members, date of birth, sex, date of commencement of service with the company, normal retirement ages and their current remuneration. The reasons for requiring these details are that the SFO will wish to ascertain who are the members of the scheme, the length of their past and future service and their current salary levels. It must be borne in mind that it is open to the SFO to check service and remuneration details with the inspectors of taxes and also with the details given in other schemes of the same employer.

9.4   Further details should be provided in the initial actuarial report of all retained benefits of the members that have to be taken into account in the funding of the scheme. These will include benefits from other schemes of the same company, or if appropriate, benefits from a scheme with another company and retirement annuity contracts. Once again the SFO will be in a position to check these retained benefits or it may be aware of other retained benefits not mentioned in the initial actuarial report and may enquire about them.

Benefits

9.5   The SFO is interested in what benefits are being provided for each member of a SSAS. This will be gathered from the initial actuarial report and the members' announcement letters. There are two basic reasons for the SFO's interest. One is to see if all members will receive the same benefits and the other is concerned with the level of funding and therefore the contributions to be paid.

9.6   It is important to demonstrate that the members will generally receive the same level of benefits at retirement or on death. The reason for this is to show that there is only one class of member in a SSAS and that a second class of members has not been brought in with derisory benefits in comparison to the others to make up the membership to more than eleven to avoid the application of JOM 58 to the scheme e.g. appointment of a pensioneer trustee, restrictions on loans and other investments etc.

Actuarial assumptions

9.7 The SFO will be looking to see what assumptions the actuary has made in a professional capacity regarding long-term increases in the value of the fund, in remuneration levels and increases in pensions in payment in determining the scheme's funding for the future. These gross yield assumptions, as they are known, are only of interest to the SFO in so far as they determine the net yield assumptions for both pre- and post-retirement. Starting with the pre-retirement net yield assumption, this is arrived at by deducting the actuary's assumed rate of increase in remuneration from the gross yield in the value of the fund. Thus if the former is 10% and the latter 10½% the pre-retirement net yield assumption will be ½%. The post-retirement net yield assumption is arrived at by deducting the actuary's assumed rate of increase in pensions from the gross yield in the value of the fund. If these are 8½% and 10½% respectively then the post-retirement net yield assumption will be 2%. Obviously there are going to be variations in the gross yield assumptions used by different actuaries and depending on the scheme membership, and there can be further factors to take into account regarding pensions increases which are mentioned later, but the SFO will be looking for net yield assumptions of ½% and 2% which are generally accepted as leading to payment of the benefits promised at the end of the scheme's life. Other net yield assumptions adopted by an actuary can lead to the same result, for instance nil and 3% will also be acceptable to the SFO, but any departure from these could lead to eventual over- or under-funding and the SFO would need to be convinced that the different assumptions were acceptable.

9.8 JOM 58 did not spell out the net yield assumptions acceptable to the SFO. However, through the experience of individual schemes and via the APT what was acceptable emerged and then following the PQ in July 1984, the SFO published its Code of practice in this area (Appendix 2). This stated that a net yield on the scheme's investments during service of at least ½% was acceptable. In addition a net yield on investments post-retirement of at least 2% would be acceptable over the rate of post-retirement increases that constituted a liability of the scheme. Where the rate of post-retirement increases is less than 6%, the assumed gross yield on investments should not be less than 8%.

9.9 It should also be noted that funding for a surviving spouse's pension payable on the death of a member is not permitted unless the member is already married. Where the husband and wife are both members, which is very often the case in a SSAS, only one surviving spouse's pension should be funded based on the entitlement of the member who would, from an actuarial point of view, die first.

Mortality assumptions

9.10 As with net yield assumptions, JOM 58 did not mention the mortality assumptions that the SFO would find acceptable. These also became apparent through the experience of individual schemes and via the APT. The SFO confirmed its practice in this area too following the PQ in July 1984 by stating it considered death in retirement mortality assumptions based on a (55) or PA (90) tables issued by the Institute of Actuaries and Faculty of Actuaries as acceptable.

Contributions

9.11 The actuary's assumptions will be used in conjunction with the length of service, the amount of remuneration and the amount of retained benefits to determine the contributions to be made to the scheme. Contributions may be recommended at a flat rate or a percentage of the member's remuneration. The following table gives examples of maximum contributions at a flat rate, expressed as a percentage of earnings in the first year:

Age Next Birthday At Entry	Male Retirement Age		Female Retirement Age	
	60	65	60	65
25	98%	82%	97%	80%
30	102%	85%	102%	83%
35	109%	89%	108%	88%
40	119%	95%	119%	93%
45	137%	104%	136%	102%
50	171%	119%	170%	117%
55	266%	149%	264%	146%
60		232%		228%

Higher amounts may be paid in the first year where members have previous service with the company. These figures are based on the following assumptions.

(a) The member is married and the husband is three years older than the wife in each case.

(b) Earnings increase at 8½% p.a. compound.

(c) The RPI increases at 7% p.a. compound.

(d) The pre-retirement yield on the fund is 9% p.a.

(e) Pensions can be purchased on annuity rates based on 9% p.a. interest and current annuitants' mortality.

(f) Pensions in payment will increase in line with increases in the RPI.

(g) The member will not be affected by the earnings cap e.g. the table is only appropriate for a male age 25 next birthday retiring at age 65 if his earnings are less than £40,900 p.a., otherwise his earnings at age 65 will be greater than the current earnings cap.

(h) Members and spouses will survive until retirement.

(j) Expenses and charges are payable in addition.

(k) The member has no retained benefits.

(l) The member has at least 20 years pensionable service by retirement age.

(m) Contributions are payable for 'n + 1' years.

These figures also give a much higher initial funding rate than if funding is based on a fixed percentage of members' earnings. The SFO is particularly concerned with what is paid by way of contributions on the establishment of a SSAS. This concern extends to special contributions and to any difference between the contribution recommended and that actually paid.

9.12 It is not permissible for a special contribution to be paid to a SSAS on its establishment or later up to the level of the recommended ordinary annual contribution to be held as a general reserve without it being justified. JOM 58(24) made that quite clear. The only justification for a special contribution in the first year would be to fund for previous service of the members. If the full amount recommended is not paid in the first year, for whatever reason, the SFO can be expected to ascertain whether it occurs again next year as the level of contribution paid may indicate the company's intention not to fund the scheme on a regular basis which would bring the scheme's *bona fides* into question. More likely though, payment of contributions below the level recommended could lead to no regular pattern of ordinary annual contributions being established and the possible spreading of contributions as deductions for corporation tax purposes may arise. This is particularly relevant where the company paid the full ordinary annual contribution and a special contribution of the same amount in the first year, because it had done well financially (which may have been the initial incentive for establishing the scheme), and in later years does not pay the full recommended contribution. The following example shows no regular pattern of OACs.

	Recommended		Paid	
	OAC	Special Contribution	OAC	Special Contribution
Year 1	£50,000	£50,000	£50,000	£50,000
Year 2	£50,000	—	£20,000	—
Year 3	£50,000	—	—	—
Year 4	£65,000	—	£40,000	—
Year 5	£65,000	—	£40,000	—

In the absence of a regular pattern of OACs the SFO may treat all the contributions paid as special contributions and spread them forward for corporation tax purposes under *section 592(6)*. The SFO would determine the amounts to be spread and assuming in this example there is no other scheme of the company the possibility is that all the contributions paid in Year 1 and in Years 4 and 5 also may be spread. Years 4 and 5 may not be spread until the pattern of contributions paid in Year 6 *et seq* has been ascertained. Advisers need to be alert to this situation so that companies are warned of the possibility of spreading where a regular pattern of ordinary annual contributions has not been established.

9.13 Finally whilst dealing with the initial application for approval, JOM 58(23) states that the SFO will ask how the contributions paid to the scheme are to be or have been invested.

Triennial valuations—Investments

9.14 Most actuarial reports provide details of the value of the investments at the valuation date. If only a total value is provided or a total is provided under a particular heading, e.g. property, the SFO is likely to request a breakdown or schedule of the investments concerned. The reasons for this are clearly to see if the investments themselves are acceptable and also if there have been any changes as the absence of an asset probably indicates its sale, and the SFO may request its details. Prior to 5 April 1991 it was possible between triennial valuations for

114

assets to be acquired and disposed of without the SFO's knowledge and this remains the case with certain assets that do not have to be reported. However, it is noticeable that the SFO has been asking recently for details of investments at intervals of less than three years.

Triennial valuations—Funding

9.15 Having checked that the actuary's net yield assumptions meet its guidelines, the SFO will look at the overall funding position including whether retained benefits and transfers into the scheme have been taken into account. It is particularly interested in whether the scheme has been under-or over-funded and what the actuary's recommendations are for dealing with such situations.

9.16 Looking at under-funding first, the reasons for the deficiency ought not to create problems with the SFO unless there has been a lack of contributions which may involve spreading, or a substantial increase in salaries the level of which the SFO can always check with the inspector of taxes. The actuary's recommendations to eliminate the deficiency will attract the SFO's attention and it will probably ask if the recommendations have been implemented. A shortfall may well be made up by an increase in contributions, but if this involves a special contribution it needs to be justified and the SFO may require the spreading forward of the contribution for relief from corporation tax.

9.17 It is however, the over-funded position which attracts the greater attention of the SFO. This is because in any self-administered scheme the Inland Revenue does not approve of the tax-free build up of assets in excess of the scheme's liabilities. Fortunately most SSASs are unlikely to become over-funded because of their nature and they have been exempted from the requirement to submit a certificate or valuation report on the prescribed basis contained in the surplus legislation enacted in 1986. The exemption is contained in regulation 3(2)(a) of the *Pension Schemes Surpluses (Valuation) Regulations 1987 (SI 1987/412)*. However, some SSASs become over-funded during their life-time or on winding-up and several aspects related to these situations will be considered in detail.

Surpluses

9.18 As the prescribed basis of valuation is not normally used for SSASs, the SFO adopts the criteria it has always used for this type of scheme if an over-funded situation is disclosed by a triennial valuation. These criteria may be summarised as follows.

9.19 *Funding and Actuarial Matters*

(a) Is the over-funding substantial.

(b) How has it arisen.

(c) What recommendations has the actuary made to reduce it.

(d) Have those recommendations been adopted?

9.19 The SFO's rule of thumb regarding the level at which a SSAS is over-funded appears to be 5% in excess of the liabilities which is coincidental to the 105% level on the prescribed basis. If the surplus is not substantial the SFO may simply ask if the actuary's recommendations have been adopted. If there is more than one member in the scheme and members have individual contribution credits calculated by the actuary, some of which are in surplus and others which disclose deficiencies, then the overall funding position should be taken into account by the SFO in determining the level of over-funding if any.

9.20 Much depends on the reason for any substantial over-funding as to whether the SFO will pursue this aspect. A drop in salary or member's cessation of service are unlikely to precipitate searching enquiries. However, an increase in the value of the fund in excess of the actuarial assumptions may generate questions from the SFO. In paragraph 6.70 above mention was made of a surplus arising because a property had increased appreciably in value or been sold following the granting of planning permission. Such a gain would be protected from taxation because of a scheme's approved status and the SFO is likely to accept the surplus has been properly dealt with if the actuary's recommendations meet its requirements (see paragraph 9.21 below), but frequent sales of property at a substantial profit could attract the attention of the inspector of taxes who may deem the trustees to be engaged in trading activities which would be taxable.

Reduction of surpluses

9.21 The actuary's recommendations for reducing a surplus should be acceptable to the SFO. The following recommendations would be acceptable to the SFO (see *schedule 22 paragraph 3(3)*).

(a) Suspension or reduction of company contributions for up to five years.

(b) Suspension or reduction of members' contributions for up to five years.

(c) Improving existing benefits.

(d) Providing new benefits.

(e)   A refund to the company.

(f)   Such other ways as may be prescribed by regulations made by the Inland Revenue.

9.22   Improving existing benefits or providing new ones may involve increases in pensions or additional benefits. Rule changes may be needed before they are implemented. New members could of course be introduced. Where a SSAS has more than one member it may be possible to reallocate the surplus in respect of a member's credit to that of another member whose credit was insufficient to provide maximum benefits. Such reallocation should usually be cleared first with the SFO. If pensions increases are to be awarded from a surplus the warning in PN 18.5 needs to be heeded. This mentions the deliberate building up of funds for the purpose of increasing pensions in payment must be restricted to schemes where the rules provide for reviews of pensions in payment and for increases. If there are no such rules, a general augmentation provision may not be sufficient in these circumstances.

9.23   In a SSAS the most common actuarial recommendation for an ongoing scheme is to reduce or suspend company contributions. It would be rare for a refund to be recommended as a first resort. Having satisfied itself on the recommendations to reduce any substantial surplus, the SFO will ask if the recommendations have been adopted. The SFO holds the trump card here, because as PN 18.6 mentions, if large surpluses are held approval may be withdrawn from the scheme unless acceptable proposals are forthcoming for dealing with the situation. This could mean approval being withdrawn from the part of the fund which is over-funded or any surplus returned to the company and taxed. This is one of the few instances where the surplus legislation applies to SSASs and it would involve a valuation on the basis prescribed in *schedule 22(2)* and possibly part approval under *schedule 22(7)*.

Winding-up

9.24   A refund of a surplus to the company from a SSAS is more likely to occur where the scheme is being wound-up rather than in an on-going situation. If a surplus is left over in this situation after all benefits up to the maximum permitted are paid out and no prospect exists of new members joining, then repayment must be made to the company and tax deducted at 40% [*section 601(1)*]. As with all schemes where refunds are to be made, the SFO must be approached first so arrangements for remittance of the tax involved can be made. Provided a scheme is not being replaced, a valuation on the prescribed basis is not required (JOM 86(25)(c)) because the amount involved is what remains in the scheme and is ascertained. If the winding-up of the scheme commenced before 18 March 1986, and there may be a few SSASs in this category, then the 40% tax charge does not apply [*section 601(3)(d)*]. In this instance the refund would be treated as a trading receipt for tax purposes as it would for an unapproved scheme and the normal rate of tax would apply.

9.25 Having mentioned unapproved schemes, it is uncommon for refunds to be made from these unless they are being wound-up because the SFO has refused to approve them or their approval has been withdrawn. The SFO refuses to allow refunds from schemes which have applied for approval, but have not yet been approved. This appears to be in line with JOM 82(20) and JOM 86(15) which require notification to the SFO in advance of any refunds.

9.26 Finally, on the tax charge of 40% itself, this is totally free-standing and cannot be set off against losses. It is deducted at source and accounted for by the trustees to the Inland Revenue.

Submission of actuarial valuations

9.27 Advisers will have noted in the past year a considerable tightening up in the SFO's attitude to delays in submitting triennial valuations and details of current investments. This arises from correspondence between the SFO and APT in 1989 regarding the SFO's practice in this area. The SFO had become increasingly concerned that in the continued absence of triennial valuations and details of current investments it could not be certain SSASs were being administered in accordance with the provisions governing approval. It therefore proposed a new procedure for pursuing valuations and obtaining current investment details at the same time.

9.28 In essence the SFO's proposals were to send reminders for triennial valuations six months after their effective date and ask for investment details. There would follow reminders depending upon whether investment details were provided or the reason for the delay was explained. Twelve months after the effective date 30 days notice would be given that the SFO would write to the managing trustees if the valuation was not forthcoming. Failure to respond would entail the managing trustees being requested to provide the outstanding valuation and a list of assets. If these details are not submitted within 30 days the scheme's approval would be seriously prejudiced or, if it was not approved, the SFO would assume the application for approval had been withdrawn. If that deadline was reached without response, approval could be expected to be withdrawn or the application for approval would be assumed to be withdrawn. These are dire consequences in view of the taxation implications for both approved and unapproved schemes. The procedure was introduced by the SFO in 1989 and it is now a familiar procedure.

9.29 Fortunately, the situation need not get so serious, although actuaries are well aware of the delays that can occur in obtaining information from trustees, companies and their accountants to enable triennial valuations to be prepared. The SFO made it plain, however, to the APT that it was in the interests of both advisers and trustees, where delay was likely in producing valuations, to inform it of the reasons and at least to provide details of the current investments in the meantime and not to wait until the valuation was prepared before doing so. The SFO further stated that its actions would depend on the particular circumstances of a scheme and this appears to have been borne out by events, especially where good reasons for delays have been provided. The SFO is also prepared to accept valuations based on unaudited accounts and to consider a valuation after four or five years if the triennial valuation is long overdue.

Chapter 10

Withdrawal of Approval

Introduction

10.1 The SFO's power to withdraw a scheme's tax exempt approval has been mentioned in several places in this book. This chapter explains what withdrawal of approval entails for SSAS and covers the most important aspects of withdrawal of approval. It should be borne in mind that any type of exempt approved scheme may have its approval withdrawn, therefore the following points do not apply solely to SSASs unless specifically mentioned.

Legislation

10.2 The Inland Revenue has discretionary powers not only to approve pension schemes, but also to withdraw that approval. The authority to withdraw approval was first contained in *section 19(3), FA 1970* on such grounds and from such date as may be specified in the notice. There were apparently some doubts as to the SFO's power to withdraw approval retrospectively. An amendment was announced in JOM 88(7) and contained in *paragraph 2 schedule 3, F(No 2)A 1987*. This legislation gave the SFO the power to withdraw approval from a date not earlier than the later of 17 March 1987 (the date of the Chancellor's Budget speech) or the date when approval ceased to be justified. These provisions were incorporated in *section 590(5)*. However, as there were apparently still some doubts regarding the SFO's power to withdraw approval, *section 590(5)* was replaced by a new provision, *section 591(B)(1)* (*FA 1991, s 36(2)*) which is the current authority for withdrawing approval. It means that if the offence giving rise to the SFO's decision to withdraw a scheme's approval occurred prior to 17 March 1987, the effective date of withdrawal would be 17 March 1987 and no earlier. It should also be noted that a scheme's approval cannot be withdrawn from a date earlier than the effective date of approval.

Reasons for withdrawal

10.3   *Section 591B(1)* states that the notice of withdrawal of approval should be sent to the administrator and that the grounds for withdrawal may be specified in the notice. It would be most unusual for the SFO not to state the reasons for withdrawing approval of a particular scheme unless they were obvious. If the reasons are not stated the SFO should be asked to justify its decision. If withdrawal of approval is on the grounds that the circumstances no longer warrant the scheme's tax exempt status details of the circumstances should be requested.

10.4   Withdrawal of approval is a serious step and one not met with too frequently. There is no exhaustive list of 'offences' that warrant withdrawal of approval, but PN 24.2 gives an indication of the circumstances that may cause a scheme's approval to be withdrawn. These are an unacceptable amendment to the rules, serious breaches of the rules, substantial over-funding and failure by the administrator to furnish information or to meet the scheme's tax liabilities. Breaches of the rules could include payment of excessive or unauthorised benefits. Failure to furnish information on a SSAS could embrace details of the investments or non-production of an actuarial report. Failure to comply with the regulations after 5 August 1991 may also lead to the loss of approval as implied by JOM 109(20). JOM 109(14)(15) also states that failure by the trustees to act in the best interests of the members regarding loans (see paragraph 5.30 above) and back-to-back loans (see paragraph 3.17 above) may also be grounds for the withdrawal of approval.

10.5   In paragraph 8.23 above it was mentioned that failure to reduce a substantial surplus could lead to loss of approval and that following tightening up by the SFO over production of investment details and triennial valuations such precipitate action might be taken. The unauthorised winding-up of a SSAS is also likely to result in removal of its tax exempt status.

10.6   PN 24.2 does not mention that approval would be withdrawn if the scheme's *bona fides* or the sole provision of the relevant benefits test were not met. However, as the SFO would not exercise its discretionary power to approve a scheme in these circumstances then it must be taken that approval would be withdrawn. This area is most relevant to a SSAS, because if it is used deliberately as a vehicle to achieve tax avoidance or non-relevant benefits are provided, e.g. loans to members (see paragraph 5.1 above) or directly linked pension mortgages (see paragraph 7.42 above), approval is likely to be withdrawn.

Effects of withdrawal

10.7 The loss of the various tax reliefs, if a scheme loses its approval, can be quite draconian. They are looked at in turn and may or may not apply depending on the nature of the scheme affected.

10.8 There would be loss of corporation tax or income tax relief under *section 592(4)* on any contributions paid between 17 March 1987 and 27 July 1989 in respect of a scheme whose approval was withdrawn from a date falling between these dates. It is possible, though unlikely, that the inspector of taxes could allow such contributions as deductions under the normal rules of Schedule D. For any contribution paid after the 27 July 1989 (the date when the *FA 1989* was enacted), *FA 1989, s 76* disallows such contributions unless the benefits payable from the scheme are taxable or the contributions are taxed under Schedule E on the member by virtue of section 591(1) (see paragraph 10.9 below).

10.9 Liability under Schedule E will arise on scheme members in respect of their share of any subsequent employer's contributions under *section 595(1)*. However, this should depend on how the inspector of taxes has treated the employer's contribution for schemes which have had their approval withdrawn from a date between 17 March 1987 and 27 July 1989. If the latter has been allowed as a deduction under the normal rules of Schedule D, Schedule E liability will arise. If the employer's contribution has been disallowed then any liability on the member should not arise.

10.10 If the scheme is contributory then the members would be penalised as they would not qualify for income tax relief on their personal contributions paid after approval was withdrawn except on the first £100 p.a. of contributions paid to secure annuities for a widow and dependents (*section 273*). Personal contributions to a FSAVCS should still qualify for tax relief unless that too has lost its approval.

10.11 Any pensions paid subsequently to members would be liable to tax under Schedule E as they are for any approved or unapproved scheme. The position is different for lump sum payments. Prior to the passing of the *Finance Act 1989* on 27 July 1989 lump sum payments made in commutation of a pension from an unapproved scheme were free from tax. This position applied following the decision of *Wales v Tilley* [*1942*] *1 All ER 455*. However, *schedule 6 paragraph 9, FA 1989* introduced *section 596A* which provides for cash lump sum payments from unapproved schemes or from schemes which were formerly approved to be taxed under Schedule E on the recipient. If a scheme's approval is withdrawn from a date between 17 March 1987 and 27 July 1989 then a cash lump sum paid from the scheme in that period in commutation of a pension would not be liable to tax. Also, under *section 189(b)* a cash lump sum paid to a member would not be taxable if the member had already been taxed under Schedule E in respect of contributions paid by the employer.

10.12 Lump sum death benefits should escape IHT if they are paid under a discretion exercised by the trustees, but they are liable to Schedule E from 27 July 1989. If a member's estate is included as a possible beneficiary under a discretionery power, an IHT gift with a reservation charge may arise.

10.13 Any income of the scheme would no longer enjoy relief from tax. This means that income received without deduction of tax would be taxable in the hands of the trustees e.g. rent from property. The trustees would not be able to claim any refund of tax deducted at source from income received. The scheme's income will, however, be exempt from an additional rate tax by virtue of *section 686(2)(c)(i)*.

10.14 CGT would arise on the disposal of assets by the trustees. The gain would arise over the whole of the period of ownership by the trustees and not from the effective date of withdrawal of approval although roll-over relief may be available. Under the *FA 1988, s 100* the rate of CGT will be restricted to the basic rate income tax.

10.15 If the scheme is insured, subsequent contributions cannot be referred to exempt pensions business. They would have to be transferred to general annuity business or the remainder of the life fund, as would the funds in which contributions have been placed.

10.16 Prior to the *FA 1989* and the advent of unapproved schemes as a result of the £60,000 cap (currently £71,400) if the employer had another approved scheme then by virtue of the former *section 590(7)* the approval of any other schemes could have been prejudiced whilst the scheme from which approval had been withdrawn remained in existence. This problem should have diminished after 27 July 1989 with the enactment of *section 590(7)–(11)*, which was introduced by *schedule 6 paragraph 3(4)* of the *Finance Act 1989*, as unapproved schemes no longer have to be considered alongside approved schemes of the employer.

10.17 Any refunds to the employer would be taxed at 40% under the surplus legislation. This is because *section 601* brings the free standing charge into effect on the refund to the employer of any funds which were held in a scheme which was formerly approved.

10.18 *Withdrawal of Approval*

10.18 Finally, tax continues to be chargeable in respect of refunds to members and commutation payments made before the scheme ceased to be exempt approved or in accordance with the rules when the scheme was last an exempt approved scheme. Tax is also chargeable on payments not authorised by the rules.

Redress

10.19 The affects are very severe and a scheme would have got into severe difficulties with the SFO to have lost its approval. Is there any action that can be taken to reverse or mitigate the SFO's action once the notification is received that approval has been withdrawn? One reaction may be to wind-up the scheme as quickly as possible, but the position should be reviewed carefully. A trust still exists with a set of rules and there may be a reason for its continuance despite the loss of tax reliefs. There is, however, no provision in the legislation for an appeal against the SFO's decision. The removal of the scheme's approval would be taken under the SFO's discretionary powers against which there is no formal appeal even if the reason for withdrawal was due to non-compliance with the regulations. It may be possible to rectify the position which has caused the withdrawal of approval, but representations would have to be made to the SFO at a high level. If redress is sought solely to reverse the SFO's decision without any rectification, then a very good case would be needed. Representations would have to be made to the controller at the SFO or to the Inland Revenue. Complaints can be made to the parliamentary ombudsman if maladministration is thought to be appropriate. The only course of action open through the courts to reverse the SFO's decision would be by way of judicial review.

Chapter 11

Requirements of the DSS

Introduction

11.1 This chapter deals with those aspects of SSASs that fall within the ambit of the DSS, such as preservation, authorisation under the *FSA 1986*, disclosure, winding-up requirements and the pension schemes' register. It also covers the proposals of the DSS announced in 1989 regarding self-investment and other measures to protect occupational pensions including the appointment of a pensions ombudsman which will impinge on SSASs when the legislation is enacted.

Preservation

11.2 Almost without exception SSASs are not contracted-out and therefore in relation to the *SSA 1973* the benefits they provide need only be the minimum required for preservation purposes for early leavers. Broadly, this means that for those members who leave service before normal retirement age they should be entitled to 'short service benefits' or to the permitted alternative benefits (see paragraph 3.42 above). Also, where a member leaves service on or after 1 January 1986 and there is at least a year between the date of leaving and normal retirement age, benefits must be revalued from the date of leaving to normal retirement date under *schedule 1A, SSA 1975*. The reason for this is to ensure early leavers are treated no less favourably as far as their benefits are concerned than those members who retire at normal retirement age.

11.3 To qualify for preservation benefits the member must have at least five years service prior to 1 April 1988 or, if leaving service occurs after that date, two years. The five or two year period of service can include service with a previous pension scheme from which a transfer payment was made to a SSAS.

Authorisation under the Financial Services Act 1986

11.4 Under the *Financial Services Act 1988 (Occupational Pension Schemes) Order 1988 (SI 1988/41)* investor protection legislation came into force on 20 February 1988 and affects the trustees of self-administered schemes who wish to manage their own investments. The intention of the Act is that everyone who advises on, or manages, investments must seek authorisation by applying for membership of one of the regulatory organisations e.g. IMRO, FIMBRA etc. The purpose of this order is to make an exception to this general rule for trustees of SSASs who are effectively managing their own investments. To qualify for this exemption under the *FSA 1986* all 'relevant members' must also be trustees or the trustees must not be involved in day-to-day decisions regarding the investment management of the SSASs.

11.5 An important point to note is that the term 'relevant member' is defined in the order as including former members who have left service and retained benefits under the scheme and retired members who still have some benefit entitlement not secured by annuities.

11.6 Generally the type of investment management in which trustees of SSASs wish to be involved relates to property purchases, loan-backs to their company, building society deposits etc. which are not caught by the *FSA 1986*. It is only where the trustees are themselves buying and selling ordinary shares and units in (say) exempt unit trusts and managed funds that they need be affected by the Act. Trustees are still permitted to make generic investment decisions affecting the mix of UK equities, UK gilts, overseas equities etc. so there is considerable scope for trustees who so wish to play an active part in the way their pension funds are managed without falling foul of the *FSA 1986* and without having to appoint all their 'relevant members' as trustees.

11.7 If a SSAS has a trustee who is not a member and that trustee does not take an active role in formulating investment policy and in taking investment decisions, then that trustee need not register under the *Financial Services Act 1986*. A trustee who is not a member and who is actively involved in investment decisions will need to take further professional advice.

Disclosure

11.8 The *SSA 1985*, the *Occupational Pension Schemes (Disclosure of Information) Regulations 1986 (SI 1986/1046)* and the *Occupational Pension Schemes (Disclosure of Information) (Amendment) Regulations*

1987 (SI 1987/1105) impose certain requirements on those who administer or are trustees of occupational pension schemes. They are popularly known as the 'disclosure' provisions. They do not apply to pension schemes with one member, so many SSASs may not have to comply. The format of accounts for a SSAS are also dealt with in SORP 1 and these details are in 12.23 below.

11.9 Under the disclosure provisions the trustees must obtain audited accounts each year and make them available on request to scheme members and former members who retain an entitlement to a benefit. The accounts should be made available within twelve months of the end of the scheme year to which they relate. It should be noted that part of the SFO's approval process requires scheme accounts to be made available (*section 605(1)(c)*). Notes on the contents of accounts as set out in *schedule 3* of *SI 1986/1046* may be found at Appendix 33. The format of accounts for a SSAS are also dealt with in the Statement of Recommended Practice (SORP 1) issued by the Accounting Standards Committee (ASC) in 1986 and these details are stated in 12.23 below. It should be noted that the auditor has to state that contributions payable to the scheme have been in accordance with the rules and the recommendations of the actuary. Alternatively the auditor must state why such a statement cannot be made. For instance, if the company pays a smaller amount than recommended by the actuary, the auditor would need to amend or qualify his statement and give a brief explanation of the reasons why the recommended rate has not been paid. Accounting and auditing requirements for companies having a SSAS are covered in Chapter 12.

11.10 The trustees must also make available on request a copy of the latest actuarial statement and certain other information regarding the scheme which is generally prepared in the form of a trustees' report. The actuarial statement is not the valuation, but is the statement prepared every time a valuation is carried out. A specimen statement was published with JOM 84 and may be found at Appendix 34. A statement does not have to be produced every year—only every three years for a SSAS— unless the actuary thinks it appropriate to issue a revised statement before the next valuation. So the latest actuarial statement need only be available. The trustees' report should be made available also within twelve months of the end of the scheme year to which it relates. The contents of the trustees' report are set out in *schedule 5* of *SI 1986/1046*.

11.11 Members of the scheme, including former members with a retained benefit entitlement, have in certain instances to be provided with information and benefit statements under *regulation 6(4)* of *SI 1986/ 1046*. Under *regulation 6(11)*, where a scheme is being wound-up, the trustees must also provide members and beneficiaries with specified information and details of benefits payable.

Insolvency and the appointment of an independent trustee

11.12 *Schedule 4 paragraph 1, SSA 1990* inserted *sections 57C, 57D* in the *SSPA 1975.* The purpose of these sections is to ensure that, if an insolvency practitioner 'commences to act' in relation to an employer who has employees in an occupational pension scheme (or if the official receiver is appointed as liquidator or provisional liquidator), one of the trustees of the scheme is 'independent'. *Section 57C* gives an insolvency practitioner or the official receiver the power to appoint or secure the appointment of an independent trustee if he is not satisfied that there is such a person among the existing trustees.

11.13 To be classed as 'independent' a person (or company) must not:

(a) be connected with an associate of the employer, the insolvency practitioner or the official receiver;

(b) have any interest in the assets of the employer or the scheme (other than as trustee);

(c) have supplied services to the trustees or managers of the scheme or to the employer within the previous three years; or

(d) be connected with or is an associate of a person or body who has an interest in the assets of the employer or of the scheme or with someone who has supplied services within the last three years.

11.14 Certain types of schemes are excluded from the provisions of *sections 57C, 57D*, namely:

(a) a scheme in which each member (including a former employee who retains benefits under the scheme) is a trustee of the scheme; or

(b) a money purchase scheme, a scheme providing benefits by means of earmarked insurance policies or a scheme providing only death-in-service benefits.

11.15 There is no requirement to have an independent trustee where the insolvency practitioner or official receiver started to act prior to the 12 November 1990.

11.16 Where the scheme is a centralised scheme, the requirement to appoint an independent trustee only applies if the employer who is in receivership or liquidation has the power to appoint and remove trustees or is itself a trustee.

11.17 In the case of a paid-up scheme with no members in pensionable service, an independent trustee has to be appointed only if the power of appointment and removal rests with the employer or the employer is a trustee.

11.18 *Sections 57C, 57D* were modified by the *Occupational Pensions Schemes (Independent Trustee) Regulations 1990 (SI 1990/2075)* and paragraphs 11.13 to 11.17 above reflect the contents of those regulations. The basic requirement for an independent trustee to be appointed in the prescribed circumstances came into force on the 12 November 1990.

11.19 In relation to SSASs, the question of whether a pensioneer trustee is automatically considered 'independent' has been raised with the DSS, but there is no special exemption for pensioneer trustees. A pensioneer trustee strictly will not be independent because it has supplied services to the trustees and the employer. It may also have an interest in the assets of the employer if there are fees outstanding. The responsibility for seeing that the regulations are complied with rests essentially with the insolvency practitioner or official receiver.

Register of occupational personal pension schemes

11.20 The *SSA 1990* made provision for the establishment of a register of occupational and personal pension schemes and for payment of an annual levy based on the number of scheme members. A detailed explanation of the legislation and the administrative arrangements of the register and the levy may be found in JOM 103. The main aspects are covered in paragraphs 11.21–11.26 below.

11.21 The regulations relating to the register and the levy came into effect on the 1 January 1991 except for the regulation which relates to the inspection of the register which was effective from 1 April 1991. The purpose of the register is to have an up-to-date central records system to enable individuals to trace their preserved pension rights. The annual levy is designed to fund the administration of the register, the pensions ombudsman (see paragraphs 11.59–11.63 below) and grants made by the OPB.

11.22 The trustees of all 'registrable schemes' are required to provide certain information about the scheme to the OPB (which is the first registrar) and, unless the scheme is frozen or paid-up, to pay the levy.

11.23 *Requirements of the DSS*

The information has to be provided on a form PR1(90) (Appendix 35). A 'registrable scheme' does not include a scheme with only one member, a scheme which provides only death-in-service benefits or a scheme which has been wound-up. Paid-up or frozen schemes, however, are registerable schemes. Those SSASs with only one member will therefore not be registerable.

11.23 Schemes with a commencement date prior to the 1 May 1991 must register and pay the levy for the registration year beginning 1 April 1991 no later than the 31 July 1991. A scheme which starts on or after 1 May 1991 must register within three months of its commencement date.

11.24 The responsibility for providing the registrar with the relevant information rests with the trustees of the scheme. They are also liable for the levy though this may be paid from the resources of the scheme or by the employer. For SSASs with two to six members the levy is £5 and with seven to twelve members £12.

11.25 The information on the register will be regularly checked. Essentially, the registrar will send the trustees a computer schedule every three years which must be returned with a note of any changes together with the payment of the appropriate levy. There are, however, transitional arrangements in the first year designed to split the schemes into three groups. Schemes which started prior to 1 May 1991 will initially pay one year's levy and will be assigned letter 'A', 'B' or 'C'. The second payment will then be for one, two or three years to establish the three-year cycle for each group.

11.26 The trustees are also responsible for notifying any changes in the relevant information within six months of the change.

DSS proposals on self-investment

11.27 The OPB report entitled 'Protecting Pensions: Safeguarding Benefits in a Changing Environment' was published on 1 February 1989. It contained various recommendations, one of which was in the area of investments of self-administered schemes. This recommended that if scheme assets, net of self-investment, did not cover winding-up liabilities, there should normally be a maximum of self-investment of 5% of scheme assets, with provision for dispensation in appropriate cases. SSASs were specifically exempted in the OPB Report from the 5% restriction on self-investment.

130

11.28 On 7 November 1989 the secretary of state for social services announced that following the OPB report the government would be making proposals for greater protection for members of pension schemes. One of the proposals was to introduce a new ceiling on self-investment for pension schemes which would allow them to invest no more than 5% of their assets in the employer's business (Appendix 29). The limit would be 5% in all cases with no dispensation to be allowed, but time would be given to meet the requirement. Nil self-investment would be recognised as good practice.

11.29 There was a considerable reaction from all those involved with SSASs when it became clear that SSASs would be affected by the proposals just as much as large self-administered schemes. The DSS explained that self-investment included loans to the company, shareholdings in the company and property let to the company and that the deadline for reducing investments of this nature to 5% of the scheme's assets would be 31 December 1991. The reasons for these measures along with other proposals were stated to be the improvement of benefit security for present and future pensioners.

11.30 The arguments for such a measure to protect the members of large self-administered schemes are well understood. Such members would be totally at arms-length from the company and the trustees and would not be able to look after their interests in the scheme. In a SSAS the members would be the directors of the company and also the trustees and therefore very much in charge of their own destiny. If their company failed they would be only too well aware that their retirement benefits could be in jeopardy if the trustees invested a substantial proportion of the assets of a SSAS in their own company's shares or in a loan to their company.

11.31 Loans to the company and property leased to the company are very common features of SSASs. They probably account for some 40% of the value of the assets of SSASs. The facility to invest in this area is a strong selling point for SSASs. However, for large self-administered schemes it would be unusual for loans to be made to the company— probably a public company—and company shares would be a small minority holding. Presumably property leased to the company was the main concern of the DSS particularly if such property had proved difficult to sell on the company's winding-up.

11.32 The proposals contrasted strongly with the SFO's practice in this area. Loans up to 50% of the assets may be made to the company. Shareholdings in the company worth up to 50% of the assets may be

131

held. The whole of the assets may be invested in commercial property and leased to the company.

11.33 The representations made on behalf of SSASs to be exempted from the proposals on self-investment were of such strength that the DSS announced concessions through a press release on 20 December 1989 (Appendix 37). The secretary of state for social services recognised that different considerations applied to SSASs in that they catered mainly and often exclusively for shareholding-directors who are themselves normally the trustees and whose investment decisions create a double risk for their own jobs and pension payments rather than those for others.

11.34 The proposals were therefore refined and one of the suggestions of the APT was adopted which is that:

'the proposed restrictions will not apply to SSASs in cases where all members are trustees, each member is a 20% director as defined for Inland Revenue purposes and trustee decisions require a nem *"con vote"*.'

'*Nem con*' means the decision was taken without any trustee dissenting.

11.35 This concession was welcome as it would exempt the majority of SSASs from the proposals. Where members were not already trustees they could probably be appointed as such before the legislation was enacted, but many SSASs would still be caught.

SSASs caught by the proposals

11.36 Those schemes with no current self-investment or with up to 5% of assets self-invested would not have been able after 31 December 1991 to make loans or lease-back property above the 5% limit.

11.37 The definition of 20% director remained to be set out by the DSS. The Inland Revenue's current definition of controlling director is given in JOM 91(3) (Appendix 10) and includes 'associates' and children of majority age of 20% directors. It was hoped that the DSS would adopt this definition as many members of SSASs are sons and daughters of the controlling director who are members of the scheme, aged over 18, but not holding over 20% of the issued share capital. Many such members were brought into SSAS by 1 June 1989 to beat the deadline for the £60,000 earnings cap which applied at that time.

11.38 Some members of SSASs did not hold 20% of the company's shares, either because they were not members of the controlling family or there were six or more of them. In either case it would not have been possible for them to become 20% directors. They could not have become members of another SSAS as the SFO will not allow more than one SSAS for the company (see paragraph 2.11 above).

11.39 The position of leavers in a SSAS also caused a problem where they had resigned as trustees and were no longer directors of the company. Unless they had taken a transfer payment to another scheme, such a SSAS would be caught by the self-investment restrictions.

11.40 Some SSASs no longer had active members. The company may have been sold or wound-up and the SSAS was paid up or being wound-up or in the five year period allowed for purchasing pensions. A few SSASs only had beneficiaries such as a minor child of a deceased member being paid an annuity whilst in full-time education.

Investment problems

11.41 If the proposals were to be enacted in their then current form then those SSASs with property, loans and shares in the self-investment areas had until 31 December 1991 to reduce such investments to below the 5% limit. This deadline was, however, set in November 1989 and therefore it is expected that the deadline would be set further forward into 1992. Those schemes that would be caught were having to consider how to comply by the deadline even though further representations might achieve some more concessions (see paragraph 11.50 below).

Property

11.42 The sale of property by the trustees before they originally intended to dispose of it to secure the members' benefits say, would cause problems. If it is leased to the company and is its main business base, the property cannot be simply re-let to another tenant. The company still needs a home. It may be possible to sell the property to the company, but if not then a sale to another purchaser with the company as a sitting tenant would not produce the best price for the trustees.

11.43 The trustees with their directors' hats on would also have been only too aware of the effects the sale would have on the financial future of the company and their employees.

Loans

11.44 This would possibly be an easier area to deal with as the trustees could reduce their investment to the 5% level albeit with difficulty. Most loans are for less than a year, so once the deadline was known, any further loans could be kept below 5%. However, if the company needed further finance a replacement loan from a bank was unlikely to be available on the scale required.

11.45 Loans of over a year and terminating beyond the deadline would cause considerable concern, especially if the capital was repayable in full at the end of the period of the loan. Many companies benefit from this source of finance and reducing this facility from 50% to 5% would have had substantial repercussions on a company's trade and employment. The trustees would be most conscious of these repercussions.

Shares

11.46 The number of SSASs which invest in shares in the company is small, but trustees faced with reducing such a holding to 5% of the assets would still have had substantial problems. There is no open market in which to sell them. There are restrictions on their sale which effectively mean the purchasers may only be the members, their relatives or the company itself. The Inland Revenue has banned member/trustee transactions from 5 August 1991 (see paragraph 7.17 above) which may mean that only the company would have been able to buy the shares.

Retrospective effect

11.47 The retrospective nature of the DSS proposals did not prove very popular. This was in stark contrast to the Inland Revenue proposals for SSASs which are prospective in line with the Inland Revenue's customary adoption of the principle that tax legislation is never retrospective. The DSS proposals would hit long-term financial arrangements made by the trustees in good faith before November 1989 in all three areas of self-investment.

11.48 They would probably have bitten hardest in relation to loans especially where the trustees had entered into (say) a five year loan agreement with the company where the company would have to repay sufficient of the loan by the deadline to ensure the SSAS met the 5% limit. Or perhaps the leasing arrangements were such that the company could not have terminated its lease earlier without a financial penalty.

Subsequent developments

11.49   The representations that led to the concessions from the DSS in December 1989 continued unabated into 1990 because of the problems and difficulties that would still have arisen for those SSASs outside the concessions. Paragraphs 11.36 to 11.48 above serve to highlight the various issues. The DSS and MPs continued to be lobbied by the representatives of the SSAS industry and by trustees, members and their companies.

11.50   In response to this further lobbying the DSS announced in March 1990 that it would conduct a survey to provide up-to-date information on the extent of self-investment, where it is concentrated and what particular problems will arise in restricting it. At Appendix 38 may be found an extract from a letter by Lord Henley (DSS) to an MP giving the background to the proposed survey.

11.51   The survey covered both SSASs and large self-administered schemes. It was undertaken by Ernst & Young for the DSS during the summer of 1990. All the usual representative bodies were given the opportunity to make further written and verbal representations. The survey team made visits to SSASs to ascertain the problems at first hand. The survey report was made to the DSS by 30 September 1990 and published in May 1991 as the 'Study of Self-Investment by Pension Funds'.

11.52   Whilst the survey was being conducted the enabling legislation was enacted. The *SSA 1990* provides at *section 14* for regulations to be made modifying the provisions of the *SSPA 1975* so that the recommendations stemming from the OPB Report may become law. *Schedule 4, paragraph 3, SSA 1990* also amends the *SSPA 1975* by introducing *section 57A*. This section deals with the restrictions to be placed on self-investment and defines the area of 'employer-related investments' that are to be restricted i.e. shares, property and loans.

11.53   At the same time as the 'Study of Self-Investment by Pension Funds' was published the DSS issued a press release (Appendix 39) and referred draft regulations to the OPB for consideration. The press release made it clear that further substantial concessions would be made for SSASs although the principle of limiting self-investment to 5% of a pension scheme's resources would be maintained. The survey recognised the considerable problems identified in paragraphs 11.36 to 11.48 above that reducing self-investment to 5% would entail and framed its recommendations accordingly. Not all the recommendations are to be adopted. There are some variations proposed by the DSS to the recommendations and the DSS has included proposals of its own.

The revised proposals for SSASs

11.54 The press release announced that SSASs would be exempt from the regulations where written agreement by all the members is provided to each act of self-investment once the regulations come into effect. The APT subsequently made it known that in these cases all members must be trustees and there is a scheme rule that all members must agree to the self-investment in writing. A member is anyone whose benefits have not been bought out. It is clear that the previous 20% director requirement (see paragraph 11.34 above) has been dropped.

11.55 If the requirements in paragraph 11.54 (above) are not met by a SSAS, this will entail self-investment being restricted to 5% of the value of the scheme's assets. If the trustees own shares in the company with a value in excess of the 5% limit and which are listed on the stock exchange (unlikely for a SSAS), these are to be reduced to the 5% limit within two years of the legislation coming into force. If loans have been made to the company and exceed the 5% limit they are to be reduced to 5% within two years also. If the trustees' shares in the company are traded on the unlisted securities market a period of five years is to be allowed for reduction to the 5% limit. The original deadline of 31 December 1991 has been considerably eased and the retrospective nature of the previous proposals has been dropped.

11.56 For those SSASs still caught by the regulations when it comes into effect, e.g. not all members are trustees, self-investment held at that date in property leased to the company and shares in the company which are unquoted may continue to be held and not sold. However, if their value exceeds the 5% limit no further self-investment may be made or if their value is less than the 5% limit further self-investment will be permissible only to the extent that it does not exceed the 5% limit taken with the current self-investment.

11.57 It is clear that any members of SSASs who are not currently trustees of the scheme need to be appointed as trustees if the restrictions are to be avoided when the legislation becomes effective. There will, however, be SSASs where this is not possible e.g. where a member has left the company's service with deferred benefits in the SSAS. Such a member may also have resigned as a trustee at the same time and re-appointment may not be possible. Advisers will need to identify these cases and perhaps suggest to their clients that the member concerned be persuaded to take a transfer value or that a deferred annuity be purchased.

11.58 At the time of writing it is not known when the regulations will be promulgated. It is to be hoped a further period of consultation on the draft regulations will be afforded to the representative bodies concerned as there are some matters that need clarification e.g. the time-scale for introducing the rule requirement that all members must agree to the self-investment in writing (see paragraph 11.54 above). Also it is not clear who will actually monitor the regulations, the OPB or SFO and what sanctions are to be applied for non-compliance.

Other DSS proposals

11.59 Following the OPB Report 'Protecting Pensions: Safeguarding Pensions in a Changing Environment' (see paragraph 11.27 above), the secretary of state also announced on 7 November 1989 (Appendix 36) several other proposals for greater protection for members of pension schemes. The remainder of this chapter explains some of the measures as they apply to SSASs and when they became effective or if they are to be enacted.

Pensions ombudsman

11.60 *Schedule 3* of the *SSA 1990* introduced *sections 59B(1), 59C(3)(5)* to the *SSA 1975* regarding the provision of a pensions ombudsman. The *Personal and Occupational Pension Schemes (Pensions Ombudsman) Regulations 1991 (SI 1991/588)* established the pensions ombudsman from 1 April 1991 and set out the guidelines within which he operates.

11.61 The ombudsman's role is that of a watchdog for people with rights under occupational or personal pension schemes. He is able to adjudicate between a member of a scheme and its trustees or manager where there is a complaint about injustice caused by maladministration or a dispute of fact or law. In relation to an SSAS it is difficult to see the ombudsman playing an adjudicating role where the potential complainant is very often also a trustee, but there are members of SSAS who are not trustees and the ombudsman will present an option for pursuing such a member's complaint. The service is free of charge.

11.62 It is expected that complainants will first raise their complaint with the trustees or managers. If they fail to get satisfaction the next step should be to ask OPAS for help. Where OPAS is unsuccessful or if the complainant is still not satisfied or where a judgment and determination are required particularly in matters of fact or law the ombudsman should be approached to resolve the issue.

11.63 In seeking the ombudsman's assistance, a complainant must apply in writing within three years from the time when the matter of the complaint or dispute arose. The ombudsman's decisions will be binding on the parties concerned subject to a right of appeal on a point of law to the high court. A booklet entitled 'The Pension Ombudsman: how he can help you' is available from the Ombudsman's office. It summarises the ombudsman's terms of reference and the procedure for someone who wants to complain. The booklet has been sent to OPAS and all Citizen's Advice Bureaux.

11.64 The ombudsman's remit does not extend to a complaint or a dispute appropriate to another ombudsman, e.g. the insurance ombudsman, to a dispute regarding a public service pension scheme, except the National Health Service Scheme for England and Wales, or to a complaint or a dispute regarding a state social security benefit. It is important also not to confuse the pensions ombudsman's role with that of the parliamentary ombudsman in the field of pension schemes. As mentioned in paragraph 11.61 (above) the pensions ombudsman deals with disputes between scheme members and the trustees. The parliamentary ombudsman, in dealing with complaints arising from pension schemes, would be concerned with the application by the SFO or OPB of the legislation which they supervise e.g. a dispute regarding the withdrawal of tax approval by the SFO as mentioned in paragraph 10.19 (above).

Increases to pensions

11.65 *Section 11(1), schedule 2, SSA 1990* introduced *section 58A, schedule 3A* to the *SSPA 1975* regarding pensions increases. Occupational schemes apart from money purchase schemes (see paragraph 4.3 above) are to be required to provide pension increases in line with the RPI up to a ceiling of 5% in respect of future pensionable service and past pensionable service out of surpluses occurring after actuarial valuations. This 'limited price indexing', as it is known, is not yet in force as the appointed day has not been set. In fact the DSS was urged from all quarters of the pensions industry to delay setting the appointed day until the decisions in the case of *Barber v Guardian Royal Exchange* [1990] *IRLR 240* were clarified with the result that the secretary of state announced in June 1991 that a final decision on when the relevant provisions in *SSA 1990* would be brought into effect is to be deferred until the present uncertainties of the *Barber* case are removed. There is presently a case before the European Court, the *Coloroll* case, where this matter is expected to be resolved.

11.66 As regards the use of the surplus, schemes are precluded from 17 August 1990 from making refunds to the company until provision has been made in the rules for every current and future pension to be increased to the level stated in paragraph 11.65 above. From the appointed day the surplus must first be used to provide the increases to pensions. This is in marked contrast to the former position where the company normally had a choice of how the surplus could be used e.g. to reduce company or member contributions.

Leavers

11.67 *Section 14(1), schedule 4 paragraph 14, SSA 1990* amended *schedule 1A paragraph 2(3), SSPA 1975* regarding the position of members who had left service before 1 January 1991. For such members their deferred pension must be revalued in the period up to normal retirement date by 5% p.a. or the increase in the RPI, if less. The pension to be revalued is that relating to service on or after 1 January 1985.

Scheme liabilities on winding-up

11.68 *Schedule 4 paragraph 2, SSA 1990* introduced *section 58B, SSPA 1975* regarding the treatment of liabilities in certain circumstances. Thus where a scheme's liabilities exceed the value of its assets, the amount of the deficiency is to be treated as a debt due from the company to the trustees. This is effective from 13 July 1990, but does not apply to money purchase schemes.

Chapter 12

Accounting and Auditing Requirements

Introduction

12.1 It was the practice to charge for pension costs in the profit and loss account the amount equal to the contribution paid by employers to the pension fund. As a result if an employer paid a special contribution to meet an actuarial shortfall in a defined benefit scheme, this would reduce profits both for tax and financial accounting purposes. These practices did not comply with the basic accounting concepts of consistency and accruals. The statement of standard accounting practice (SSAP 24) which was introduced to remedy this, however, affords a lot of latitude in presenting pension costs resulting in affecting several pence of a quoted company's earnings per share. However, it is expected that valuation methods and assumptions used for costing may not be at variance from those used for funding in the long-term. As for defined contribution schemes (see paragraph 4.3 above), SSAP 24 affects only disclosure and the amount funded and the amount charged in the profit and loss account usually will coincide, ignoring the year end adjustment, if any. In general terms this would apply to all SSASs.

A detailed exposition of SSAP 24 is given in Tolley's Accounting for Pension Costs.

12.2 Discussions have taken place between the actuarial and accounting professions for a number of years, but it took considerable time for a standard to emerge because pension costs for defined benefit schemes do not lend themselves readily to standard accounting procedures due to the uncertainty of the eventual liability. However, as a result of the application of SSAP 24, a company's management may now understand for the very first time the mystique of the work of the actuary and as a result appreciate the effects of a funding plan in relation to the population mix of the scheme, salary and merit increases, pension in payment increases, inflation and investment returns. These factors are influenced by the underlying nature of pensions which have the following characteristics:

(a) Pensions liabilities are long-term in nature and allocation of pension costs built up over a number of years between each accounting year is at best a guestimate and not always straightforward.

(b) Pension liabilities are uncertain in amount since they are linked to final salaries.

(c) Different benefits are paid out in different instances depending on whether the member:

    (i) retires;
    (ii) dies; or
    (iii) leaves service.

(d) Some benefits are discretionary e.g. pensions in payment being increased from time to time.

12.3 A company may try, in the future, to match the funding basis with the costing basis so as to achieve equality thereby eliminating large balance sheet entries e.g. prepayments or provisions. Ultimately a neutral position may well be achieved, but the fact that the funding basis is based on conservative methods and assumptions and the costing basis may be based on the 'best estimate' will militate against this and may well result in surpluses being accumulated and prepayments arising in the company's balance sheet. However, the company's strategy will be to achieve equality so as to present a neutral position both for financial and tax purposes subject, of course, to the constraints of trustees/members' requirements as to prudence in funding.

Consistency

12.4 As the SSAP 24 permits alternate methods as to assumptions and does not compel any one method to be used, it would be well nigh impossible for these to be consistency in the treatment of pensions between one company and another even if they belong to the same industry. Astute financial directors will examine the alternatives under SSAP 24 to obtain the best profile of pension costs for defined benefit schemes to meet their own objectives. It is, however, desirable for the same basis to be used consistently by a company so as to avoid distortions. The trend of pension costs are best observed as a percentage of payroll for a period of ten years rather than on cash figures.

Post-retirement benefits

12.5 SSAP 24, paragraph 75 states that 'although this statement primarily addresses pensions, its principles may be equally applicable to the cost of providing other post-retirement benefits'. The ASC states that this paragraph is indicative only and that it is intended to suggest to companies how they might account for other post-retirement benefits. The ASB has no plans to develop a statement on accounting for other post-retirement benefits and until they do so there is no obligation to apply SSAP 24 to such benefits although companies may consider it appropriate to do so. (See TR 756 'Statement by the ASC on the application of the principles of SSAP 24 'Accounting for pension costs' to other post-retirement benefits'.)

Discounting

12.6 It is well understood that a sum of money receivable at a future date is worth less to the recipient than the same money receivable immediately even after allowing for changes in the purchasing powers of the money. Equally an obligation to make a payment in the future is less onerous for the payer than one to make an immediate payment of the same amount. Money has therefore a time value and discounting is a technique that gives recognition to the time value of money. (This is dealt with in detail in TR 773 'The use of discounting in financial statements'.) This technique is not currently used extensively in the preparation of financial statements although it is accepted practice to discount long-term assets and liabilities in certain specialised cases. SSAP 24 provisions dealing with balance sheet items are cases in point as are the provisions in the ASC discussion paper 'Fair value in the context of acquisition accounting'.

Pension surplus

12.7 To whom does a surplus belong? Where assets and liabilities pertaining to pension funds are reworked or there are parallel calculations and a surplus occurs it is relevant to question its destination. Does it belong to the company, the members of the scheme or to the pensioners? The answer to this question largely depends on the terms of the trust deed and rules made thereunder. If these are silent, then from 17 August 1990 schemes are prevented from making refunds to the company until provision has been made in the rules for every current and future pension to be increased in line with the RPI with a ceiling of 5%. This is not yet in force (see paragraphs 11.65 and 11.66 above).

Valuations

12.8 SSAP 24 offers a choice on implementation of the standard. The last available actuarial valuation (provided always that it is consistent with the requirements of the standard) or a special valuation for purposes of implementation of the standard could be used. A reason for obtaining a new valuation is that it may be decided to change the method and/or assumptions used in the previous valuation in order to produce a result more compatible with the objectives of the standard.

12.9 There must be a rigid timetable for valuations so as not to delay the preparation of accounts. Also the methods and assumptions must be consistent—one valuation taken with the next. It would, of course, be desirable for industry-wide consistency to be achieved so that the different company results can be judged from a uniform standpoint. SSAP 24 makes it clear that actuarial valuations are required no more frequently than triennially and that a special valuation is not necessary on its implementation. The figures can be based on the most recent valuation although appropriate adjustments will be required if there have been major changes since the earlier valuation.

Takeovers and mergers

12.10 Since disclosure is required of the market value of pension fund assets and the percentage solvency level, the existence of surplus resources in the pension scheme will become public knowledge. Companies whose funds are in surplus will feel exposed and the remedy will be for rapid and effective action to be taken to deal with the surplus. Although earlier drafts contained a section on accounting for pensions in takeover and merger situations the final version of SSAP 24 is silent on this topic. The reason for this is that a new standard for fair value accounting, which will include the pensions accounting requirements, is expected soon.

The role of the auditor

12.11 Whereas in other aspects of company accounts the directors and the auditors have to co-operate to achieve a true and fair view in presenting accounts and to comply with accounting standards, in the case of pensions both these parties must rely to a large extent on the actuary to provide appropriate information to comply with the requirements of SSAP 24.

12.12 Normally actuaries only report to the trustees of a scheme, but it may be desirable to extend this to cover a report to the company and/or the auditor in relation to the requirements of SSAP 24 (see also paragraph 12.20 below).

The application of SSAP 24 to SSASs

12.13 In general terms most SSASs would be treated as defined contribution schemes and the SSAP 24 requirements are as follows:

'In the case of a defined contribution scheme the employer's obligation at any point in time is restricted to the amount of the contributions payable to date. The pension cost is, therefore, the amount of the contributions payable in respect of the particular accounting period' (SSAP 24, paragraph 17).

12.14 The disclosure requirements for defined contribution schemes (see paragraphs 11.8 to 11.11 above) are that it will usually suffice to indicate the nature of the scheme and the amounts disclosed in the profit and loss account and balance sheet (SSAP 24, paragraph 46). SSAP 24, paragraph 87 specifies the disclosure requirements of a defined contribution scheme as:

(a) the nature of the scheme (i.e. defined contribution);

(b) the accounting policy;

(c) the pension cost charge for the period; and

(d) any outstanding or prepaid contributions at the balance sheet date.

12.15 The charge against profits for such schemes should be the amount of contributions payable to the pension scheme in respect of the accounting period (SSAP 24, paragraph 78). However, it should be noted that the pension cost should be paid as contributions in the accounting period if it is to be allowed as a charge against profits for corporation tax purposes.

12.16 As the rationale for most SSASs is that pension costs depend on the cash flow requirements of the company, it is possible for directors of companies to arrange for a smoothing over of pension costs over accounting periods. In these cases it is only the pension cost paid to the scheme that will be shown in the accounts. The Inland Revenue may arrange for special contributions to be allocated over several chargeable accounting periods. This may have deferred tax consequences in the company's accounts to allow for the timing differences between the contributions being paid and the tax allowances being given.

12.17 SSAP 24, Appendix 1(a) gives an example of disclosure for a defined contribution scheme as:

'The company operates a defined contribution pension scheme. The assets of the scheme are held separately from those of the company in an independently administered fund. The pension cost charge represents contributions payable by the company to the fund and amounted to £500,000 (1986 £450,000). Contributions totalling £25,000 (1986 £15,000) were payable to the fund at the year-end and are included in creditors.'

12.18 It should be noted that in an SSAS it is extremely unlikely that the contributions of successive years have any correlation with each other as regards the amount of the pension contribution or that there would be unpaid contributions or prepayments at the end of an account year.

12.19 Some schemes (and some SSASs could fall into this category) are not easy to be categorised as to whether they are defined contributory schemes or defined benefit schemes. These may be hybrid schemes (see paragraph 1.9 above) and in such cases the rules or the trust deed should be carefully studied and the operation of the scheme in practice has some bearing on the accounting treatment to be accorded it. With regard to SSASs, such schemes may involve the benefits being underwritten by LOs and the trust deed in question will often be a model deed produced by the LO. It is necessary in such cases to get expert opinion as to whether it is to be accorded accounting treatment as a defined benefit or defined contribution scheme. The perils of such a scheme being treated as a defined benefit scheme will result in the full rigour of SSAP 24 being applied to it.

The audit of an SSAS

12.20 The issue by the ASC in 1986 of SORP 1 'Pension Scheme Accounts', the *Occupational Pension Schemes (Disclosure of Information) Regulations (SI 1986 No 1046)*, the *Occupational Pension Schemes (Auditors) Regulations (SI 1987 1102)* together with the publishing of an 'Audit Brief' entitled 'The work of a pension scheme actuary' and a PN issued by the APC in June 1990 titled 'Auditing for pension costs under SSAP 24 — Liaison between the actuary and the auditor' clearly brought the audit of pension schemes into the full glare of publicity. The auditing practices committee also issued an auditing guideline 'Pension Schemes in the United Kingdom' in May 1988 to clarify the factors to be taken into account by the auditor in relation to the scheme audit and disclosure requirements.

12.21 The level of audit work and audit procedures will depend on the complications of a SSAS. The auditor will have to watch the level of self-investment, the type of investment etc. He will have to consider carefully the guidelines and requirements issued by the SFO in relation to SSASs and to ascertain the validity of the valuations of fund assets.

12.22 Where a scheme does not comply with the disclosure requirements or actuarial recommendations on levels of contributions are not followed the auditor will have to consider qualifying the audit report. Breach of self-investment limits or other requirements applicable to a SSAS by the DSS or Inland Revenue regulations or guidelines may lead to the qualification of the audit report where 'approval status' is jeopardised.

12.23 The disclosure regulations (see paragraphs 11.8 and 11.9 above) apply to all occupational schemes and therefore include SSASs except for those with only one member or those that only provide death-in-service benefits (*SI 1986/1046(3)(1)*). SORP 1 applies to all pension schemes except those with only one member. It therefore follows that a SSAS with one member is outside the scope of the disclosure regulations and SORP 1.

SORP 1 contains a format for the accounts of a pension scheme and they are shown below. The disclosure regulations require disclosure of any material departure from SORP 1 and therefore effectively require the principles and format of SORP 1 to be followed. It will be noted that some of the items shown below also appear in Appendix 26 which covers the contents of accounts under the disclosure regulations. There are also very specific accounting disclosure requirements in Appendix 3 to the regulations which must be shown.

The accounts of a pension scheme, and the notes thereto, should contain the items listed below where they are material. These lists are not intended to be recommendations on either the layout or the order of these items.

Revenue account

1. Contributions receivable:
    1.1 from employers:
         1.1.1 normal;
         1.1.2 additional;
    1.2 from members:
         1.2.1 normal;
         1.2.2 additional voluntary (see paragraphs 63 and 64);
    1.3 transfers in:
         1.3.1 group transfers in from other schemes;
         1.3.2 individual transfers in from other schemes.

2. Investment income:

    2.1   income from fixed interest securities;
    2.2   dividends from equities;
    2.3   income from index-linked securities;
    2.4   income from managed or unitized funds;
    2.5   net rents from properties. Any material netting-off should be separately disclosed;
    2.6   interest on cash deposits;
    2.7   share of profits/losses of trading subsidiary companies and joint ventures.

3. Other income:

    3.1   claims on term insurance policies;
    3.2   any other category of income which does not naturally fall into the above classification, suitably described and analysed where material.

4. Benefits payable:

    4.1   pensions;
    4.2   commutation of pensions and lump sum retirement benefits;
    4.3   death benefits;
    4.4   payments to and on account of leavers:
          4.4.1   refunds of contributions;
          4.4.2   state scheme premiums;
          4.4.3   purchase of annuities to match preserved benefits,
          4.4.4   group transfers out to other schemes;
          4.4.5   individual transfers out to other schemes.

5. Other payments:

    5.1   premiums on term insurance policies;
    5.2   any other category of expenditure which does not naturally fall into the above classification, suitably described and analysed where material.

6. Administrative and other expenses borne by the scheme, with suitable analysis where material.

    Where the administrative expenses are borne directly by a participating employer, that fact should be disclosed.

Net assets statement

7. Investment assets:

7.1 fixed interest securities (analysed between public sector and other);

7.2 equities;

7.3 index-linked securities;

7.4 managed funds (analysed between property and other);

7.5 unit trusts (analysed between property and other);

7.6 trading subsidiary companies and joint ventures;

7.7 freehold and leasehold property;

7.8 cash deposits;

7.9 insurance policies;

7.10 other investments, such as works of art;

7.11 debtors and creditors in respect of investment transactions where these form part of the net assets available for investment within the investment portfolio;

7.12 other assets and liabilities directly connected with investment transactions (e.g. financial futures, options and forward dealings in currencies and, where appropriate, tax recoverable).

Investments should be further analysed between 'UK' and 'foreign' and between 'quoted' and 'unquoted', and freehold and leasehold property should be further analysed between 'short leasehold' and 'other'.

8. Fixed assets held primarily for reasons other than investment potential.

9. Long-term borrowings:

9.1 sterling; and

9.2 foreign currency.

10. Current assets and liabilities:

10.1 contributions due from employer;

10.2 unpaid benefits; and

10.3 other current assets and liabilities (other than liabilities to pay pensions and other benefits in the future).

Appendix 1 to the SORP states that although it is desirable for freehold and leasehold property to be valued annually, such annual valuations can be carried out by the trustees provided a professional valuer carries out a valuation at regular intervals (say) every five years in the absence of unusual circumstances. The disclosure regulations require all assets to be shown at market value. As actuarial valuations are carried out every three years for a SSAS, a professional valuation of the property at the date of the actuarial valuation is often undertaken.

Appendix 2 states that all investments of the pension scheme (including long-term insurance policies) should be included in the net assets statement at market value. As the market value of long-term insurance policies is not available between the triennial valuation of the policies by the insurance company, the excess of the premiums paid over the pensions paid or *vice versa* must be added to or deducted from the pension policy asset shown in the balance sheet in those years. In the year the actuarial valuation is carried out, the market value is the actuarial value and it is therefore only in that year that there will be a change in the value of the insurance policy. This situation will only arise in the case of a hybrid SSAS set up by a LO or where, an unlikely situation, the SSAS assets consist of an insurance policy which is taken out to satisfy the obligation to set up pensions for the beneficiaries. Where, however, an annuity or pension policy has been taken out for a specific beneficiary at pension date this can be removed from the balance sheet.

Glossary

The descriptions of the terms which appear in this glossary are not intended to be comprehensive definitions. They are intended as guides for ease of reference to the particular paragraphs in the book where the term or concept is defined and/or discussed in more detail.

Additional voluntary contributions (AVC) — Additional payments to an occupational pension scheme made by a member up to 15% of his remuneration per tax year (see 4.3).

Administrator — The person or persons having the management of the scheme and who is or are responsible to the Inland Revenue for fulfilling certain statutory duties (see 3.66 *et seq*).

Buy-out policy or Section 32 buy-out policy — A single life deferred annuity on the life of the member taken out with an insurance company to satisfy the rights of an early leaver who selects this option on the termination of his pensionable service (see 3.38, 3.42 and 4.3).

Common trust fund — Investments made under trust where the interests of the beneficiaries (members in a pension scheme) lie against all the assets of the trust and not against any specific asset (see 3.10).

Commutation — The right to convert part of an income pension entitlement into a cash lump sum. Permissible within certain limits for all forms of Inland Revenue approved pension provision (see 4.11–4.14, 4.36 and 4.40).

Contracting-out/Contracted-out money-purchase scheme (COMP) — The OPB may permit an occupational pension scheme, including with effect from 6 April 1988 a money-purchase scheme, to contract-out of the SERPS provided broadly that equivalent basic protected rights are guaranteed under the occupational scheme (see 11.2).

Contribution credit — Such an amount as calculated by the actuary as represents the member's interest in the scheme (see 3.10).

Defined benefit scheme — A type of pension scheme under which the amount of pension and related benefits of the member is defined by reference to final remuneration. Also known as a 'Final salary scheme' (see 4.4).

151

Glossary

Defined contribution scheme — A type of pension scheme under which the pension and related benefits of the members depend entirely on the amount of contributions paid into the scheme by the company and by the employee/members themselves, albeit subject to final salary limitations. Also known as a money-purchase scheme (see 4.3).

Definitive deed — Comprehensive deed setting out the powers and duties of the trustees to which will commonly be attached the full rules of the scheme (see 3.15–3.43). To be distinguished from the interim deed (see 3.3–3.7).

Dynamisation — A means of increasing final remuneration for particular basis periods in line with the increase in RPI (see 3.26).

Earnings Cap — The limit imposed on pensionable earnings by the *FA 1989* (£60,000 p.a) and on pensionable service with companies within a trading group (currently £71,400 pa) (see 4.36–4.40).

Equal access — The requirement imposed under *section 53, SSPA 1975* that membership of a pension scheme must be open to both men and women on equal terms (see 3.43).

Final remuneration — The term commonly used to describe what pay of an employee/member and over what period is to count in the calculation of pensionable pay. Subject to numerous restrictions (see Chapter 4).

Fluctuating emoluments — Remuneration received by an employee on an irregular basis or not as part of basic remuneration which may be included in final remuneration (see 4.22, 4.25 and 4.35).

Free-standing AVC (FSAVC) — A contract between an individual who is a member of an occupational pension scheme and an independent pension provider under which the member can make additional voluntary contributions up to the general limit of 15% of his remuneration per tax year (see 4.3 and 10.10).

Hybrid scheme — A partly insured, as opposed to fully self-administered, occupational pension scheme under which up to, usually, 50% of the fund is invested in an insurance policy and the remainder is self-invested (see 1.9, 12.19 and 12.23).

Interim deed — Deed between the company and the trustees under which the scheme is established. To be distinguished from the definitive deed (see 3.3–3.7).

152

Model deed — A definitive deed agreed by a practitioner with the standards section of the SFO for use on that practitioner's SSAS (see 3.44–3.50).

Occupational Pensions Board (OPB) — Body responsible for enforcement of the following legislation:

(a)   The preservation requirements (see 11.2–11.3).

(b)   Contracting-out procedure and practice (see 11.2).

(c)   The equal access provisions (see 3.43).

Ordinary annual contributions — The regular contributions made by the company in line with the actuary's recommendations to the trustees of its pension scheme and is to be distinguished from a special contribution (see 9.11–9.13).

Pensioneer trustee — An individual or body corporate widely involved with occupational pension schemes and approved to have dealings with the SFO (see 2.24–2.32).

Personal pension scheme — A form of pension for the self-employed and for those in employment whose employer does not have an occupational scheme, other than a death-benefit only scheme, or who choose to opt out of that scheme (see 3.30, 3.38, 4.49 and 11.20).

Preservation — Broadly the requirements imposed under *section 63* and *schedule 16 SSA 1973* that certain early leavers are to be no less favourably treated in the way in which their pension and related benefits are calculated than those who retire at normal pension age. The term also refers to the statutory revaluation of deferred pensions (see 11.2–11.3).

Regulations — The statutory provisions contained in *SI 1991/1614* restricting or banning certain features and investments of SSAS and laying down reporting requirements effective from 5 August 1991 (see 2.2 and Appendix 4).

Relevant benefits — Broadly these are the permitted classes of benefit which an occupational pension scheme may provide (see Chapter 4).

Retirement annuity contract — A pension policy providing certain pension and related benefits, principally for the self-employed (see 1.3).

Retained benefits/Retained death benefits — The benefits and death benefits payable under separate pension arrangements which members of an occupational scheme, or their dependants as the case may be, must take into account when determining whether the total level of benefits from the occupational pension scheme exceeds Inland Revenue maxima (see 4.44–4.45, 9.4 and 9.15).

Self-investment — Investment by the trustees in loans to the company, in property and land leased to the company and in shares of the company (see 11.27–11.53).

SERPS — The state earnings-related pension scheme applicable to those in employment who are not members of contracted-out occupational pension schemes or (after June 1988) of personal pension schemes contracted-out of SERPS.

SFO — The Superannuation Funds Office of the Inland Revenue — a special department of the Inland Revenue which deals with, *inter alia*, the grant of exempt approved status to occupational pension schemes including SSAS.

Special contribution — A contribution made by a company to the trustees of its pension scheme which is not part of the regular pattern of contributions. It may be made in order to fund for a particular liability, e.g. an increase in pension entitlement, or to meet a deficiency in the assets of the fund (see 9.11–9.13).

Transfer payment — The amount paid by the trustees of one scheme to the trustees of another scheme or personal pension scheme when members change employer from one company to another and at the same time join the new company pension scheme or a personal pension scheme (see 4.49). A transfer payment could also take place where a member leaves one scheme and joins another scheme of the same employer.

Unit trust scheme — An authorised unit trust within the meaning of *section 468(6)* or where all the unit holders are wholly exempt from CGT or corporation tax (otherwise than by reason of residence) if they dispose of their units (see 6.28).

List of Appendices

Appendix

1. Joint Office Memorandum No 58.

2. Notes on Practice by the Inland Revenue issued to the Association of British Insurers and the Association of Pensioneer Trustees.

3. Occupational Pensions: Small Self-Administered Schemes Consultative Document.

4. Statutory Instrument 1991 No 1614.

5. Memorandum No 109.

5A. Model Rules for Small Self-Administered Pension Schemes.

6. Board Minute Resolving to Establish a Small Self-Administered Scheme.

7. Clause for Insertion in the Memorandum of Association of a Company Authorising the Establishment of a Pension Scheme.

8. Specimen Investment Power.

9. Specimen Power of Amendment.

10. Definition of 20% Director — PN 6.15 & JOM 91(3).

11. Power to Make and Receive Transfer Payments.

12. Specimen Deed of Adherence.

13. Standard Documents: Finance Act 1989 Provisions: Extract from SFO Controller's letter of 1 November 1989.

14. Specimen Winding-up Provision for Interim Trust Deed.

15. Occupational Pension Schemes Application for Approval — Form SF 176 (11/87).

16. Documentation Certificate — SF5 (2/91).

17. Documentation Certificate — SF6 (2/91).

18. Inland Revenue Undertakings Schemes Open to More than One Member — Form SF176(U) (1989) (12/89).

19. JOM 87(12) Transitional Arrangements — Circumstances where Finance (No 2) Act 1987 does not apply.

20. Expression of Wish Form.

21. Specimen Loan Document.

155

22. Particulars of Loans to Employers and Associated Companies — Form SF192 (6/89).

23. Scheme Investments — Loans to Employer and Associated Companies — Form SF7013.

24. Particulars of Property or Land Transactions — Form SF191 (6/89).

25. Particulars of Shares in Private Employer Company or Associated Company — Form SF7012.

26. Scheme Investments — Shares in an Employer Company (or Associated Company) or an Unlisted Company — Form SF193 (6/89).

27. Particulars of Non-Income Producing Assets — Form SF7014.

28. Scheme Investments — Non-Income Producing Assets — Form SF194 (12/87).

29. Scheme Investments — Miscellaneous Acquisitions and Disposals — Form SF7016.

30. Scheme Borrowing — Form SF7015.

31. Inland Revenue Statement of Practice SP 4/88, 22 July 1988 — Tax Treatment of Transactions in Financial Futures and Options.

32. GN9: Retirement Benefit Schemes — Actuarial Reports.

33. Schedule 3 — Disclosure Regulations Contents of Accounts.

34. Form of Actuary's Statement — Appendix 5 to JOM 84.

35. Occupational Pension Scheme Registration — Form PR1(90).

36. Social Security Press Release: New Measures to Protect Occupational Pensions.

37. Social Security Press Release: Small Self-Administered Pension Schemes Exempted from 5% Self-Investment Limit.

38. Extract from Lord Henley's (DSS) letter to Local MP.

39. Social Security Press Release: Investment of Resources by Pension Schemes.

40. Summary of Main Changes Introduced by SI 1991 No 1614.

Appendix 1

Joint Office Memorandum No 58

MEMORANDUM NO 58

Joint Office of
Inland Revenue Superannuation Funds Office and
Occupational Pensions Board

February 1979

Lynwood Road
Thames Ditton
Surrey KT7 0DP

01-398 4242

SMALL SELF-ADMINISTERED SCHEMES

Issued by the Inland Revenue Superannuation Funds Office

INTRODUCTION

1   Following about 3 years' experience with applications for tax approval of small self-administered schemes, it is now opportune for the Superannuation Funds Office (SFO) to publish more guidance on this subject. As will be seen from what follows, such schemes cannot be treated in the same way as either self-administered schemes catering for large numbers of rank and file employees, or as insured schemes. Employers have been encouraged by press articles referring to "tax havens" and "captive funds" to regard a small self-administered scheme as more than just an arrangement "for the sole purpose of providing relevant benefits" (see section 19(2) Finance Act 1970) and the progressively more critical approach adopted by the SFO in individual cases has followed inevitably from proposals which seem designed either for tax avoidance or to benefit the employer's business financially, rather than as straightforward arrangements for providing financial support for the members in old age.

2   This memorandum, which supersedes the existing short leaflet on form SF 133, outlines the special considerations applicable to small self-administered schemes. In other respects, normal Inland Revenue practice applies to them and benefits for 20% directors should satisfy the conditions described in Memorandum No 25. It has been assumed that such schemes will not be contracted-out under the Social Security Pensions Act 1975, but if, exceptionally, contracting-out is involved, the Occupational Pensions Board guidance on self-investment in Memorandum No 43 will apply.

Meaning of "small" scheme

3   Since it is necessary for practitioners to know which schemes will be subject to this memorandum, "small" generally means "with less than 12 members". But the SFO has taken the view that a scheme primarily for a few family directors, to whom were added some relatively low-paid employees with entitlement only to derisory benefits, included as a make-weight to bring the total membership to 12 or slightly more, was nevertheless "small". Conversely it might not be necessary to apply "small scheme" treatment to one, albeit with fewer than 12 members, where all the members were at arm's length from each other, from the employer and the trustees. No special action under the memorandum will normally be required in respect of a self-administered scheme already approved under the Finance Act 1970 in the ordinary way, merely because at a later date the membership fortuitously falls below 12. A small insured scheme, which becomes self-administered after approval will of course need to comply with the memorandum, except that the question whether a "pensioneer trustee" (see paragraph 4) needs to be appointed in place of, or in addition to, the existing trustee, will be considered in the light of the facts of the case.

Pensioneer trustee

4   It is necessary for the trustee to be, or the trustees to include, an individual or body widely involved with occupational pension schemes, and having dealings with the SFO, who is prepared to give an undertaking to the SFO that he will not consent to any termination of a scheme of which he is trustee, otherwise than in

157

accordance with the approved terms of the winding-up rule. Such a trustee is customarily described as a "pensioneer trustee". For the avoidance of doubt, it is worth stating that the undertaking has no hidden implications; a pensioneer trustee is not a "watchdog" for the Inland Revenue in any area other than the improper termination of the scheme.

5   If the trust instrument establishing the scheme provides for the trustees to act on majority rather than unanimous decisions, this provision must be qualified so that it does not apply where the question for decision relates to the termination of the scheme.

6   Where a corporate body wishes to act as a pensioneer trustee, it is normally essential that the directors, or a majority of them, should be acceptable as pensioneers in their own right, and that the acceptable directors should have the power to determine how the corporate body will vote in any proceedings of the pension scheme trustees.

7   The object of the Revenue's insistence on the appointment of a pensioneer trustee is that he should be able to block any request from the members of the scheme, or some of them, that the trust should be terminated and the funds distributed among them, subject perhaps to their giving the trustee an indemnity against the contingency of a claim by a remoter beneficiary having an interest on a member's death. It is accepted that the opposition of one trustee, or even of all, would be immaterial if all the persons having an interest under the trust were agreed in requiring the termination of the scheme (cf Saunders v Vautier, 1841). But such a consensus is unlikely in the context of a typical pension scheme except where all the members have retired and all interests have vested.

8   It has recently been suggested that as an alternative to the appointment of a pensioneer trustee, a trustee corporation, qualified by rules made under the Public Trustee Act 1906 to act as a custodian trustee, should be appointed as such. The trust deed would include provisions to prevent any payment out of the trust fund to the managing trustees apart from sums required from time to time to finance benefits as they fall due. Without commitment, the SFO will consider any proposal on these lines.

Investment of funds

9   It is not necessary to include in the trust deed any special restrictions on the investment powers of the trustees, except for a prohibition on loans to members of the scheme or to any other individual (for example, relatives of members) having a contingent interest under the scheme. This restriction is considered necessary in small schemes in particular, because of the possibility (arising from the less than arm's length relationship of all the parties) that such loans would become, in reality, a charge on the retirement benefit, and that the pension scheme would be used in this way so as to avoid the tax liability arising on loans direct from close companies to their "participators".

10   Where schemes have already been approved, or draft documents have been agreed, without any prohibition on loans to members, the matter may remain in abeyance until some other rule change is being introduced. Meanwhile, however, if the financial information obtained (see paragraph 23 below) shows that such loans have actually been made, the SFO may need to ask about the conditions of the loan, the rate of interest being paid and the arrangements for repayment.

11   On the other hand there is no outright objection to loans out of scheme funds to the employer on commercially reasonable terms, provided that –

    (a)   employer's contributions are not returned to him in this way with such frequency, or

    (b)   the proportion of the total assets lent to the employer is not so great,

as to suggest that a scheme which is being presented as a funded scheme is in reality an unfunded or partly unfunded one.

12   The SFO is unlikely to question the *bona fides* of a scheme on the grounds mentioned in paragraph 11 if the loans to the employer do not exceed one-half of the assets, unless, exceptionally, this situation appears to be inconsistent with the imminent cash needs to the scheme for purchasing annuities (see paragraph 17 below).

13 It does not follow from the reference in paragraph 9 to the terms of the trustees' investment powers, that the SFO will necessarily regard any form of investment, however unconventional, as consistent with approval of the scheme just because it is not *ultra vires*. Obviously it is not for the Inland Revenue to interfere in the way the trustees invest trust monies, except where tax avoidance is in point, or where the investment appears to be irreconcilable with the *bona fides* of the scheme having regard to its cash needs for purchasing annuities. Investment in land or buildings may be a good long-term investment for a scheme where the members are many years from retirement, but even so, questions would need to be asked if the property purchased appeared to be an important part of the employer's own commercial premises, and thus potentially difficult to realise.

14 If assets are acquired from the employer, the SFO will generally need to consult the Inspector of Taxes dealing with the employer's tax affairs to determine whether tax avoidance is involved, and particularly whether the acquisition is part and parcel of a "transaction in securities" to which section 460 Income and Corporation Taxes Act 1970 might apply. It goes without saying that a retirement benefit scheme used in this way will not be approved, and indeed it would probably be appropriate to withdraw any existing approval. Even where section 460 is not in point, similar consultation will be necessary if the scheme is to acquire shares or debentures in the employing company whether by subscription, bonus issue, or by purchase from existing shareholders. The possibility of capital transfer tax avoidance may be grounds for withholding tax approval of the scheme.

15 It is unlikely that the SFO will be prepared to approve a small self-administered scheme which invests a significant amount of its funds in works of art or other valuable chattels or non-income producing assets, which could well be made available for the personal use of scheme members and lead to transactions between the trustees and the members otherwise than on a purely commercial basis. In any event, if such an asset were placed at the disposal of a member or of his family or household, he would be assessable to income tax under Schedule E by virtue of section 63(4) and (5) Finance Act 1976 on an annual sum equal to 10% of the market value of the asset.

16 Purchases of commodities, dealings in commodity futures, or the acquisition of plant and machinery for hiring out, may result in the trustees becoming assessable to tax on trading profits or profits from "an adventure in the nature of trade" (see Wisdom v Chamberlain 45 TC 92); such income is not exempt from tax under section 21(2) Finance Act 1970. The SFO is not competent to give any information as to whether the income from specified activities will be regarded as trading income or not, and it is not normally the practice of Inspectors of Taxes to discuss transactions not yet carried out.

17 It was previously Inland Revenue practice to require the rules to provide for any member's pension to be secured immediately on becoming payable by the purchase of a non-commutable non-assignable annuity from a Life Office, subject to certain exceptions for impaired lives and pension increases. This requirement was intended primarily as a safeguard against a situation in which, under the principle in Saunders v Vautier, the members would be able to demand the termination of the scheme in any way they chose, since, as indicated in paragraph 7 above, this situation is more likely to occur where all or most of the members have retired. But it is now accepted that a risk of this kind is no more significant during the first 5 years of retirement than it was during service, if the pension is guaranteed for 5 years minimum and there is a lump sum guarantee payment prospectively distributable to the dependants or legal personal representatives of the deceased pensioner. Thus, in such a case the SFO will be content for the rules to provide for the purchase of an annuity at some time during the first 5 years of a member's retirement. This easement is intended to enable the trustees to choose a financially opportune time for the transaction, and to avoid having to purchase at a moment when Life Office annuity rates may be relatively unfavourable, or the market value of the scheme's investments depressed.

18 Where the rules provide for pension increases linked with prospective increases in the cost of living (but not where the pension increases are to be at a fixed rate of 3% per annum (see PN 7.2(a)) money to finance the increases may be retained in the fund.

19 Where there is a prospective widow's reversionary pension, the rules may provide either that the widow's pension shall be purchased simultaneously with the member's pension, whenever that may be (as may be desirable on grounds of cost) or that the purchase of the widow's pension shall be deferred until the husband dies. If the latter method is adopted the rules should normally provide for the widow's pension to be payable to whichever woman is the member's wife at the time he dies.

159

Appendix 1

20   The newer practice set out in paragraph 17 above makes it inappropriate to continue exempting schemes from purchasing annuities for members with impaired lives. The directors of family companies for whom many small self-administered schemes cater, often postpone retirement to an advanced age; if purchase of an annuity is then deferred for 5 more years, the individual will be of an age when the dividing line between an impaired and an unimpaired life is often blurred. A dispensation in those instances where life is considered to be impaired, from the normal requirement to purchase an annuity would, it is feared, often be misused.

Death benefits

21   All death in service benefits should be insured from the outset insofar as they exceed the value from year to year of the employee's interest in the fund based on his accrued pension and other retirement benefits. In order to reduce the risks of the principle in Saunders v Vautier applying, the scheme rules should provide that lump sum benefits payable on death in service and lump sum guarantee payments should be distributable at the trustees' discretion among the usual wide range of individuals customarily designated for this purpose in the rules of pension schemes, *except* where general SFO practice precludes discretionary distribution of a benefit payable on death on or after age 75 — see, for example Memorandum No 41 paragraph 8.

Full commutation of pension

22   Where scheme rules contain a provision for the full commutation of pension where the employee is "in exceptional circumstances of serious ill-health", it has always been Inland Revenue practice to leave the application of the rule in particular cases to the trustees. In large schemes the arm's length relationship, and in insured schemes the interest of the Life Office, provide a reasonable guarantee that the facility will not be abused. Neither factor is present in the context of small self-administered schemes and the rules should therefore provide for full commutation on serious ill-health grounds to be subject to the agreement of the Inland Revenue. The SFO does not intend to do more than confirm that proper medical evidence has been obtained (see PN 8.11) and that its terms appear to warrant a conclusion that the member's expectation of life is very short.

Funding, actuarial reports and other information

23   As a condition of approval the SFO will expect actuarial reports to be made at intervals not greater than 3 years, and will examine the assumptions that have been used as a basis for funding the scheme. In view also of the significance attaching to the investment policy of the trustees (see paragraphs 11–15 above) the SFO will need to know, when the application for approval is first considered, and in conjunction with the examination of later actuarial reports, how the funds are to be or have been invested.

24   There seems to be a widely-held view that irrespective of the needs of the scheme, SFO general practice allows an employer, when money is available, to make a special contribution equal to one year's ordinary annual contribution, to be held as a general reserve. This is a misconception. The SFO will question the payment of special contributions not justified by the recommendations of the actuary and the liabilities of the scheme.

General enquiries

25   Every effort has been made to make the explanation of practice in this memorandum as informative as any general statement on this subject can be. It is an area where the facts of the particular case are all-important, and the treatment of the scheme from the tax-approval viewpoint cannot be infallibly deduced in advance from abstract propositions and "rules of thumb". It is unlikely therefore that the SFO will be able to enlarge on what is said in paragraphs 9–16, and 23–24, above in reply to hypothetical or general enquiries which do not disclose the title of the scheme to which they relate and other relevant facts and figures.

Appendix 2

Notes on Practice by the Inland Revenue issued to the Association of British Insurers and the Association of Pensioneer Trustees

Small self-administered schemes

Application of Memo No 58

1. *Purchase by Trustees of Residential Property*

The purchase of residential property for leasing to a director/shareholder or to the employer will not normally be regarded as consistent with scheme approval because of the likelihood of beneficial use by or for the benefit of members.

2. *Holiday property*

The investment of scheme monies in the purchase of holiday cottages and the like is normally regarded as inconsistent with approval.

3. *Purchase at arm's length of shares in the employer company*

This may be acceptable in principle subject to consideration of all the circumstances but the value of such holdings must be aggregated with loans to the employer for the purpose of the 50% self investment maximum laid down in paragraph 12 of Memorandum No 58.

4. *One man schemes*

In cases where the employer is providing for one employee only we are prepared to approve a one man small self-administered scheme. If, however, more than one employee is to be pensioned all should be included in one self-administered scheme.

5. *Borrowing by Trustees to facilitate purchase of property etc.*

Each case will need consideration on its own merits but excessive borrowing by Trustees may give rise to doubts as to the 'sole purpose' of the arrangements and lead to difficulty over approval. Any significant proposed borrowing should therefore be cleared with the SFO in advance.

6. *Purchase of pension increases*

Where the rules provide for pension increases linked to prospective increases in the cost of living, such increases should be secured with a Life Office as soon as they are awarded unless the guarantee period has not expired and the basic pension has not been so secured at that time. If that is the case then all COL increases awarded since the pension commenced must be secured at the appropriate time along with the basic pension.

7. *Employer going into liquidation without successor*

The scheme documentation should provide that in these circumstances the scheme will be wound up, or partially wound up if appropriate, and the proceeds used in accordance with the documentation to purchase or transfer accrued benefits of members. Any surplus being returned to the employer.

Any other course should be subject to the specific approval of the Board of Inland Revenue.

Appendix 3

Occupational Pensions: Small Self-Administered Schemes.

Consultative Document

Introduction

1. The Inland Revenue press release published on Budget Day (17 March 1987) announced a change in the present tax regime for occupational pensions (*section 19 et seq. Finance Act 1970*). Paragraph 26 of the Background Document which accompanied the press release stated that the purpose of this change was to clarify the scope and extent of the discretionary powers conferred on the Board by *section 20* of that Act. In particular, the amendment to the legislation would enable additional conditions for tax exempt approval to be prescribed in Regulations e.g. in the case of small self-administered pension schemes.

2. Such an amendment was considered necessary because recently obtained legal advice suggested that the discretionary powers conferred by *section 20* were in practice unfettered. If the Board were to exercise their discretion properly, they must therefore be prepared, in an individual case, to consider *any* request for concessionary treatment in respect of *any* of the conditions for tax approval. This was so even if such a concession had never been allowed in the past. This advice raised the unwelcome prospect of an increase in the already considerable volume of correspondence relating to scheme approvals – particularly where small self-administered schemes were involved.

3. In consequence, paragraph 3(5) of Schedule 3 to the *Finance (No 2) Act 1987* adds three new subsections (*4*) to (*6*) to *section 20* of the 1970 Act. The substantive change is made by the new *section 20(5)*, which enables the Board to limit its discretion to approve a scheme by Regulations relating to:

'the benefits provided by the scheme, the investments held for the purposes of the scheme, the manner in which the scheme is administered, or any other circumstances whatever'.

163

4. The purpose of this note is to give a broad outline of what these Regulations will contain and to invite written comments by 25 September. It is hoped that draft Regulations will subsequently be available in time to allow further consultations.

Present position

5. The present discretionary practice in relation to small self-administered schemes evolved following the lifting, in 1973, of the statutory ban on membership of an approved scheme by a controlling director. In view of the obvious danger that such schemes might be used for purposes other than *bona fide* provision for retirement, it has always been considered necessary to impose special conditions for tax approval. These were codified in a Joint Office Memorandum (JOM) 58, issued by the Superannuation Funds Office (SFO) in February 1979 (Annex A). Since then practice has developed on a number of minor detailed aspects (Annex B).

6. It must be emphasised that JOM 58 has always been regarded only as a general guide to the tax approval of small self-administered schemes. The Inland Revenue has continually made it clear that, in a particular case, additional conditions might be imposed if the facts warranted this.

Proposed changes in current practice

7. In general, no major changes are envisaged in the general approach underlying the requirements in JOM 58. Many features of the existing rules—for example, the meaning of 'small' scheme—will remain substantially the same as now. But it is proposed to make a few detailed changes, including some changes of emphasis. The main aspects are as follows:

(i) The Regulations will proscribe completely certain types of investment which hitherto have almost invariably been refused under present practice and they will specify the conditions which currently attach to loans by the scheme to the employer, and to self-investment in the employer's company. Two new conditions will be introduced (paragraphs 9 to 15 below).

(ii) The Regulations will require the automatic provision of full information about certain prescribed transactions and investments by the scheme (paragraphs 16 to 20 below).

(iii) The Regulations will set out the conditions applicable to 'pensioneer trustees'. In general, a much wider range of individuals and companies will be able to act in this capacity (paragraph 21 below).

8. At present, these aspects are all areas of current practice which, in a minority of cases, generate considerable work, both for SFO and pensions advisers. The purpose of reducing the degree of flexibility in current practice is to cut out the, frequently protracted, correspondance to which each of these aspects can give rise, while in no way inhibiting the activities of the majority of schemes whose sole purpose is the provision of retirement benefits for their members.

I. Investment of scheme funds

9. No general restriction is proposed on the investment powers of trustees, except for the general prohibition on loans to members of the scheme or to any other persons who have a contingent interest (e.g. relatives of members)—as already applies under paragraph 9 of JOM 58.

10. As regards loans to the employer, the conditions outlined in paragraphs 11 and 12 of JOM 58 will continue to apply. In future, however, those conditions will apply to all loans. Furthermore, two additional conditions will apply:

(i) all loans must be properly secured; and

(ii) in the first two years after the establishment of the scheme, all loans to the employer should not exceed 25 per cent (as opposed to 50 per cent, as now) of the scheme's assets excluding the value of transfer payments and assigned policies.

11. The question of scheme *investment in property* gives rise to a great amount of protracted correspondence between SFO and pension advisers. The effect of the Regulations will be as follows:

(*a*) *Commercial property*
The conditions outlined in paragraph 13 of JOM 58 will continue to apply.

(*b*) *Residential property*
Although not expressly covered in JOM 58, practice in recent years has normally been not to approve the purchase of residential property for use by, or leasing to, a director/shareholder or to the employer. The same has applied for investment in holiday homes etc. These restrictions – which are necessary because of the real

165

danger that such property could be used for the benefit of members before retirement – are frequently the subject of disputes. The Regulations will therefore provide that no such investment will be approved unless the property is occupied by an arm's length employee (such as a caretaker) who is required to live close to the employer's premises.

12. The purchase by a scheme of shares in the employer's company will continue to be subject to the conditions outlined in paragraph 14 of JOM 58, and the further requirement will also continue to apply that the value of such holdings must be aggregated with any loans to the employer for the purpose of the 50 per cent (and the new 25 per cent) rules.

13. Paragraph 15 of JOM 58 states that 'significant' investment in works of art, valuable chattels etc. is unlikely to be acceptable. As a rough rule of thumb, 'significant' has generally been taken to mean 5 per cent of scheme assets. But the reason for the restriction is the same as for the restriction on investment in residential property (see 11. above). For this reason the Regulations will provide that in no case will such pride in possession assets be approved.

14. It is not uncommon for a scheme to borrow money to help finance the purchase of investments. As a general rule such borrowings have been regarded as acceptable if they did not exceed three times the amount of the employer's ordinary annual contributions to the scheme. This limit on borrowings will be included in the Regulations.

15. As a transitional measure, where a scheme currently holds assets that will be prohibited by the Regulations, those assets may be retained (provided that they were consistent with existing practice). But once such assets are disposed of they should not be replaced by assets of a similar nature.

II Provision of information

16. One of the greatest sources of unproductive work for SFO is the monitoring of the activities of small self-administered schemes after they have received tax approval. Serious difficulties frequently arise in:

— finding out about particular types of transaction and obtaining full details; and

— investigating individual transactions when there is *prima facie* reason to suspect an infringement of current requirements

17. This often gives rise to lengthy and time-consuming correspondence, even where the scheme trustees are willing to provide all the information requested. But in a minority of cases it is apparent that the trustees are anxious to conceal the true nature or purpose of a given transaction—thereby making even more difficult the task of getting at all the facts.

18. Paragraph 23 of JOM 58 requires the trustees of small self-administered schemes to provide actuarial valuations every three years at least. The Regulations will include this requirement; and in addition they will require schemes to volunteer certain other information, which will be prescribed in the Regulations. In particular, automatic notification will be required of any transaction in the categories described in paragraphs 9 to 14 above. together with an undertaking that the transaction does not infringe current requirements and any further material to support such an undertaking.

19. The Regulations will also require the automatic notification of any transaction between the scheme and a connected person. For this purpose the following will be regarded as a connected person:

— the principal employer;

— another participating employer;

— a company associated with the principal employer or participating employer because it is a subsidiary or it shares a common trade, shareholdings or directorships;

— a scheme member, the member's husband or wife, a relative of the member or the relative's spouse.

20. The Regulations will provide for this information to be furnished at the time of, and preferably before, the date of the transaction. Failure to comply with these requirements is likely to result in withdrawal of tax approval.

III Pensioneer trustees

21. The present requirements which SFO impose on 'pensioneer trustees' have been reviewed, and the following changes in emphasis are proposed.

(*a*) The Regulations will require all small self-administered schemes to appoint a 'pensioneer trustee'. Failure to do so will result in a refusal to approve the scheme, or a withdrawal of approval if already granted.

Appendix 3

(*b*) If the 'pensioneer trustee' resigns or is dismissed or has his status withdrawn the Regulations will stipulate that a suitable successor must be appointed within 30 days.

(*c*) The main function of the 'pensioneer trustee' will continue to be the prevention of a premature winding-up of the scheme (paragraph 4 of JOM 58).

(*d*) However, the Regulations will impose a new requirement, which is that the 'pensioneer trustee' must undertake to notify SFO of any transaction undertaken by the scheme which, in his opinion, is likely to infringe the requirements for approval. Failure to do so is likely to lead to withdrawal of 'pensioneer trustee' status.

(*e*) The conditions for SFO approval of an application for 'pensioneer trustee' status will be considerably simplified. In general, any reputable professional person with pensions experience will be regarded as competent to act as a 'pensioneer trustee'.

Appendix 4

Statutory Instrument 1991 No 1614

1991 No. 1614
INCOME TAX
The Retirement Benefits Schemes (Restriction on Discretion to Approve) (Small Self-administered Schemes) Regulations 1991

Made - - - -	*15th July 1991*
Laid before the House of Commons	*15th July 1991*
Coming into force	*5th August 1991*

The Commissioners of Inland Revenue, in exercise of the powers conferred on them by section 591(6) of the Income and Corporation Taxes Act 1988(**a**), hereby make the following Regulations:

Citation and commencement

1. These Regulations may be cited as the Retirement Benefits Schemes (Restriction on Discretion to Approve) (Small Self-administered Schemes) Regulations 1991 and shall come into force on 5th August 1991.

Interpretation

2.—(1) In these Regulations unless the context otherwise requires–

"Act" means the Income and Corporation Taxes Act 1988;

"actuary" means–

    (a) a Fellow of the Institute of Actuaries,

    (b) a Fellow of the Faculty of Actuaries, or

    (c) a person with other actuarial qualifications who has been approved as a proper person to act for the purposes of regulation 8 of the Occupational Pension Schemes (Disclosure of Information) Regulations 1986(**b**) in connection with the scheme;

"administrator" in relation to a scheme means the trustees of the scheme or any person appointed by them to have the management of the scheme;

"the Board" means the Commissioners of Inland Revenue;

"business" includes a trade or profession and includes any activity carried on by a body of persons, whether corporate or unincorporate, except the activity of making or managing investments where those investments do not consist of shares in 51 per cent. subsidiaries of the body of persons which do not themselves carry on the activity of making or managing investments;

"close company" has the meaning given by sections 414(**c**) and 415 of the Act;

"company" means any body corporate or unincorporated association, but does not include a partnership;

(**a**) 1988 c.1; section 591(6) was amended by the Finance Act 1988 (c.39), section 146 and Schedule 13, paragraph 6.
(**b**) S.I. 1986/1046.
(**c**) Subsections (2) to (2D) were substituted for subsection (2) by the Finance Act 1989 (c.26), section 104(1) and (4); subsection (3) was repealed by the Finance Act 1989, sections 104(2) and (4) and 187 and Schedule 17, Part V; and subsection (5) was amended by the Finance Act 1989, section 104(3) and (4).

"control", in relation to a body corporate or partnership, shall, subject to paragraph (2), be construed in accordance with section 840 of the Act; and the like construction of "control" applies (with the necessary modifications) in relation to an unincorporated association as it applies in relation to a body corporate;

"controlling director" means a director to whom subsection (5)(b) of section 417 of the Act (read with subsections (3), (4) and (6) of that section) applies;

"director" means a director within the meaning of section 612(1) of the Act;

"employer" in relation to a scheme means an employer who, by virtue of the governing instrument, is entitled to pay contributions to the scheme;

"governing instrument" in relation to a scheme means a trust deed, or other document by which the scheme is established, and any other document which contains provisions by which the administration of the scheme is governed;

"pensioneer trustee" means a trustee of a scheme who–
    (a) is approved by the Board to act as such, and
    (b) is not connected with–
        (i) a scheme member,
        (ii) any other trustee of the scheme, or
        (iii) a person who is an employer in relation to the scheme.

"relative" means brother, sister, ancestor or lineal descendant;

"residential property" means property normally used, or adapted for use, as one or more dwellings;

"scheme" means a retirement benefits scheme as defined in section 611(1) of the Act;

"small self-administered scheme" means a scheme–
    (a) some or all of the income and other assets of which are invested otherwise than in insurance policies, and
    (b) which, if a scheme member is connected with–
        (i) another scheme member,
        (ii) a trustee of the scheme, or
        (iii) a person who is an employer in relation to the scheme,
        has less than 12 members;

"scheme member" in relation to a scheme means a member of the scheme to whom benefit is currently accruing as a result of service as an employee;

"shares" includes stock;

"the trustees" in relation to a scheme includes any person having the management of the scheme;

"unlisted company" means a company which is not officially listed on a recognised stock exchange within the meaning of section 841 of the Act;

"51 per cent. subsidiary" has the meaning given by section 838 of the Act.

(2) The interpretation of "control" in paragraph (1) does not apply in relation to a body corporate which is a close company and in relation to such a body corporate "control" shall be construed in accordance with section 416(**a**) of the Act.

(3) For the purposes of these Regulations any question whether a person is connected with another shall be determined in accordance with paragraphs (4) to (8) (any provision that one person is connected with another being taken to mean that they are connected with one another).

(4) A person is connected with an individual if that person is the individual's husband or wife, or is a relative, or the husband or wife of a relative, of the individual or of the individual's husband or wife.

(5) Without prejudice to paragraph (4) a person, in his capacity as a scheme member, is connected with an employer in relation to a scheme if–
    (a) where the employer is a partnership, he is connected with a partner in the partnership, or

---

(**a**)   Words in subsection (2) were repealed by the Finance Act 1989 (c.26), section 187 and Schedule 17, Part V.

(b) where the employer is a company, he or a person connected with him is, or at any time during the preceding 10 years has been, a controlling director of the company.

(6) A company is connected with another company–

(a) if the same person has control of both, or a person has control of one and persons connected with him, or he and persons connected with him, have control of the other, or

(b) if a group of two or more persons has control of each company, and the groups either consist of the same persons or could be regarded as consisting of the same persons by treating (in one or more cases) a member of either group as replaced by a person with whom he is connected.

(7) A company is connected with another person if that person has control of it or if that person and persons connected with him together have control of it.

(8) Any two or more persons acting together to secure or exercise control of a company shall be treated in relation to that company as connected one with another and with any person acting on the directions of any of them to secure or exercise control of the company.

(9) For the purposes of these Regulations a company is associated with an employer if (directly or indirectly) the employer controls that company or that company controls the employer or if both are controlled by a third person.

Restrictions on the Board's discretion

3. The Board shall not exercise their discretion to approve a scheme by virtue of section 591 of the Act in circumstances where the scheme is a small self-administered scheme and–

(a) the Board have previously approved such a scheme–

(i) of which an employee of any employer in relation to the scheme has at any time been a scheme member, and

(ii) to which any such employer was entitled to pay contributions, and

(iii) which has not been wound up; or

(b) subject to regulation 11, the governing instrument of the scheme does not contain provisions of a description specified in regulations 4 to 10.

Provisions as to borrowing

4.—(1) The description of provision specified in this regulation is a provision to the effect that at the time of any borrowing the trustees of the scheme in their capacity as such shall not have borrowed an aggregate amount, including the amount of that borrowing but excluding any amount which has been repaid before that time, in excess of the total of–

(a) three times the ordinary annual contribution paid by employers;

(b) three times the annual amount of contributions paid by scheme members as a condition of membership in the year of assessment ending immediately before that time;

(c) 45 per cent. of the market value of the investments held for the purposes of the scheme.

(2) In this regulation "ordinary annual contribution" means the amount which is the smaller of–

(a) the amount found by dividing the amount of the contributions paid by employers in the period of three years which ended at the end of the previous accounting period of the scheme by the number of those years or, if the scheme has been established for less than three years at the time of any borrowing, by the number of the years since the scheme was established (a period of less than one year since that time being counted as one year), and

(b) the amount of the annual contributions which, within the period of three years immediately before the date of any borrowing, an actuary has advised in writing would have to be paid in order to secure the benefits provided under the scheme.

171

Appendix 4

Provisions as to investments

5.—(1) The description of provision specified in this regulation is a provision to the effect that the trustees of the scheme in their capacity as such shall not directly or indirectly hold as an investment–

(a) personal chattels other than choses in action (or, in Scotland, movable property other than incorporeal movable property);

(b) residential property other than that specified in paragraph (2);

(c) shares in an unlisted company which–

    (i) carry more than 30 per cent. of the voting power in the company, or

    (ii) entitle the holder of them to more than 30 per cent. of any dividends declared by the company.

(2) The residential property specified in this paragraph is–

(a) property which is, or is to be, occupied by an employee who is not connected with his employer and who is required as a condition of his employment to occupy the property; and

(b) property which is, or is to be, occupied by a person who is neither a scheme member nor connected with a scheme member in connection with the occupation by that person of business premises held by the trustees of the scheme in their capacity as such.

(3) For the purposes of paragraph (1), trustees shall not be regarded as indirectly holding as an investment residential property other than that specified in paragraph (2) where they hold as an investment units in a unit trust scheme–

(a) which is an authorised unit trust within the meaning of section 468(6) of the Act, or

(b) where all the unit holders would be wholly exempt from capital gains tax or corporation tax (otherwise than by reason of residence) if they disposed of their units,

and the trustees of the scheme hold such property as an investment subject to the trusts of the scheme.

Provisions as to lending and the acquisition of shares

6.—(1) The description of provision specified in this regulation is a provision to the effect that the trustees of the scheme in their capacity as such shall not directly or indirectly lend money–

(a) to a member of the scheme or a person connected with him, other than an employer in relation to the scheme or any company associated with that employer, or

(b) to an employer in relation to the scheme, or any company associated with that employer, unless the lending is within the exception contained in paragraph (2).

(2) Lending is within the exception contained in this paragraph–

(a) only if the amount lent is utilised for the purposes of the borrower's business, and

(b) if it is–

    (i) for a fixed term,

    (ii) at a commercial rate of interest, and

    (iii) evidenced by an agreement in writing which contains the provisions specified in paragraph (3) and all the conditions on which it is made.

(3) The provisions specified in this paragraph are provisions to the effect that the amount lent shall be immediately repayable–

(a) if the borrower–

    (i) is in breach of the conditions of the agreement,

    (ii) ceases to carry on business, or

    (iii) becomes insolvent; or

(b) if it is required to enable the trustees to pay benefits which have already become due under the scheme.

(4) Subject to paragraphs (5) and (6), for the purposes of this regulation a borrower shall be taken to have become insolvent if–

    (a) he has been adjudged bankrupt or has made a composition or arrangement with his creditors;

    (b) he has died and his estate falls to be administered in accordance with an order under section 421 of the Insolvency Act 1986(**a**) or Article 365 of the Insolvency (Northern Ireland) Order 1989(**b**);

    (c) where the borrower is a company, a winding-up order or an administration order has been made with respect to it, or a resolution for voluntary winding-up has been passed with respect to it, or a receiver or manager of its undertaking has been duly appointed, or possession has been taken, by or on behalf of the holders of any debentures secured by a floating charge, of any property of the company comprised in or subject to the charge, or a voluntary arrangement is approved under Part I of the Insolvency Act 1986 or Part II of the Insolvency (Northern Ireland) Order 1989.

(5) Until the coming into operation of Article 365 of the Insolvency (Northern Ireland) Order 1989, paragraph (4) above shall have effect in its application to Northern Ireland subject to the following modifications–

    (a) in sub-paragraph (b) of that paragraph for the reference to that Article there shall be substituted a reference to section 30(1) of, and Part I of Schedule 1 to, the Administration of Estates Act (Northern Ireland) 1955(**c**); and

    (b) in sub-paragraph (c) of that paragraph the words from "or an administration order" to "to it" (where those words first occur) and the words from "or a voluntary arrangement" onwards shall be omitted.

(6) In the application of this regulation to Scotland, for sub-paragraphs (a), (b) and (c) of paragraph (4) above there shall be substituted the following sub-paragraphs–

    (a) an award of sequestration has been made on his estate, or he has executed a trust deed for his creditors or has entered into a composition contract;

    (b) he has died and a judicial factor appointed under section 11A of the Judicial Factors (Scotland) Act 1889(**d**) is required by the provisions of that section to divide his insolvent estate among his creditors; or

    (c) where the borrower is a company, a winding up order or an administration order has been made, or a resolution for voluntary winding-up is passed with respect to it, or a receiver of its undertaking is duly appointed, or a voluntary arrangement for the purposes of Part I of the Insolvency Act 1986 is approved under that part.

(7) For the purposes of this regulation and of regulation 8 a member of a scheme includes–

    (a) a scheme member;

    (b) a person who is in receipt of a pension from the scheme;

    (c) a person who has left the service of the employer but was a scheme member during that service;

    (d) a person who is in the service of the employer but is no longer a scheme member.

7.—(1) The description of provision specified in this regulation is a provision to the effect that at the time that any money is lent, or any shares in an employer or any company associated with that employer are acquired, the aggregate of–

    (a) the total amount outstanding of money lent to an employer and any company associated with him in accordance with regulation 6(2) and (3), and

    (b) the market value of shares in an employer and any company associated with him held by the trustees in their capacity as such,

shall not, where that time is during the period of two years from the date on which the scheme was established, exceed the figure specified in paragraph (2) or, where that time is after the end of that period, exceed the figure specified in paragraph (3).

(**a**) 1986 c.45.
(**b**) S.I. 1989/2405 (N.I. 19).
(**c**) 1955 c.24 (N.I.).
(**d**) 1889 c.39; section 11A was inserted by the Bankruptcy (Scotland) Act 1985 (c.66), section 75(1) and Schedule 7, paragraph 4.

(2) The figure specified in this paragraph is 25 per cent. of the market value of the assets of the scheme which are derived from contributions made by an employer and by employees since the scheme was established.

(3) The figure specified in this paragraph is 50 per cent. of the market value of all the assets of the scheme.

Provisions as to transactions with scheme members and others

8.—(1) The description of provision specified in this regulation is a provision to the effect that the trustees of the scheme in their capacity as such shall not directly or indirectly purchase, sell or lease any asset–

    (a) from or to a member of the scheme or a person connected with him, other than an employer in relation to the scheme or any company associated with that employer, or

    (b) from or to an employer, or any company associated with that employer, except in accordance with paragraph (2).

(2) A purchase, sale or lease is in accordance with this paragraph only when it is made–

    (a) after the trustees have obtained independent professional advice in writing, and

    (b) in accordance with that advice.

(3) For the purpose of this regulation–

    (a) a purchase by the trustees shall not be regarded as a purchase indirectly from a member of the scheme, or a person connected with him, if the purchase by the trustees took place three years or more after the sale by the member or person connected with him; and

    (b) a sale by the trustees shall not be regarded as a sale indirectly to a member of the scheme, or a person connected with him, if the purchase by the member or person connected with him took place three years or more after the sale by the trustees.

Provisions as to pensioneer trustees

9. The description of provision specified in this regulation is a provision to the effect that–

    (a) one of the trustees of the scheme shall be a pensioneer trustee, and

    (b) if a pensioneer trustee ceases to be qualified to act as such or ceases to be a trustee, the trustees or the remaining trustee or trustees shall–

        (i) within 30 days after that cessation notify the Board in writing;

        (ii) within 60 days after that cessation appoint a successor to him as a pensioneer trustee;

        (iii) within 30 days after that appointment notify the Board in writing of the name of the successor.

Provisions as to furnishing of information and documents

10.—(1) The description of provisions specified in this regulation are provisions to the effect that the administrator of a scheme shall, within 90 days after any transaction by the trustees in their capacity as such as is specified in paragraph (2), furnish to the Board such information and documents as may be specified on the relevant form to be supplied by the Board.

(2) The transactions specified in this paragraph are–

    (a) the acquisition or disposal of land,

    (b) the lending of money to an employer or any company associated with him,

    (c) the acquisition or disposal of shares in an employer or any company associated with him,

    (d) the acquisition or disposal of shares in an unlisted company,

    (e) the borrowing of money,

    (f) the purchase, sale or lease from or to an employer, or any company associated with him, of any asset other than one specified in sub-paragraph (a), (c) or (d).

Schemes awaiting approval

11.—(1) Where at the date of coming into force of these Regulations a scheme which is a small self-administered scheme is in existence and either–

(a) has not yet been submitted to the Board for approval, or

(b) is before the Board for approval,

the Board shall not be prevented from approving it by virtue of section 591 of the Act by reason only that it contains a provision or provisions of a description specified in any of sub-paragraphs (a), (b) and (c) of paragraph (2).

(2) The description of provisions specified in this paragraph is–

(a) a provision which authorises the trustees of the scheme to retain an investment of a description mentioned in sub-paragraph (a), (b) or (c) of regulation 5(1) which is held by them immediately before the day on which these Regulations were made;

(b) a provision which authorises the trustees of the scheme to continue to lend money, or retain shares in an employer or any company associated with that employer, which was being lent or held by them immediately before the day on which these Regulations were made, where at the time the money was first lent or the shares were acquired the aggregate referred to in paragraph (1) of regulation 7 exceeded the figure specified in paragraph (2) of that regulation, but did not exceed the figure specified in paragraph (3) of that regulation, notwithstanding that the loan was made or the shares were acquired during the period of two years from the date on which the scheme was established;

(c) a provision which authorises the trustees of the scheme to sell assets held by them immediately before that day to a member of the scheme or a person connected with him.

A. J. G. Isaac
T. J. Painter
15th July 1991   Two of the Commissioners of Inland Revenue

Appendix 4

Section 591(6) of the Income and Corporation Taxes Act 1988 provides that regulations made by the Board for the purposes of that section may restrict the Board's discretion to approve a retirement benefits scheme ("a scheme") by reference to the benefits provided by the scheme, the investments held for the purposes of the scheme, the manner in which the scheme is administered or any other circumstances whatever; and these Regulations, which come into force on 5th August 1991, impose restrictions in relation to small self-administered schemes.

Regulation 1 provides for citation and commencement.

Regulation 2 contains definitions and provides for the determination for the purposes of the Regulations of any question whether a person is connected with another and whether any company is associated with an employer.

Regulation 3 restricts the Board's discretion in relation to small self-administered schemes where–

(a) the Board have previously approved such a scheme of which an employee of the employer who would be entitled to make contributions to the scheme is a member;

(b) subject to regulation 11, the governing instrument of the scheme does not contain provisions of a description specified in regulations 4 to 10.

Regulation 4 specifies provisions which restrict the power of the trustees of a scheme to borrow money.

Regulation 5 specifies provisions which restrict the power of the trustees of a scheme to hold certain assets as investments.

Regulations 6 and 7 specify provisions which restrict the power of the trustees of a scheme to lend money and to acquire shares.

Regulation 8 specifies provisions which restrict the power of the trustees of a scheme to purchase, sell or lease property.

Regulation 9 specifies provisions concerning pensioneer trustees.

Regulation 10 specifies provisions for the furnishing of information and documents to the Board by the administrator of a scheme.

Regulation 11 contains transitional provisions with regard to schemes which had not yet been submitted for the Board's approval, or were awaiting the Board's approval, when these Regulations were made.

Appendix 5

Memorandum No 109

MEMORANDUM NO 109

Inland Revenue Superannuation Funds Office

August 1991

Lynwood Road
Thames Ditton
Surrey
KT7 0DP

081-398 4242

SMALL SELF-ADMINISTERED SCHEMES

INTRODUCTION

1   The Inland Revenue's discretionary practice in relation to the approval of Small Self-Administered Schemes (SSAS) has continued to develop since the mid-1970s when such schemes first began to emerge. General guidance as to the special requirements for the approval of these schemes was set out in Memorandum No 58 which issued in February 1979. The Memorandum is only a general guide as to how the Inland Revenue is likely to exercise its discretion in particular circumstances. It has always been made clear that further conditions could be imposed to meet the facts of particular cases or more generally in the light of further experience in dealing with such schemes.

2   The fact that the Inland Revenue has discretionary powers under the law means that it is not possible to lay down hard and fast rules of general application. Strictly each case requires individual consideration based on its own facts and merits. This is particularly burdensome in the area of SSAS where, because of the usual close identity of interests between the employer, the trustees and the scheme members, it is necessary to monitor carefully transactions between the parties and to establish that the purpose of a particular investment is bona fide for the sole purpose of providing relevant benefits. Parliament has therefore approved Regulations to limit the Board's discretion and to specify certain requirements for the approval of SSAS.

3   These Regulations, The Retirement Benefit Schemes (Restriction on Discretion to Approve) (Small Self-administered Schemes) Regulations 1991 [SI 1991 No 1614] were made on 15 July 1991 and came into force on 5 August 1991. Copies are obtainable from HM Stationery Office. In this Memorandum references to Regulations are to these Regulations.

4   The effect of the Regulations is to restrict the power of the trustees of a SSAS to borrow money and to make and dispose of certain investments. They also require the scheme administrator to provide information and documents to the Superannuation Funds Office (SFO).

5   The purpose of this Memorandum is to highlight the main points of the Regulations and explain some other aspects of SFO practice in relation to SSAS. Memorandum No 58 has not yet been cancelled (see however paragraph 21). Where the Regulations or this Memorandum overlap Memorandum No 58 the new provisions will prevail.

177

Appendix 5

DEFINITION OF A SMALL SELF-ADMINISTERED SCHEME

6.   Regulation 2 contains definitions of terms used in the Regulations including "small self-administered scheme". This is defined as a self-administered scheme with less than 12 members.

For this purpose, a scheme is defined as self-administered if some or all of the income and other assets are invested otherwise than in insurance policies. Scheme monies held in a current account (whether interest-bearing or not) with a bank, building society, etc, for incidental purposes will not be treated as an investment "otherwise than in insurance policies".

The second leg of the definition provides that a scheme will not be regarded as a SSAS unless at least one of the members is related

   (i)   to another member, or

   (ii)   to a trustee of the scheme, or

   (iii)   (where the employer is a partnership) to a partner, or

   (iv)   (if the employer is a company) where a member or a person connected with that member has been a controlling director of the company at any time during the preceding 10 years.

Notwithstanding this definition the SFO may, under their discretionary powers, apply the same restrictions and requirements to a self-administered scheme with 12 or more members (for example where rank and file employees have been introduced into the scheme as "makeweight" members with insignificant benefits, simply to increase the number of members to 12 or more).

Some small schemes (generally administered by life offices) are documented to permit self-administration but scheme monies are wholly invested in insurance policies from the outset. These schemes have commonly been known as wholly insured LOSSAs or as deferred SSASs. Such schemes do not fall within the Regulation definition of a SSAS. As soon as the trustees of such a scheme invest other than in insurance policies, then the scheme will immediately become a SSAS and subject to the requirements of the Regulations. The SFO must be notified at once if this happens and details of the non-insured investment should be supplied.

Previously those schemes described in the previous paragraph have not been required to submit full-scale actuarial valuations provided their only investments were insurance policies with one life office. This dispensation was given on the understanding that a short report was provided every 3 years covering remuneration and contribution details of each member in the preceding 3 year period and also confirmation that the scheme remained fully insured with one life office. Such reports and confirmation are no longer required. As explained above when such a scheme becomes self-administered the SFO must be informed.

PENSIONEER TRUSTEE

7   Regulation 2 also defines "pensioneer trustee". The criteria for being accepted as a pensioneer trustee remain as set out in Memorandum No 58. Regulation 9 requires that in the event of a scheme ceasing to have a pensioneer trustee the SFO must be notified in writing within 30 days and a replacement pensioneer trustee must be appointed within 60 days. The Regulation also requires that the SFO should be given written notification of the name of the new pensioneer trustee within 30 days of appointment. A copy of the document(s) removing and appointing pensioneer trustees should be sent to the SFO.

RESTRICTION OF BOARD'S DISCRETION

8   Regulation 3 prohibits the approval of a further SSAS of a particular employer if one has previously been approved but not wound up. If an employer has an approved SSAS that is being wound up the SFO cannot approve another SSAS for that employer until winding up is complete and the scheme has ceased to exist. If an employer who wishes to establish a SSAS has been participating in another employer's approved SSAS, it will be necessary for him to withdraw from the latter before his own SSAS can be approved. Regulation 3 also sets out the general restriction of discretion to approve a SSAS unless its rules conform with Regulations 4 to 10.

SCHEME BORROWING

9 Regulation 4 restricts any borrowing by the trustees of a SSAS to not more than 45% of the market value of the scheme investments plus 3 times the ordinary annual contribution and 3 times the annual amount of the contributions paid by scheme members (excluding AVCs).

For this purpose "ordinary annual contribution" means the smaller of:

(i) the average annual amount of the contributions paid to the scheme by the employer in the 3 scheme accounting periods preceding the date on which the ordinary annual contribution is to be ascertained (or, where at that date the scheme had been established less than 3 years, the total amount of contributions paid to the scheme by the employer divided by the number of years since the scheme was established (a part year counting as one year)), and

(ii) the amount of the annual contribution which has been advised by an actuary in writing within 3 years of the date on which the ordinary annual contribution is to be ascertained, as that necessary to secure the benefits payable under the scheme.

The borrowed money must be used to benefit the scheme. If the money is on-lent to the employer (or any associated company) the trustees must receive a higher rate of interest than they have to pay to obtain the finance.

Purely as a work saving measure the SFO will not require to be notified of temporary borrowings for a period not exceeding 6 months where the aggregate amount borrowed does not exceed the lesser of 10% of the market value of the fund or £50,000 and the borrowing is repaid at or before the due date. If a borrowing is "rolled over" into a further term it is outwith the concession and must be reported (see paragraph 19).

SCHEME INVESTMENTS

10 Regulation 5 prohibits among other things investment by trustees in personal chattels other than choses in action. A "chose in action" is something which is not corporeal, tangible, movable or visible and of which a person has not the present enjoyment but merely a right to recover it (if withheld) by action. Choses in action are permitted investments and include:

Company shares	Financial futures
Copyrights	Commodity futures
Deposit Accounts	Traded options

The following assets are personal chattels which are NOT choses in action and are therefore prohibited investments:

Antiques	Furniture
Works of Art	Fine wines
Rare books	Vintage cars
Rare stamps	Yachts
Jewellery	Gold bullion
Gem stones	Krugerrands
Oriental rugs	

The above lists are given simply by way of example and are not comprehensive. Trustees who are uncertain as to whether a particular investment is a chose in action should consult their professional advisers before making the investment.

RESIDENTIAL PROPERTY

11 Regulation 5 prohibits investment in residential property except where it is for occupation by:

(i) an unconnected employee as a condition of employment (eg a caretaker), or

(ii) someone unrelated to the members of the scheme (or to a person connected with a scheme member) in connection with his or her occupation of business premises (eg a shop, with an integral flat above) where those business premises are held by the trustees as a scheme asset.

179

Appendix 5

SHARES IN UNLISTED COMPANIES

12   Regulation 5(1)(c) limits a scheme's investment in an unlisted company to not more than 30% of the shares (as defined) in that company. This restriction is intended to limit the scope for tax avoidance which exists when an exempt approved pension scheme operates through its "own" company. Any attempt to circumvent the effect of the 30% limit, for example by means of dividend waivers by other shareholders will prejudice the approval of the scheme.

TRANSACTIONS WITH SCHEME MEMBERS

13   Regulation 6 bans loans to scheme members or anyone connected with a scheme member and Regulation 8 prohibits the purchase, sale or lease of any assets from or to scheme members or anyone connected with a scheme member.

LOANS TO THE EMPLOYER AND ASSOCIATED COMPANIES

14   These are permitted subject to the conditions contained in Regulations 6 and 7.

(i)   **amount**

First the 50% limit on self-investment (viz loans to and shares in an employer company and any associated company) has been reduced to 25% for the first 2 years of the scheme's existence. And second the 25% is to be applied to the value of the fund exclusive of transfers received from other schemes ie the 25% relates to the funds contributed by the employer and scheme members and any investment income or gains from the investment of these contributions. The 25%/50% test is to be applied at the date that money is loaned (or shares acquired).

(ii)   **purpose**

The borrower must use the borrowed money only for business purposes. In other words the money must be used to benefit the borrower's trade or profession. The money should not be on-lent nor should it be used for some purely speculative purpose such as the purchase of shares or other investments. A holding company is however permitted to make or manage share investments in its 51% trading subsidiaries.

(iii)   **term**

The loan must be for a fixed term. The length of the term is a matter for the parties to the loan agreement but it should be realistic. It is not acceptable for a series of 364 day loans to be made (simply to enable the interest to be paid to the trustees gross without deduction of tax) when in reality there is no real intention to repay the loan for say 3 years. Nor is it acceptable for the term to be longer than necessary - scheme funds should not lodge unnecessarily with the employer.

(iv)   **rate of interest**

Loans must be at a commercial rate of interest. Commercial rate is not defined in the Regulations. The SFO will maintain its long established practice and accept an interest rate equivalent to Clearing Bank Base Rate (CBBR) plus 3% as satisfying the "commercial rate" test. This rate will be accepted for both secured and unsecured loans. The SFO will be prepared to consider a lower rate of interest only if written evidence is produced to show that the borrower can obtain a loan on similar terms from a bank or other arm's length financial institution at a rate below CBBR + 3%.

(v)   **loan to be on commercial basis**

It is a Revenue requirement that the commercial rate of interest (see (iv) above) must be charged and paid. It is also a requirement (Regulation 6(3)) that the loan document must provide for the loan to be repaid immediately in certain circumstances including that where the borrower is in breach of the conditions of the agreement.

180

The Regulations apart, the SFO require pension scheme trustees to act in the best interests of scheme members in their capacity as members of the pension scheme and not as employees, shareholders etc. If they fail to do so the SFO are likely to take the view that the scheme is not being properly administered and that exempt approval should be withdrawn. Examples of the sort of actions which might lead to withdrawal of approval are:

(a)   loans solely to keep an ailing business afloat,

(b)   loans to employers who are technically insolvent,

(c)   the failure of trustees to take all legal steps open to them to enforce the repayment of a loan to an employer in the circumstances described in Regulation 6(3).

As a rule loans should not be made to the employer (or any associated company) unless the trustees would be prepared to lend the same amount on the same terms to an unconnected party of comparable standing.

(vi)   **"roll over" of loan**

The Regulations do not preclude an outstanding loan from being "rolled over" into a fresh loan agreement. For the future the SFO will not, however, agree to a loan being "rolled over" more than twice. Where a loan is "rolled over" after the Regulations have taken effect the new loan will be subject to the conditions in Regulations 6 and 7. The "roll over" of unpaid interest into a new loan will not be permitted.

BACK TO BACK LOANS

15   Any attempt to circumvent the longstanding ban on loans to members or the restrictions on loans to employers by entering into arrangements by which the scheme loans money to an unconnected party on the understanding for instance that reciprocal loans will be made by that party (or an associate) to the employer or a scheme member will have serious consequences. The SFO will enquire about loans to allegedly unconnected companies or individuals. If it comes to light that the parties are indulging in back to back loans or other arrangements to avoid the restrictions on loans the SFO will not hesitate to withdraw approval, if necessary retrospectively, from the schemes involved.

APPLICATION OF THE REGULATIONS

16   **New schemes and schemes not yet approved**

(i)   From 5 August 1991, the date on which the Regulations came into force, the SFO cannot approve a SSAS unless its governing documentation takes account of the requirements of the Regulations.

(ii)   However as a transitional measure a SSAS established before, but not approved by, 5 August 1991 may retain investments made before 15 July 1991 provided they are acceptable under previous SFO practice. Such investments may be disposed of by the trustees in due course to whoever they wish (including scheme members and their relatives) provided that the disposal is on an arm's length basis at full market value in accordance with current SFO discretionary requirements. It is emphasised that in all other respects the requirements of the Regulations must be fully observed with effect from 5 August 1991. The scheme rules must be amended to take account of the Regulations, before approval can be granted.

Existing approved schemes

(iii)   Under section 591A Income and Corporation Taxes Act 1988 (introduced by section 35 of the Finance Act 1991), those SSAS approved before 5 August 1991 have 3 years from that date to amend their rules to accord with the Regulations otherwise they will cease to be approved. Investments made before 15 July 1991 may be retained provided they are acceptable under previous SFO practice. Such investments may be disposed of by the trustees in due course to whoever they wish (including scheme members and their relatives) provided that the disposal is on an arm's length basis at full market value in accordance with current SFO discretionary requirements. It is emphasised that in all other respects the requirements of the Regulations must be fully observed with effect from 5 August 1991. For the future the Board's discretionary practice will be adapted to reflect the spirit and content of the Regulations.

Appendix 5

MODEL RULES

17   The Standards Section of SFO has produced a package of model rules that may be used to incorporate the requirements of the Regulations into scheme documents. These rules may be used by any SSAS irrespective of whether or not it has been documented using agreed model rules. The package does not include a provision for retaining assets acquired before the Regulations came into effect. Where such a provision is appropriate it should be individually drafted to meet the particular circumstances of the scheme.

Copies of the package will be issued to all practitioners who are negotiating or have agreed model SSAS rules with SFO. Copies are also available free of charge by writing to the Standards Section of SFO.

RULE AMENDMENTS

18   Rule amendments to take account of the Regulations should be submitted to SFO in the normal way. If the amendments are entirely in accordance with the package of model rules (see paragraph 17) this should be stated. Use of the SFO package will avoid detailed rule examination and should lead to earlier agreement.

INFORMATION AND DOCUMENTS

19   The Regulation 9 requirement to notify the removal and appointment of pensioneer trustees is covered at paragraph 7 above. Regulation 10 provides that the scheme administrator must, within 90 days of certain specified transactions, furnish information and documents to the SFO. The information and documents are as specified on the relevant forms supplied by the SFO. Copies of the relevant forms are attached. Supplies of the new forms are being issued automatically to large users. Otherwise supplies may be obtained by writing to the Supplies Section, Room 0407 at the above address or by telephoning extension 4254. The SFO have no objection to practitioners producing their own supplies of these forms. The forms are as follows:

SF 7012   details of the acquisition or disposal of land (this term includes buildings and other structures),

SF 7013   lending of money to an employer (including associated companies),

SF 7014   acquisition or disposal of shares in the employer, associated companies or unlisted companies,

SF 7015   the borrowing of money,

SF 7016   purchase from an employer or associated company of any asset other than land or shares, or the sale of any asset of the scheme to an employer or associated company.

The SFO will continue to issue forms SF 191/4 when making enquiries concerning investments made before the Regulations take effect.

COMPLIANCE

20   Failure to comply with the Regulations in any way, including arrangements to circumvent particular conditions or requirements, and failure to provide information or documents by the due dates will jeopardise a scheme's tax approved status.

PRACTICE NOTES

21   The revised Practice Notes when published later this year will contain a detailed explanation of both the effect of the Regulations and Inland Revenue practice in relation to SSAS. Memorandum No 58 will then be cancelled.

Appendix 5A

Model Rules for Small Self-Administered Pension Schemes

[1] Notwithstanding anything to the contrary in the Scheme provisions the following rules [2 to 9] shall have full effect except that they may not be construed as conferring powers on the Trustees which they do not otherwise have by virtue of the Trust Deed and Rules.

See Note 1

(1) In these rules the following expressions shall have the meanings ascribed to them:

    a.   "Business" includes:

        (i)   a trade or profession, or

        (ii)   any activity other than investment carried on by a body of persons, whether corporate or unincorporate, or

        (iii)   any activity carried on by a holding company for a trading group.

    b.   "Close company" has the meaning given by sections 414 and 415 of the Act.

    c.   "Company" means any body corporate or unincorporated association, but does not include a partnership.

    d.   "Control" in relation to a body corporate (other than a close company) or partnership shall be construed in accordance with section 840 of the Act and in relation to an unincorporated association that section shall be applied as it applies to a body corporate.

In relation to a close company "control" shall be construed in accordance with section 416 of the Act.

    e.   "Employer" means an employer participating in the Scheme.

    f.   "Ordinary annual contribution" means for the purpose of Rule [2] the smaller of:

        (i)   the average annual amount of the contributions paid to the Scheme by the Employers in the three accounting periods preceding the date on which the ordinary annual contribution is to be ascertained [or, where at that date the Scheme had been established less than 3 years, the total amount of contributions paid to the scheme by the Employers divided by

See Note 2

the number of years since the Scheme was established (a period of less than a year being counted as one year)], and

        (ii)   the amount of the annual contribution which has been advised by an Actuary in writing within 3 years of the date on which the ordinary annual contribution is to be ascertained, as that necessary to secure the benefits payable under the Scheme.

Note 1   It is assumed that the rules will contain acceptable definitions of the terms Act (to mean the Income and Corporation Taxes Act 1988), Actuary, Administrator, Controlling Director and Trustees. Care is required to ensure that terms defined for the purpose of these rules do not conflict with terms defined for the purposes of the Scheme generally.

Note 2   The words in square brackets may be excluded where this rule is adopted more than 3 years after the establishment of the scheme.

g. "Pensioneer trustee" means a Trustee of the Scheme who:

    (i)   is approved by the Board of Inland Revenue to act as such, and

    (ii) is not connected with a Scheme Member, another Trustee or an Employer.

h. "Private company" means a company which is not officially listed on a recognised stock exchange within the meaning of section 841 of the Act.

i. "Relative" means a brother, sister, ancestor or lineal descendant.

j. "Residential property" means property normally used, or adapted for use as one or more dwellings.

k. "Scheme member" means a member of the Scheme to whom benefit is currently accruing by virtue of service as an employee.

(2) For the purpose of these rules any question of whether a person is connected with another shall be determined as follows:

a. a person is connected with an individual if that person is the individual's spouse or is a Relative or the spouse of a Relative of the individual or of the individual's spouse;

b. a Scheme Member is connected with an Employer if:

    (i)   the Employer is a partnership and the Scheme Member is connected with a partner, or

    (ii) the Employer is a Company and the Scheme Member or any person connected with him or her is, or has been during the last 10 years a Controlling Director of the Company;

c. a Company is connected with another Company if:

    (i)   the same person has Control of both, or

    (ii) a person has Control of one and persons connected with that person have Control of the other, or

    (iii) a person has Control of one and that person and persons connected with that person have control over the other;

d. a Company is connected with another person if that person has Control of it or if that person and a person or persons connected with him or her together have Control of it;

e. any two or more persons acting together to secure or exercise Control of a Company shall be treated in relation to that Company as connected one with another and with any person acting on the directions of any of them to secure or exercise Control of the Company.

(3) For the purpose of these rules a company is associated with an Employer if (directly or indirectly) the Employer controls that company or that company controls the Employer or if both are controlled by a third person.

(4) For the purpose of these rules a member of the Scheme includes:

    a.   a Scheme Member,

    b.   a person in receipt of a pension from the Scheme, or

    c.   a person who has been a Scheme Member.

[2] Provisions as to borrowing

Any power of the Trustees to borrow shall be restricted so that, at the time of any borrowing, the Trustees shall not have borrowed and not repaid an aggregate amount including the amount of that borrowing in excess of the total of:

    a.   three times the Ordinary Annual Contribution, and

    b.   three times the annual amount of contributions paid or payable as a condition of membership by Scheme Members in the year of assessment ending immediately before the borrowing takes place, and

    c.   forty-five per cent of the market value of investments held for the purposes of the Scheme.

[3] Provisions as to investment

The Trustees' powers of investment shall be restricted to preclude investment either directly or indirectly in:

See Note 3   a.   personal chattels other than [choses in action] [moveable property other than incorporeal moveable property]; or

    b.   Residential Property other than that:

      (i)   which is, or is to be, occupied by an employee who is not connected with his or her Employer and who is required as a condition of employment to occupy that property, or

      (ii)   which is integral to a commercial property which is not and is not to be occupied by a Scheme Member or a person connected with a Scheme Member; or

    c.   Stock or shares in a Private Company which:

      (i)   carry more than thirty per cent of the voting power in the Company, or

      (ii)   entitle the holder to more than thirty per cent of any dividends declared by the Company.

Note 3   The second alternative should be substituted for the first in schemes subject to the law of Scotland.

For the purposes of this rule the Trustees are not regarded as holding a Residential Property where they hold as an investment units in a unit trust scheme:

(i)   which is an authorised unit trust scheme within the meaning of section 468(6) of the Act, or

(ii)   an exempt unit trust within the meaning of section 96 of the Capital Gains Tax Act 1979, and

(iii)   that unit trust scheme holds Residential Property as an investment.

[4]   The Trustees in that capacity shall not directly or indirectly lend money:

a.   to a member of the Scheme or to a person who is connected with a member of the Scheme other than an Employer or any Company associated with an Employer; or

b.   to an Employer or a Company associated with an Employer unless the loan is:

(i)   utilised for the purpose of the borrower's Business, and

(ii)   for a fixed term, and

(iii)   at a commercial rate of interest, and

(iv)   evidenced by an agreement in writing which contains all the conditions on which it is made and, in particular, the provisions specified in paragraph c. below;

c.   the provisions specified in this paragraph are that the lending shall be repaid before the expiration of the term for which is was made if:

(i)   the borrower is in breach of the conditions of the agreement; or

(ii)   the borrower ceases to carry on business; or

(iii)   the borrower becomes insolvent within the meaning defined for the purposes of Regulation 6 of the Retirement Benefit Schemes (Restriction on Discretion to Approve) (Small Self-administered Schemes) Regulations 1991; or

(iv)   the money is required to enable the Trustees to pay benefits which have already become due under the Scheme.

[5]   The amount of the aggregate of:

a.   the amount outstanding of any lending to an Employer and/or a Company associated with an Employer made in accordance with Rule [4]b. and c. above, and

b.   the market value of stock and shares in an Employer and/or a Company associated with an Employer held by the Trustees in that capacity

shall not at the time of any lending under Rule [4] or the purchase of any shares in the Employer or a company associated with an Employer exceed fifty per cent of the market value of the total assets of the Scheme. [If the lending or purchase takes place within 2 years of the establishment of the Scheme the amount shall not exceed twenty five per cent of the market value of the total assets of the scheme excluding the value of any transfer values received.]

See Note 4

Note 4   The words in square brackets may be excluded where the rule is adopted more than 2 years after the establishment of the scheme.

[6] **Provisions as to transactions with members of the Scheme**

The Trustees in that capacity shall not directly or indirectly purchase, sell or lease any investment or asset from or to a member of the Scheme or a person (other than an Employer or a company associated with an Employer) connected with a member. A purchase will not be construed as being an indirect purchase from a member of the Scheme or a connected person if at the time of purchase 3 or more years have elapsed since the investment or asset was owned by the member or connected person. A sale will not be construed as an indirect sale to a member of the Scheme or a connected person if the purchase by the member or connected person takes place 3 years or more after the sale by the Trustees.

[7] **Provisions as to transactions with Employers and associated companies**

The Trustees in that capacity shall not directly or indirectly purchase, sell or lease any investment or asset from or to an Employer or a Company associated with an Employer except in accordance with independent professional advice obtained in writing.

[8] **Provisions as to Pensioneer Trustees**

One of the Trustees shall be a Pensioneer Trustee and should that Trustee cease to be a Trustee or cease to be qualified to act as a Pensioneer Trustee the remaining Trustee or Trustees shall within 30 days notify the Board of Inland Revenue in writing and within 60 days appoint a successor who is a Pensioneer Trustee. The Trustees shall within 30 days of the appointment of the successor notify the Board of Inland Revenue in writing of the name of the successor.

[9] **Provision of information to Inland Revenue**

(1)   Within 90 days of any transaction by the Trustees such as is specified in paragraph (2) below the Administrator will furnish the Board of Inland Revenue with such information and documents as the Board requires.

(2)   The transactions specified are:

a.   the acquisition or disposal of land (including buildings or other structures);

b.   the lending of money to an Employer or a Company associated with an Employer;

c.   the acquisition or disposal of shares in an Employer or a Company associated with an Employer;

d.   the acquisition or disposal of shares in a Private Company;

e.   the borrowing of money; or

f.   the purchase, sale or lease from or to an Employer or a Company associated with an Employer of any investment or asset.

Appendix 6

Board Minute Resolving to Establish a Small Self-Administered Scheme

ABC LIMITED

Minutes of a meeting of the board of directors of the company held on .... at ....
Present ....

....

....

There was produced to the meeting an initial actuarial costing report from Messrs. .... advising of the cost to the company of establishing an occupational pension scheme for the controlling directors.

Directors D, E and F disclosed their interests and it was resolved that the company should proceed to establish such a pension scheme and that the company's advisers be instructed to prepare the requisite documentation and to apply to the Inland Revenue for the approval of the scheme.

It was further resolved that Messrs. D, E and F would be the first trustees of the scheme together with the pensioneer trustee.

Chairman

Appendix 7

Clause for Insertion in the Memorandum of Association of a Company Authorising the Establishment of a Pension Scheme (paragraph 3.2)

'To establish, maintain, participate in or contribute to or produce the establishment and maintenance of, participation in or contribution to any pension, superannuation, benevolent or life assurance fund, scheme or arrangement (whether contributory or otherwise) for the benefit of, and to give or procure the giving of donations, gratuities, pensions, allowances, benefits and emoluments to, any persons who are or were at any time in the employment or service of the company or any of its predecessors in business, or of any company which is a subsidiary of the company or is allied to or associated with the company or with any such subsidiary or who may be or have been directors or officers of the company, or of any such other company as aforesaid, and the wives, widows, widowers, families and dependants of any such persons'.

Appendix 8

Specimen Investment Power

Trustees shall have the power to invest any monies forming part of the Scheme in the purchase of or at interest upon the security of such stocks funds shares securities annuities or other investments or property of whatsoever nature and wheresoever situate and whether involving liability or not and whether producing income or not or upon such personal credit with or without security and to raise or borrow any sum or sums of money and secure the repayment thereof in such manner and upon such terms as the Trustees think fit and charge the sums so raised or borrowed or any part thereof on all or any investments of the Scheme as the Trustees shall in their absolute discretion without being liable to account think fit to the extent that the Trustees shall have the same full and unrestricted powers of investing and transposing investments in all respects as if they were absolutely and beneficially entitled to the assets of the Scheme and without prejudice to the generality hereof trust money may (i) be placed or retained upon deposit or current account at such rate of interest (if any) and upon such terms as the Trustees shall think fit with any bank investment company building society local authority or finance company or any United Kingdom office or branch of an insurance company (ii) be invested in any type of Unit Trust which is empowered to transact business with the trustees of pension schemes designed to satisfy the provisions of Part XIV Chapter I of the Income and Corporation Taxes Act 1988 be invested in underwriting or sub-underwriting new issues of stocks and shares (iii) be used to pay the premiums on any insurance policy the proceeds of which will fall to meet any benefit payable pursuant to the Rules or part thereof and (iv) be invested in or upon any stocks shares or securities of the Principal Company and Associated Companies (as hereinafter defined) and may be lent to or placed on deposit with any of the said Companies on such normal commercial terms and at such commercial rate of interest as the Trustees may arrange with the said Companies PROVIDED THAT no loan shall be granted to any member or to any individual having a contingent interest under the Scheme.

Appendix 9

Specimen Power of Amendment

(i)   The Principal Company may at any time, and subject only to the following Rules of this Section, by deed, alter or repeal this Deed and all or any of the Rules whether retrospectively or otherwise for the time being in force or make any new Rules to the exclusion of or in addition to all or any of the existing Rules, and any Rules so made shall be deemed to be Rules of the same validity as if originally made and shall be subject in the same way to be altered or modified.

(ii)   There shall be no alteration without the consent in writing of the Trustees.

Appendix 10

Definition of 20% Director — PN 6.15 & JOM 91(3)

(a) A member who retired before 17 March 1987 if he is a director who, either alone or together with his/her spouse and minor children, is or becomes the beneficial owner of shares which, when added to any shares held by the trustees of any settlement to which the director or his/her spouse had transferred assets, carry more than 20% of the voting rights in the company providing the pension or in a company which controls that company.

(b) A member who retires on or after 17 March 1987 if he has, at any time after 16 March 1987 and within 10 years of retirement, been a director and either on his own or with one or more associates* beneficially owned or been able to control directly or indirectly or through other companies 20% or more of the ordinary share capital of the company. In scheme rules this should be described as a director as defined in Section 612 (1) ICTA 1988 who is within paragraph (b) of Section 417 (5) ICTA 1988.

*   (i) 'Associates' means in relation to a director, any relative (i.e. spouse, forebears, issue and siblings) or partner, the trustees of any settlement in relation to which the director is, or any relative of his (living or dead) is or was, a settlor, and, where the director is interested in any shares or obligations of the company which are subject to any trust, or are part of the estate of a deceased person, any other person interested therein.

  (ii) The expression 'either on his or with one or more associates' requires a person to be treated as owning or, as the case may be, controlling what any associate owns or controls, even if he does not own or control share capital on his own.

Appendix 11

Power to Make and Receive Transfer Payments

[   ] The Trustees may, with the consent of the Principal Company, accept in respect of any Member a transfer from the trustees or administrator of another fund, scheme or arrangement approved under the Act or for the purpose of this Rule [   ] by the Board of Inland Revenue (referred to in this Rule [   ] as 'the other scheme') of all or any of the assets of the other scheme upon the footing that the Member's Credit shall be increased by the amount of value of the assets transferred, provided that:

(a)   no such transfer shall be made if the Actuary advises that it would cause any benefit payable under the Scheme to exceed the limits set out in Rule [   ], and

(b)   such part of the assets transferred as is derived from the contributions (if any) made to, or treated under it as having been made to, the other scheme (but only such part) shall be treated under the Scheme as having been derived from contributions made by the Member to the Scheme and shall be subject to such restrictions as to refunds and otherwise as are notified to the Trustees by the trustees or administrator of the other scheme on such transfer being made and as is necessary for the purpose of the continued approval of the Scheme under the Act.

[   ] The Trustees may, at the request of a Member, transfer to the trustees or administrator of any fund, scheme or arrangement which is certified by the trustees or administrator thereof to be approved under the Act or which is approved for the purposes of this Rule [   ] by the Board of Inland Revenue and in which the Member's employer participates (any such fund, scheme or arrangement being referred to in this Rule [   ] as 'the other Scheme') assets equal in value to the Member's Credit at the date of transfer upon the footing that such assets shall be applied under the other scheme in providing benefits (consistent with approval of the Scheme under the Act) in respect of the Member. The Trustees shall supply the trustees or administrator of the other scheme with such information relating to the Service of the Member and any contributions made by him as may be requested

by them. Upon any such transfer being made, the Member's Credit shall be extinguished with all entitlement relating thereto.

Appendix 12

Specimen Deed of Adherence

DEED OF ADHERENCE

DATED [   ]

PARTIES

(1)   J. BLACK AND SONS LIMITED
30 The Common
Anytown
Blankshire AN1 2ZQ   ('the Principal Company')

(2)   JAMES BLACK
4 London Road
Anytown
Blankshire AN1 5PQ

JESSICA BLACK
4 London Road
Anytown
Blankshire AN1 5PQ

[THE PENSIONEER TRUSTEE]

                                            ('the Trustees')

(3)   J. BLACK AND SONS (CARDIFF) LIMITED
34 High Street
Cardiff CF2 1NS   ('the New Participating
                                      Company')

WHEREAS

(A)   By an Interim Pension Trust Deed ('the Interim Deed') dated
[   ] and made between (1) the Principal Company and (2)
the Trustees there was established with effect from that date the

J. Black & Sons Ltd Pension Scheme ('the Scheme') for providing relevant benefits (as defined in Section 612(1) of ICTA 1988) for certain employees of the Principal Company and certain other companies which might thereafter agree to participate in the Scheme

(B) There was executed on [   ] by (1) the Principal Company and (2) the Trustees a Definitive Pension Trust Deed ('the Definitive Deed') in accordance with the provisions of which and of the Rules scheduled thereto the Scheme is administered

(C) The Principal Company pursuant to the provisions of Clause [   ] of the Definitive Deed may with the consent of the Trustees extend the benefits of the Scheme to companies subsidiary to or associated with the Principal Company

(D) The Principal Company wishes to extend the benefits of the Scheme to employees of the New Participating Company and the Trustees consent is indicated by their execution hereof

NOW THIS DEED WITNESSES AS FOLLOWS:-

1. The benefits of the Scheme are hereby extended to the New Participating Company and the participation of the New Participating Company in the Scheme is deemed to be effective from the [   ]

2. The New Participating Company agrees to comply with the provisions of the Definitive Deed and the said Rules and any amendments thereto.

IN WITNESS WHEREOF etc.

Appendix 13

Standard Documents: Finance Act 1989:
Extract from SFO Controller's letter

 Inland Revenue

R G LUSK Controller

SUPERANNUATION FUNDS OFFICE
Lynwood Road   Thames Ditton
Surrey   KT7 0DP

Telephone 01-398 4242 ext

Our ref: SF 73/15

November 1989

Dear Sir

STANDARD DOCUMENTS: FINANCE ACT 1989 PROVISIONS

1. I am writing concerning the future use of previously agreed forms of standard rules for schemes approvable under Chapter I Part XIV ICTA 1988.

2. The Finance Act 1989 and Memoranda 99 and 100 set out the changes in the tax rules for retirement benefit schemes. It is clear that your existing standard sets of rules can no longer be used in their present form for, for example, schemes set up on or after 14 March 1989 and not approved before 27 July 1989. To enable the previously agreed standard rules to be re-introduced into the Joint Office without re-examination we have prepared the enclosed packages A and B.

3. Package A is intended to be incorporated into your previously agreed standard rules so as to make them suitable for schemes which commenced on or after 14 March 1989, were not approved before Royal Assent (27 July 1989) and which do not have members with transitional rights to the old regime ie, the new basis of benefits will apply to all members.

4. Previously agreed standard rules into which are incorporated package B will be suitable for use with schemes which commenced on

or after 17 March 1987 and before 14 March 1989 (not 27 July 1989 as stated in paragraph 58 of Memorandum 100) and which were not approved before 27 July 1989. Such rules will also be suitable as replacement rules for those schemes which were approved under the terms of paragraph 55 of Memorandum 100.

5. If you wish to avail yourself of the package procedure you should first notify the Standards Section of this Office, and forward final prints of the revised documents together with a certificate to the effect that these consist of the previously agreed standards amended only to the extent necessary to incorporate the relevant package wording and, if appropriate, changes in the DSS legislation.

6. The revised document should be given a revised code. The phrase "to the extent necessary" in the certificate may be interpreted as giving scope to use different terminology for defined terms and/or to place the definitions used in a separate rule which defines terms for the purposes of the whole scheme provided that the essence of the new rules remains intact.

7. These procedures will not be available where rules have been amended in any other way.

8. These procedures may also apply in respect of model rules for small self-administered schemes.

Appendix 14

Specimen Winding-Up Provision for Interim Trust Deed

If at any time before the definitive deed is executed the principal company shall determine that the scheme be discontinued the principal company shall (subject as hereinafter provided) or if there be no principal company or other employers the trustees alone shall forthwith execute the definitive deed and rules and the trustees shall deal with the assets of the scheme affected by the discontinuance in the manner described therein PROVIDED ALWAYS that if there is a complete discontinuance of the scheme and if the confirmation of the Commissioners of Inland Revenue is obtained that treatment of the scheme as an exempt approved scheme for the purposes of Part XIV Chapter I would not thereby be prejudiced the definitive deed and rules may contain no provisions other than those relating to the disposal by the trustees of the said assets and upon the trustees disposing of the said assets in the manner prescribed by the definitive deed and rules the trusts consituted by this deed shall thereupon be determined in relation to those assets and those beneficiaries affected by the discontinuance.

Appendix 15

Occupational Pension Schemes Application for Approval

Inland Revenue
Superannuation Funds Office

OCCUPATIONAL PENSION SCHEMES
APPLICATION FOR APPROVAL

SCHEME OPEN TO MORE THAN ONE EMPLOYEE

Notes on completion

1 Each application for approval of a scheme for more than one employee under Chapter II Part II Finance Act 1970 must be made on this form which should be completed and returned to SFO.

2 All questions should be answered in full; "None" or "Not applicable" should be entered where appropriate; blank spaces or "to be advised" are not acceptable, except where stated. Ticks should be used where indicated (√).

3 Reference to other documents giving the information is not acceptable as an answer, except where stated.

4 *To be read in connection with Section III Question No 11.* A policy is Standard if it is in a standard form appropriate to the scheme and agreed, or in course of being agreed, with the Inland Revenue as satisfying section 323(4)(aa) Income and Corporation Taxes Act 1970.

5 *To be read in connection with Section III Question Nos 15 and 16.* Where exceptionally the agreed wording of a standard document has been added to or amended, the applicant should supply, in addition to the copy of the executed document, a copy of the coded standard print marked up in a distinctive way to show all the differences between it and the formal instrument.

SECTION I   GENERAL

1	Name of principal (or only) employer	
2	Address of employer (registered office if a company or principal place of business if a partnership or individual)	
3	Name of scheme (as in governing document)	
4	Date of commencement	

SECTION II   PRINCIPAL (OR ONLY) EMPLOYER INFORMATION

1	Status of employer (eg Registered Company, Partnership etc)				
2	Employer's accounting date				
3	Nature of business				
4	Schedule D Tax District and Reference (NOT Collector)				
5	Schedule E Tax District and Reference (if known) (NOT Collector)				
6	Are there any other schemes of the employer of which the employees are or may become members? (√)	No	Yes	If YES complete Section VI	
7	Approximate percentage of scheme contributions (excluding employees' AVCs) expected to be paid by the employer	%			

200

Appendix 15

SECTION III SCHEME INFORMATION

1	Administrator Name and address	
2	Trustee Name and address	
3	Benefits eg 60ths, uplifted 60ths etc (reference to document in question 9 below will be sufficient where scale benefits provided)	

4	Indicate NRA range (√)	(M) 60–70	(F) 55–65	Other (please specify)

5	Number of Members		6	Date first employee notified	
7	Amount of all employers' ordinary annual contributions		8	Date first premium/contribution paid	

9	Method of publicity (please attach (√) relevant document)	Booklet	Letter	Other (please specify)

10	Funding Please indicate (√)	Self-administered (include Deposit Administration and Managed Fund Schemes where appropriate (PN 18.9))	Insured

11	If insured: is the policy Standard? (see note 4) (√)	Yes	Code	No	If NO please attach a copy of the policy if available

12	Date(s) of any special contributions (all employers)		13	Amount(s) of special contributions	
14	Reason for special contribution				

Full details of all contributions both ordinary and special to all schemes of the employer should be given at the end of the accounting period where the total special contributions exceed £20,000.

Nature of Documentation *(see note 5)*

15	Interim (√)	Agreed Standard Code	Agreed Standard Code .... plus amendments	Non-standard
16	Final (if attached) (√)	Agreed Standard Code	Agreed Standard Code .... plus amendments	Non-standard

Page 2

201

Appendix 15

SECTION IV EMPLOYEE INFORMATION

1	Does current membership include 20% Directors or former Controlling Directors? *(see PN 6.15 and 6.28)* (✓)	No	Yes	If YES complete Section V
2	Expected approximate amount of employee contribution (including AVCs) to this scheme as a percentage of salary			%
3	Pensionable earnings of highest paid scheme member			

SECTION V 20% AND FORMER CONTROLLING DIRECTORS INFORMATION *(See PN 6.15 and 6.28)*
(Continue on separate sheet if necessary)

1	Name			
2	Date of birth			
3	Date of joining firm			
4	Anticipated current year remuneration including fluctuating emoluments			
5	Benefits: as shown in Sect III.3? (✓) (If not, please specifiy, eg pension, lump sum, DIS benefit, expressed as anticipated fraction of final remuneration.			
6	Retained benefits (expressed as at 5 above) *(see PN 6.26 to 28 and PN 8.7)*			

SECTION VI OTHER SCHEMES OF THE PRINCIPAL (OR ONLY) EMPLOYER

In respect of all other schemes of the employer, including individual arrangements, discretionary schemes and service agreements, under which the employee benefits or may benefit.

NOTE To be completed in full *(continue on separate sheet if necessary)*

1	Name of scheme			
2	SFO Ref No			
3	Date of commencement			
4	NRA as at III.4 above? (✓) If not, please specify (M) (F)			
5	How is this scheme affected by the new one? (✓)	Closed / Paid-up / Wound-up / Other or unaffected *(State below)*	Closed / Paid-up / Wound-up / Other or unaffected *(State below)*	Closed / Paid-up / Wound-up / Other or unaffected *(State below)*

FURTHER "OTHER" SCHEME INFORMATION

SECTION VII PARTICIPATING EMPLOYER INFORMATION

NOTE To be completed in full for each participating employer other than the principal employer *(continue on separate sheet if necessary)*

1	Name of participating employer			
2	Address of participating employer			
3	Status (eg registered company, partnership etc)			
4	Nature of business			
5	Schedule D Tax District and Reference			
6	Schedule E Tax District and Reference (if known)			
7	Contributions to this scheme paid by participating employer			
8	Degree of association (See PN 16.7 and 8)			
9	Other schemes of participating employer of which the employees are or may become members? (√)	No	Yes	If YES please complete 10—12 below
10	SFO Ref No			
11	NRA as at III.4 above? If not (√) please specify (M) (F)			

12	How is this scheme affected by participation? (√)	Closed	Closed	Closed
		Paid-up	Paid-up	Paid-up
		Wound-up	Wound-up	Wound-up
		Other or unaffected *(Give separate details)*	Other or unaffected *(Give separate details)*	Other or unaffected *(Give separate details)*

SECTION VIII DOCUMENTS TO ACCOMPANY APPLICATION

For SFO use

A copy of the instrument establishing the scheme	
A copy of the Deed and/or rules governing the scheme (where prepared)	
A copy of the explanatory booklet or announcement to employees about the scheme	
When the scheme is self-administered; — a copy of the actuarial report or advice on which the funding of the scheme is based (PN 22.5) — if small self-administered, a list of the current investments of the scheme.	

SECTION IX DECLARATION

I/We hereby apply for approval of the retirement benefits scheme named in Section I of this form under Chapter II Part II of the Finance Act 1970. I/We declare that to the best of my/our knowledge and belief the information given in this application is correct and complete.

Signed (by or on behalf of Administrator) ....

Capacity in which signed   ....

Name   ....

Address ....

....

Date .... 19 ....

Page 4

203

Appendix 16

Documentation Certificate

 Inland Revenue
Superannuation Funds Office

DOCUMENTATION CERTIFICATE

Certificate for the purposes of approval under Chapter I Part XIV ICTA 1988

Name of Employer ....

Name of Scheme ....

....

Scheme Ref No SF........ /...
(if already known)

I certify

    a.   that the above Scheme was established by trust deed/exchange letter dated ...., and

    b.   has adopted Standard/Model rules which accord in *all* respects with standard/model documents agreed under reference SF └─┴─┴─┴─┴─┴─┴─┴─┴─┴─┴─┴─┘ (1), and

    c.   that, in my opinion, the rules adopted by the Scheme are appropriate(2).

In addition, I undertake

    d.   to notify the SFO of any alteration to the Scheme of which I become aware.

Signature ....

Name ....
and professional qualification (if any)

Capacity ....
(administrator or practitioner)

Name of Practitioner Company (if appropriate)

....

....

Position in Company ....

Date ....

[This certificate must be signed by one of the following:
(i) the Scheme administrator
(ii) a director of the Life Office with whom the scheme funds are wholly or partly insured, or an employee of that company who is authorised to sign such a certificate on its behalf
(iii) a legal practitioner
(iv) a Fellow of the Institute or Faculty of Actuaries
(v) a fellow of the Pensions Management Institute.]

Notes:

1.   Enter SF reference number of standard/model document.

2.   *Appropriate* rules means those used for the purpose designated, as agreed with the Standards Section of SFO.

3.   This certificate must accompany the application for approval of the Scheme in lieu of the Scheme rules where those rules accord with agreed standard or model documentation.

4.   The Superannuation Funds Office reserves the right to call for copies of the documentation of any particular scheme.

5.   A false declaration or facts concerning the Scheme or its administration may result in the non-approval of the scheme or withdrawal of approval.

SF 5 *(2/91)*

Appendix 17

Documentation Certificate

Inland Revenue
Superannuation Funds Office

DOCUMENTATION CERTIFICATE

Certificate for the purposes of approval/continued approval under Chapter I Part XIV ICTA 1988

Name of Employer ....

Name of Scheme ....

....

Scheme Ref No   SF .... / ....

I certify

a.   that the above Scheme was amended on .... by a Standard/Model rule amendment which accords in *all* respects with the standard/model amendment document agreed under reference SF ⌊ ı ı ⌊ ı ı ı ⌊ ı ı ı ı ⌋ [1], and

b.   that, in my opinion, the rule amendment adopted by the Scheme is appropriate[2].

In addition, I undertake

c.   to notify the SFO of any further alteration to the Scheme of which I become aware.

Signature ....

Name ....
and professional qualification (if any)

Capacity ....
(administrator or practitioner)

Name of Practitioner Company (if appropriate)

....

....

Position in Company ....

Date ....

[This certificate must be signed by one of the following:
(i)   the Scheme administrator
(ii)   a director of the Life Office with whom the scheme funds are wholly or partly insured, or an employee of that company who is authorised to sign such a certificate on its behalf
(iii)   a legal practitioner
(iv)   a Fellow of the Institute or Faculty of Actuaries
(v)   a fellow of the Pensions Management Institute.]

Notes:

1.   Enter SF reference number of standard/model rule amendment.

2.   An *appropriate* amendment means one adopted for the purpose designated, as agreed with the Standards Section of SFO.

3.   This certificate must accompany any notification of alteration to the scheme based on an agreed standard or model amendment in lieu of the amending documentation.

4.   The Superannuation Funds Office reserves the right to call for copies of the documentation of any particular scheme.

5.   A false declaration or facts concerning the Scheme or its administration may result in the non-approval of the scheme or withdrawal of approval.

SF 6 (2/91)

Appendix 18

Inland Revenue Undertakings Schemes Open to More than One Member

INLAND REVENUE UNDERTAKINGS

SCHEMES OPEN TO MORE THAN ONE MEMBER

TO: THE BOARD OF INLAND REVENUE

Name of Retirement Benefits Scheme ....

....

SF Ref No *(where known)* SF .... / ....

I/We, as Administrator(s) of the above pension scheme for the purposes of Chapter I Part XIV Income and Corporation Taxes Act 1988, as amended, hereby undertake to refer to the Inland Revenue *before* taking any action under paragraphs 1 to 11 and *after* taking any action under paragraphs 12 - 14 below. I/We further undertake to bring this undertaking to the notice of any new administrator of the scheme.

Signed ....

....

.... Date ....

1. Admission of any other employer to participate in the scheme or the retention of any employer when the circumstances which justified his participation change.

2. Admission of any member who is (or has since 16 March 1987 and within 10 years of his retirement been) a 20% Director of any of the participating employers and retention of any member who becomes a 20% Director – Note A.

3. Admission of any member who before 6 April 1973 was a controlling director, as defined in Section 624(3) ICTA 1988, of any of the participating employers and who has retirement annuity contracts in respect of that period.

4. Admission of any member to whom a pre-89 basis of calculation is to apply under transitional arrangements -- Note B.

5. Acceptance of any donations, bequests, etc.

6. Provision of benefits which exceed the amounts set out in the table in the Appendix to this Undertaking, other than pensions which do not exceed, when taken together with any retained benefits, £1,000.

7. Payment of lump sum benefits in respect of funds transferred into the scheme unless within the amount certified by the administrator(s) of the transferring scheme, increased by no more than the cost of living (measured by reference to the Retail Price Index) during the period of deferment and to no greater extent than the increase on total deferred benefits.

8. Provision of added years of service in the scheme in respect of a transfer payment where

    (a) remuneration exceeds £10,000 pa, and

    (b) prospective service to normal retirement date is 15 years or less, and

    (c) added years will exceed one half of that prospective service.

9. Provision of benefits in respect of a transfer payment received from a scheme of a Relevant employer in the case of

    (a) an 87 Member, or

    (b) an 89 Member if that scheme was not a Connected scheme (Note B and Definitions in Appendix).

10. Provision of benefits where there has been a change from part-time to full-time service (or vice versa) if part-time service is to be converted to its full-time equivalent (or vice versa) for the purpose of calculating benefits – Note C.

11. Refund of any scheme funds (eg surplus assets, excess policy proceeds) to the Employer – Note D.

12. Repayment of contributions to an employee – Note E.

13. Repayment of surplus voluntary contributions to an employee – Note E.

14. Commutation of an entire pension on grounds of triviality or in exceptional circumstances of serious ill-health -- Note E.

SF 176(U)(1989) *12/89*

NOTES

General: Full details should be submitted with all reports in accordance with these undertakings.

The expressions used in these notes will in most cases be defined in the Scheme rules. If further clarification is required you should refer to the Practice Notes, IR12, issued by the Superannuation Funds Office, Lynwood Road, Thames Ditton, Surrey, KT7 0DP. Tel: 01-398 4242.

A.   "20% Director" means a director who either on his own or with one or more associates beneficially owns or is able to control directly or indirectly or through other companies 20% or more of the ordinary share capital of the company. "Associates" for this purpose has the meaning given by Section 417 ICTA 1988.

B.   A Member who has joined the Scheme on or after 17 March 1987 or 14 March 1989/1 June 1989 in circumstances which did not involve a change of employment, eg as a result of corporate reorganisation or scheme reconstruction. Full details of the circumstances are given in Memoranda 87 and 99 obtainable from the SFO (see also Definitions in Appendix).

C.   A leaflet explaining Revenue requirements in these circumstances is available on request from the SFO.

D.   You are required to deduct tax at source under Section 601 and 602 ICTA 1988. Full details should be submitted to the SFO who will issue the necessary payslip and instructions for payment.

E.   There is a charge to tax in these circumstances under Section 598, Section 599 and Section 599A ICTA 1988 as appropriate. Reports should be made to the SFO unless particulars are submitted annually to HMIT on a return form I-SF or repayment claim form R63N (usually on schemes with 20 or more initial entrants). The appropriate tax should be retained until instructions are received from HM Inspector of Taxes.

Appendix 18

APPENDIX

Aggregate Pension before commutation

The greater of (A) N/60 x FR (Capped in the case of an 89 Member),
and
(B) the amounts in the following chart:

	Pre-17.3.87 Member	87 Member	89 Member
At NRD	Up to 5 years N/60 x FR 6 years 8/60 x FR 7 years 16/60 x FR 8 years 24/60 x FR 9 years 32/60 x FR 10 years or more 40/60 x FR Provided that pension plus RBs do not exceed 2/3 x FR (capped in case of 89 Member)	N/30 x FR Up to 20/30 maximum (including benefit derived from any transfer payment from schemes of Relevant employers)	N/30 x FR (capped) Up to 20/30 maximum
Before NRD (on incapacity grounds)	N/NS x P (Pension as calculated at NRD with NS substituted for N)	N/NS x P	N/30 x FR (capped) up to 20/30 maximum provided pension plus RBs do not exceed 2/3 x FR (capped)
After NRD	The greater of (i) pension at NRD but substituting date of retirement for NRD, (ii) pension at NRD plus N/60ths (maximum 5/60ths) for further service over 40 years after NRD, and (iii) pension at NRD increased by greater of increase in RPI since NRD or actuarial increase since NRD. (ii) and (iii) are not available to 20% Directors other than in respect of service after age 70.		N/30 x FR (capped) up to 20/30 maximum, provided pension plus RBs do not exceed 2/3 x FR (capped)

Aggregate Lump Sum on commutation

The greater of (A) 3N/80ths x FR (Capped in the case of an 89 Member),
and
(B) the amounts in the following chart:

At NRD	Up to 8 years 3N/80 x FR 9 years 30/80 x FR 10 years 36/80 x FR 11 years 42/80 x FR 12 years 48/80 x FR 13 years 54/80 x FR 14 years 63/80 x FR 15 years 72/80 x FR 16 years 81/80 x FR 17 years 90/80 x FR 18 years 99/80 x FR 19 years 108/80 x FR 20 years or more 120/80 x FR Provided that lump sum plus lump sum RBs do not exceed 1.5 x FR (capped in case of 89 Member)	Formula $\left[\left(\frac{a-b}{c-b} \right) \times (d-e) \right] + e$, where a = scheme pension before any commutation or allocation b = N/60 x FR c = N/30 x FR d = uplifted/80 x FR, according to pre-17.3.87 maximum table e = 3N/80 x FR	2.25 x initial pension (before commutation or allocation)
Before NRD (on incapacity grounds)	N/NS x LS (Lump sum as calculated at NRD with NS substituted for N)	N/NS x LS	2.25 x initial pension before commutation or allocation provided lump sum plus lump sum RBs do not exceed 1.5 x FR (capped).
After NRD	The greater of (i) lump sum at NRD but substituting date of retirement for NRD, (ii) lump sum at NRD plus 3N/80ths (maximum 15/80ths) for further service over 40 years after NRD, and (iii) lump sum at NRD plus interest (ii) and (iii) are not available to 20% Directors other than in respect of service after age 70.		2.25 x initial pension before commutation or allocation provided lump sum plus lump sum RBs do not exceed 1.5 x FR (capped).

Aggregate Non-commutable pension where lump sum given separately

At NRD	Up to 5 years N/80 x FR 6 years 8/80 x FR 7 years 16/80 x FR 8 years 24/80 x FR 9 years 32/80 x FR 10 years 40/80 x FR Provided that pension plus RBs do not exceed 0.5 x FR (capped in case of 89 Member)	N/40 x FR Up to 20/40 maximum	N/40 x FR (capped) Up to 20/40 maximum

Aggregate Lump Sum where lump sum given separately - as for commuted lump sum limits, EXCEPT

(At NRD)		b = N/80 x FR c = N/40 x FR	3 x number of 80ths comprising non-commutable pension up to 120/80ths maximum

208

Spouses and Dependants Pensions

(The following limits are approximate; more may be given where the deceased but not the dependant has RBs.)

ONE   -   2/3 x Member's pension calculated as above as appropriate
TWO OR MORE - 1 x Member's pension calculated as above as appropriate, provided that neither/none exceeds
                2/3 x Member's pension.

Definitions in Appendix

Pre-17.3.87 Member	-- A member who joined the scheme before 17.3.1987 or who is treated as such under transitional arrangements by virtue of his membership of a previous scheme of this or a Relevant employer.
87 Member	-- A member who joined the scheme on or after 17.3.1987 but who is not an 89 Member, either by reason of his date of entry or transitional arrangements.

89 Member	-- (a) A member who has joined
	    (i) a scheme established on or after 14.3.1989, or
	    (ii) a scheme in existence prior to 14.3.1989, on or after 1.6.1989
	(b) A member who has elected or opted to be treated as an 89 Member.

Relevant employer	-- means an Associated employer, or
	an employer
	    (i) who has acquired, or who has been acquired by, or who has merged with, another employer, or
	    (ii) who has taken over the whole or part of the business of such an employer.

Aggregate	-- means the aggregate benefits under all approved schemes of the employer, including free-standing AVC schemes. For 89 Members it also includes benefits under Connected schemes of Associated employers.
Associated employer	-- Employers are associated employers if (directly or indirectly) one is controlled by the other or if both are controlled by a third person.
Connected schemes	-- Approved schemes of Associated employers which have provided benefits during periods of concurrent employment.
NRD	-- Normal Retirement Date.
FR	-- Final Remuneration. This means final remuneration as defined in the scheme rules. (Otherwise, it means the average annual remuneration of the last three years' service.)
Capped	-- This means FR limited to the permitted maximum prescribed: £60,000 for 1989/90, increased annually by a formula reflecting price inflation.
N	-- Actual service with the employer with a maximum of 40 years. In the case of an 89 Member, total actual service with all Associated employers who have provided benefits under a Connected scheme but with concurrent service counted only once.
NS	-- Notional service with employer to NRD.
P	-- The maximum pension permissible had the member served until NRD.
LS	-- The maximum lump sum permissible had the member served until NRD.
RBs	-- Retained Benefits: Benefits under approved occupational pension schemes relating to earlier employments and under retirement annuity contracts and personal pension schemes relating to this or earlier employments. Benefits derived from transfer payments received from schemes of non-Relevant employers are treated as RBs but in the case of pre-17.3.87 Members, all benefits derived from transfer payments are treated as RBs.

Appendix 19

JOM 87 (12) Transitional Arrangements — Circumstances where Finance (No 2) Act 1987 does not apply

JOM 87(12) Transitional Arrangements for employees in service and members of a scheme before 17 March 1987 and who remain with the same employer. The following situations will not normally be regarded as caught by Finance (No.2) Act 1987:

(a) Restructuring of a business (or re-organisation of pension arrangements) resulting in employees moving from one employer's scheme to another's, provided that both employers are within the same group and that such changes do not give accelerated rates of accrual under the pre-17 March rules where these were not previously available.

(b) A move (e.g. on promotion) from one scheme of an employer to another scheme of that same employer, or of another employer in the same group.

(c) The joining (e.g. on promotion) of a separate top-up scheme which provides additional benefits to those under the main scheme in respect of which the individual remains a member.

(d) A move to a new or existing scheme of a new employer who has taken over the old employer (or all or part of his business), provided that the individual was a member of the old employer's scheme.

(e) Changes in the benefits structure of an existing scheme, provided that such changes do not give accelerated rates of accrual under the pre-17 March rules where these were not previously available.

(f) The exercise of a power of augmentation under the rules of an existing scheme to improve the benefits available to a member who joined before 17 March 1987, provided that the rules contained such a power before that date.

(g) Schemes or arrangements established before 17 March 1987, even if by then all the relevant documentation had not been finalised or no application for tax approval had been made. This will usually depend on the facts of a particular case but, as a general rule, a scheme will be in this category if, before 17 March 1987, the employer had entered into a contractual obligation to provide benefits.

(h)   Changes to an existing scheme to permit it to contract-out of SERPS or the establishment of a new scheme to enable existing members to contract-out.

(i)   Employees who leave their employer's scheme as a result of a temporary posting or secondment to another employer (whether in the United Kingdom or abroad), provided that at the time of leaving the scheme there was a definite intention to return and that on return they rejoin a scheme of the original employer, or of another employer in the same group.

(j)   Individuals not covered by (i) above who cease to be members of their employer's scheme (whether or not they leave the employer's service), provided that they rejoin the scheme within one month. Where absence is due to maternity leave, temporary lay-off or redundancy, a longer period may be appropriate.

(k)   Employees serving a waiting period before becoming full members of the employer's scheme, provided that they were regarded as members before 17 March 1987, for preservation purposes.

Appendix 20

Expression of Wish Form

TO: The Trustees of

Name of Member . . . .
        (Surname)   **(First Names)**

I understand that under the Rules of the Scheme a lump sum will be payable if I die while still in the service of the Company and, in certain circumstances, on death after retirement. I also understand that the Trustees have discretionary powers to pay the lump sum to such one or more of my relatives and dependants as they shall decide or to my legal personal representatives.

For the guidance of the Trustees in such circumstances I would like the following person or persons to receive the benefits in the proportions shown.

Name   *Relationship with Member*   *Proportion of lump sum*

I understand that this expression of wish does not in any way bind the Trustees or fetter the exercise of their discretionary powers.

Signature . . . . Date . . . .

NOTES

1. To ensure confidentiality you may wish to place this Form in a sealed envelope when you return it. The envelope will then only be opened by the Trustees in the event of your death.

2. Your 'legal personal representatives' are, if you leave a will, your Executors; if not, the administrators of your estate.

3. If your personal circumstances change and you wish to alter this expression of wish, you should ask for the return of this Form and complete a further form in its place.

Appendix 21

Specimen Loan Document

1. Name of Pension Fund...............................

2. Name of company to whom loan is granted................

3. Amount of Loan £ ....

4. Purpose of the Loan...............................

....

5. The loan is *Secured/*Unsecured

6. Date from which loan is to run....................

7. Date on which loan is due for repayment ....

8. Interest is due annually on the anniversary of the loan, or on earlier repayment at a rate of 3 % above [the Clearing Bank's] base lending rate ruling on the due date.

9. The Trustees and the company have agreed that the loan may be repaid at the option of the company prior to the date due for repayment. The loan may be recalled by the Trustees giving the Company one month's notice. The loan shall be immediately repayable if the Company breaches the conditions of this agreement, ceases to carry on business or becomes insolvent, or the loan is required by the Trustees to pay benefits which have become due under the Pension Fund.

10. Subject to the agreement of the Trustees, this loan may be renewed for a further period on similar terms.

11. The terms and conditions set out above have been accepted by the company.

12. We hereby confirm that the terms of this loan set out above have been approved by a majority of the trustees acting in accordance with their powers of investment as conferred by the Trust Deed.

214

Signature .... Signature ....
         Trustee   Trustee

Date .... Date ....

Signature ....
    On Behalf of the Company

Date ....

* Delete as appropriate

Appendix 22

Particulars of Loans to Employers and Associated Companies

 **Inland Revenue**

Superannuation Funds Office

Lynwood Road
Thames Ditton
Surrey KT7 0DP
GTN 3017
Telephone 01-398 4242
ext

Please reply to the Controller

Your reference

Our reference

Date

Dear Sir/Madam

Scheme ....
....

Please complete this questionnaire and return it to this office. The information is required in respect of all completed loans made in the last 5 years, all current loans, and any proposed loan, unless this office has already been notified - in which case you should state the date and amount of the loan, and the date of notification. A copy of the loan agreement in each case should be enclosed (unless already provided).

SCHEME INVESTMENTS

Loans to Employer and Associated Companies		
1	Date of Loan		
2	Amount		
3	Rate of Interest		
4	Purpose of Loan *(full details are required "cash flow" is not sufficient)*		
5	Term of Loan and any repayment conditions		
6	Total value of fund at date of loan		
7	The amount invested in loans and shares in the employer and associated companies, at date of loan. *(Note: The 50% limit applies to loans and shares combined.)*		

(continue on a separate sheet if necessary)

Yours faithfully

SF 192 *(6/89)*

Appendix 23

Scheme Investments — Loans to Employer and Associated Companies

 Inland Revenue

Superannuation Funds Office

Lynwood Road
Thames Ditton
Surrey KT7 0DP
GTN 3017
Telephone 081-398 4242

SMALL SELF-ADMINISTERED SCHEMES

Information required under The Retirement Benefit Schemes (Restriction on Discretion to Approve) (Small Self-administered Schemes) Regulations 1991

Name of Principal Employer ....

Name of Scheme   ....

SFO reference   SF .... / ....

SCHEME INVESTMENTS: Loans to employer and associated companies	
1	Name of borrower	
2	Date of loan	
3	Amount	
4	Rate of interest	
5	Purpose of loan *(full details are required "cash flow" is not sufficient)*	
6	Term of loan and any repayment conditions	
7	Total value of fund at date of loan	
8	The amount invested in loans and shares in the employer and associated companies, at date of loan. *(Note: The 25%/50% limit applies to loans and shares combined.)*	

Signed (by or on behalf of administrator) ....

Capacity in which signed   ....

Notes on completion

1. Administrators of small self-administered schemes are required to furnish to the Board of Inland Revenue the relevant information and documents within 90 days after the trustees in their capacity as such have loaned money to an employer (or any associated company).

2. A copy of the loan agreement is required and this should be submitted with the completed questionnaire.

SF 7013

Appendix 24

Particulars of Property or Land Transactions

 Inland Revenue

Superannuation Funds Office

Lynwood Road
Thames Ditton
Surrey KT7 0DP
GTN 3017
Telephone 01-398 4242
ext

Please reply to the Controller

Your reference

Our reference

Date

Dear Sir/Madam

Scheme ....

....

Would you please complete this questionnaire in full and return it to this office.

SCHEME INVESTMENTS

	Property or land transactions	
1	Date of purchase	
2	Address of property	
3	Description of property	
4	Purchase price and interest in property (freehold or leasehold)	
5	Name of vendor and whether "connected" ie a scheme member, relative etc	
6	If property purchased leasehold, and vendor is "connected", was any part of the vendor's interest in the property retained by him?	
7	Name of tenant (if any) and whether "connected"	
8	Length of lease and rent payable	
9	Details of any associated agreement concerning the property or otherwise involving any member of the scheme or any connected person	
10	Details of any trustees' borrowing to finance the purchase	

If the vendor is "connected" (see question 5) please enclose a copy of an independent valuation of the property. Similarly, if the lessee in "connected", a copy of an independent valuation of the rental value will be required.

Yours faithfully

218

Appendix 25

Particulars of Shares in Private Employer Company or Associated Company

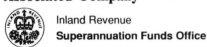 Inland Revenue

Superannuation Funds Office

Lynwood Road
Thames Ditton
Surrey KT7 0DP
GTN 3017
Telephone 081-398 4242

SMALL SELF-ADMINISTERED SCHEMES

Information required under The Retirement Benefit Schemes (Restriction on Discretion to Approve) (Small Self-administered Schemes) Regulations 1991

Name of Principal Employer ....

Name of Scheme   ....

SFO reference   SF .... / ....

	SCHEME INVESTMENTS: Property or land acquisitions (or disposals)	
1	Date of purchase/sale *(state which)*	
2	Address of property	
3	Description of property	
4	Purchase/sale price and interest in property (freehold or leasehold)	
5	Name of vendor/purchaser and whether "connected" ie a relative or business associate of a member, trustee or employer	
6	If property purchased leasehold, and vendor is "connected", was any part of the vendor's interest in the property retained by him?	
7	Name of lessee (if any) and whether "connected"	
8	Length of lease and rent payable	
9	Details of any associated agreement concerning the property or otherwise involving any member of the scheme or any connected person	
10	Details of any trustees' borrowing to finance the purchase (see also form SF 7015)	

Signed (by or on behalf of administrator) ....

Capacity in which signed   ....

Notes on completion

1. Administrators of small self-administered schemes are required to furnish to the Board of Inland Revenue the relevant information and documents <u>within 90 days</u> after the trustees in their capacity as such have acquired (or disposed of) any land or buildings.

2. If the vendor/purchaser is "connected" (see question 5) please enclose a copy of an independent valuation of the property Similarly, if the lessee is "connected", a copy of an independent valuation of the rental value is required, and a copy of the lease. As a concession further time may be allowed for production of the copy of the lease.

SF 7012

Appendix 26

Scheme Investments — Shares in an Employer Company (or Associated Company) or an Unlisted Company

Inland Revenue

Superannuation Funds Office

Lynwood Road
Thames Ditton
Surrey KT7 0DP
GTN 3017
Fax: 081-398 4242 ext 4253
Telephone 081-398 4242
ext

Please reply to the Controller

Your reference

Our reference

Date

Dear Sir/Madam

Scheme ....

....

Would you please complete this questionnaire in full and return it to this office.

SCHEME INVESTMENTS

	Shares in private employer company or associated company	
1	Date of purchase	
2	Type and number of shares concerned	
3	Purchase price	
4	Name of vendor and whether scheme member relative or associated person (ie connected with member, relative, directors or trustees)	
5	Total Issued Share Capital (ISC)	
6	Vendor's beneficial interest (as a % of ISC) prior to sale	
7	Trustees' reason for acquiring shares	
8	Date and reference number of any clearance under s.707 ICTA 1988	
9	Total amount invested in loans to or shares in the employer company or associated company (prior to this purchase) *(Note: The 50% limit applies to both loans and shares)*	

Please also provide:-

(a) Full details of the calculations used in valuing the shares, and a copy of any professional valuation or advice obtained.

(b) Copies of the most recent accounts of the scheme, and the last 3 years accounts of the company.

(c) Details of any associated agreement with any member of the scheme, any relative or other person connected with the scheme to purchase or sell shares in the company.

Yours faithfully

220

SF 193 *(6/89)*

Appendix 27

Particulars of Non-Income Producing Assets

 Inland Revenue

Superannuation Funds Office

SMALL SELF-ADMINISTERED SCHEMES

Lynwood Road
Thames Ditton
Surrey KT7 0DP
GTN 3017
Telephone 081-398 4242

Information required under The Retirement Benefit Schemes (Restriction on Discretion to Approve) (Small Self-administered Schemes) Regulations 1991

Name of Principal Employer ....

Name of Scheme ....

SFO reference SF .... / ....

SCHEME INVESTMENTS:	Shares in an employer company (or associated company) or an unlisted company	
1	Name of company	
2	Type and number of shares concerned	
3	Date of purchase/sale (state which) and purchase/ sale price	
4	Name of vendor/purchaser and whether "connected" ie a relative or business associate of a member, trustee or employer	
5	Total Issued Share Capital (ISC)	
6	Where shares purchased by scheme, vendor's beneficial interest (as a % of ISC) prior to sale	
7	Trustees' reason for acquiring shares	
8	Date and reference number of any clearance under s.707 ICTA 1988	
9	Total amount invested in loans to or shares in the employer company or associated company prior to this transaction *(the 25%/50% limit applies to loans and shares combined)*	

Signed (by or on behalf of administrator) ....

Capacity in which signed ....

Notes on completion

1. Administrators of small self-administered schemes are required to furnish to the Board of Inland Revenue the relevant information and documents <u>within 90 days</u> of any acquisition (or disposal) by the trustees in their capacity as such of shares in an employer, associated company or unlisted company.

2. "Unlisted company" means a company which is not officially listed on a recognised stock exchange within the meaning of section 841 ICTA 1988.

3. If the vendor/purchaser is "connected" (see question 4) and the shares were purchased/sold privately, the following are required:-

   (a) Full details of the calculations used in valuing the shares, and a copy of any professional valuation or advice obtained.

   (b) Copies of the most recent accounts of the scheme, and the last 3 years accounts of the company.

   (c) Details of any associated agreement with anyone connected with the scheme to purchase or sell shares in the company.

SF 7014

Appendix 28

Scheme Investments — Non-Income Producing Assets

Inland Revenue

Superannuation Funds Office

Lynwood Road
Thames Ditton
Surrey KT7 0DP
GTN 2017
Telephone 01-398 4242
ext

Your reference

Our reference

Date

Dear Sir

Scheme ....

....

Would you please complete this questionnaire and return it to this office.

QUESTIONNAIRE XIII

SCHEME INVESTMENTS

Non income-producing assets	
1	Nature of asset	
2	Name of vendor and whether a scheme member, relative or associated person (ie connected with member, relative, directors or trustees)	
3	Price paid and proportion of fund represented *(Note: a copy of any valuation should be supplied)*	
4	Where is asset normally kept?	
5	Can the asset be readily sold when required for pension etc purposes NB Any proposal to sell the asset to a member of the scheme or any "connected person" is likely to give rise to non-relevant benefits and may put the approval of the scheme in jeopardy.	

Yours faithfully

SF 194 *(12/87)*

Appendix 29

Scheme Investments — Miscellaneous Acquisitions and Disposals

Inland Revenue
Superannuation Funds Office

Lynwood Road
Thames Ditton
Surrey KT7 0DP
GTN 3017
Telephone 081-398 4242

SMALL SELF-ADMINISTERED SCHEMES

Information required under The Retirement Benefit Schemes (Restriction on Discretion to Approve) (Small Self-administered Schemes) Regulations 1991

Name of Principal Employer ....

Name of Scheme   ....

SFO reference   SF .... / ....

SCHEME INVESTMENTS: Miscellaneous acquisitions and disposals	
1 Description of asset	
2 Date of purchase/sale (state which) and purchase/sale price	
3 Name of vendor/purchaser and whether "connected", ie a relative or business associate of a member, trustee or employer	
4 If the asset has been leased to anyone please give brief details and state whether the lessee is "connected"	

Signed (by or on behalf of administrator) ....

Capacity in which signed   ....

Notes on completion

1. Administrators of small self-administered schemes are required to furnish to the Board of Inland Revenue the relevant information and documents <u>within 90 days</u> after the trustees in their capacity as such have acquired, leased or disposed of any asset from or to an employer or associated company. Transactions involving property and shares should not be reported on this form.

2. If the vendor/purchaser is "connected" (see question 3) please enclose a copy of an independent valuation of the asset. Similarly, if the lessee is "connected", a copy of an independent valuation of the rental value is required, and a copy of the lease.

SF 7016

Appendix 30

Scheme Borrowing

 **Inland Revenue**
Superannuation Funds Office

Lynwood Road
Thames Ditton
Surrey KT7 0DP
GTN 3017
Telephone 081-398 4242

SMALL SELF-ADMINISTERED SCHEMES

Information required under The Retirement Benefit Schemes (Restriction on Discretion to Approve) (Small Self-administered Schemes) Regulations 1991

Name of Principal Employer ....

Name of Scheme ....

SFO reference   SF .... / ....

SCHEME BORROWING		
1	Date of borrowing	
2	Amount	
3	Rate of interest	
4	Purpose of borrowing	
5	Repayment date	
6	Name and address of lender	
7	Total value of fund at date of borrowing	
8	Total amount of employer contributions to the above scheme in the last 3 completed accounting years of the scheme (or since commencement, if the scheme has not been in existence for 3 years).	
9	Total amount of employee contributions to the scheme (as a condition of membership) in the year ended 5 April prior to the date of borrowing.	

Signed (by or on behalf of administrator) ....

Capacity in which signed   ....

Notes on completion

1. Administrators of small self-administered schemes are required to furnish to the Board of Inland Revenue the relevant information and documents <u>within 90 days</u> after the trustees in their capacity as such have borrowed money for any reason.

2. If the lender is "connected", a copy of the loan agreement should be submitted with the completed questionnaire.

3. As a concession, no report need be made of temporary borrowings for a period not exceeding 6 months where the aggregate amount borrowed does not exceed the lesser of 10% of the market value of the fund or £50,000 and the borrowing is repaid at or before the due date. If a borrowing is rolled over into a further term it is outwith the concession and must be reported.

SF 7015

Appendix 31

Inland Revenue Statement of Practice

SP 4/88 22 JULY 1988

Tax treatment of transactions in financial futures and options

1. This Statement sets out the Inland Revenue's views on the tax treatment of transactions in financial futures and options carried out by investment trusts, unit trusts, pension funds, charities, and companies which either do not trade or whose principal trade is outside the financial area. The principles set out apply to all futures and options, whether traded on an exchange or otherwise.

2. Section 72, Finance Act 1985 provides, broadly, that transactions in commodity and financial futures and traded options on recognised exchanges will be treated as capital in nature unless they are regarded as profits or losses of a trade. Section 81 Finance Act 1987 extends this treatment to other transactions in futures and options. If, under normal statutory and case law principles, profits or losses fall to be treated as trading in nature then Sections 72 and 81 have no application to those profits or losses. It is therefore necessary first to determine whether or not a taxpayer is trading in futures or options without reference to the provisions of Sections 72 and 81.

3. Whether or not a taxpayer is trading is a question of fact to be determined by reference to all the facts and circumstances of the particular case. Consideration is given to the 'badges of trade'. Generally a person will not be regarded as trading if the transactions are infrequent or to hedge specific capital investments. An individual is unlikely to be regarded as trading as a result of purely speculative transactions in options or futures.

4. If the taxpayer in question is a company, which would include an investment trust or authorised unit trust, it is necessary to consider not only the normal case law defining trading but also the case of *Lewis Emanuel and Son Ltd v White (42 TC 369)*. The broad effect of the judgment in this case is that generally a company cannot speculate and that any

transactions carried out by a company must either be trading or capital in nature.

5. If a transaction in financial futures or options is clearly related to an underlying asset or transaction, then the tax treatment of the futures or options contract will follow that of the underlying asset or transaction. In general, the Inland Revenue take the view that this relationship exists where a futures or options contract is entered into in order to hedge an underlying transaction, asset or portfolio by reducing the risk relating to it; and the intention of the taxpayer in entering into a transaction is of considerable importance. Where the underlying transaction is itself treated as giving rise to a capital gain or loss, the related futures or options contract will also be treated as a capital matter and not as trading.

6. The basic conditions which have to be met if the transaction is to be treated as hedging in this sense are:

(1) the transaction must be economically appropriate to the reduction in risk of the underlying transaction, asset or portfolio; and

(2) the price fluctuations of the options and futures must be directly and demonstrably related to the fluctuations in value or composition of the underlying transaction, asset or portfolio at the time the hedging transaction is initiated.

7. This applies equally to long and short positions, and is not dependent upon the form of the eventual dispostion of the position. In other words it will apply whether the futures position is closed out or held to maturity, or in the case of an options position, closed out, exercised or held to final expiry.

Examples

8. Transactions would be treated as giving rise to capital gains or losses in the following circumstances:

(1) A taxpayer who holds gilts sells gilt futures to protect the value of his capital in the event of a fall in the value of gilt-edged securities generally.

(2) A taxpayer purchases an asset in two stages by purchasing a foreign currency future in advance of the purchase of an asset denominated in that currency, or by purchasing an option in respect of an underlying asset as a first step towards the acquisition of the asset itself.

(3) A taxpayer who holds a broadly based portfolio sells index futures or purchases index put options to protect himself against the risk

to the value of the portfolio from a fall in the market, (provided the fall in the index futures or options is directly and demonstrably correlated to the loss on the portfolio as it was constituted at the date the hedge was initiated).

9. But even if a transaction is not a hedging transaction in the sense of paragraph 8 above, it may, nevertheless, be regarded as capital in nature, depending on all the facts and circumstances. To take two specific examples—

(1) If a taxpayer is committed to making a bond issue in the near future and enters into an interest rate future or option with a view to protecting himself against rises in interest costs before he is able to make the issue, the Revenue will regard the transaction as being of a capital nature.

(2) If a taxpayer sells or buys options or futures as an incidental and temporary part of a change in investment strategy, (e.g., changing the ratio of gilts and equities), that transaction is likely to be treated as being of a capital nature, if the transaction in the assets themselves would be a capital matter.

10. A further uncertainty may arise if a transaction is originally undertaken as a capital hedge but the underlying transaction or motive falls away. If the futures or options transaction is closed out within a reasonably short period after the underlying motive falls away then the transaction will continue to be treated as capital in nature in accordance with the principles outlined above. If however the transaction is not closed out at that time it may be arguable that any profit or loss arising subsequently is of a trading nature. In practice the Revenue would not normally take this point in view of the original intentions of the taxpayer and the practical difficulties of making the necessary calculation.

11. Where a company enters into these transactions as incidental to its trading activity, for example a manufacturer entering into transactions to hedge the price of his raw materials, then the profits and losses from these transactions would be taken into account as part of the profits and losses of the trade.

Appendix 32

GN9: Retirement Benefit Schemes—Actuarial Reports

[This guidance note was first issued to members in April 1984 and revised in April 1987 and April 1988].

1. INTRODUCTION

1.1 When a retirement benefit scheme is to be set up, and at intervals thereafter, an actuarial report should be prepared.

1.2 These guidelines apply to such reports, including those on valuations which are required under the Occupational Pension Schemes (Disclosure of Information) Regulations 1986 (SI 1986 No. 1046) - as amended by the Occupational Pensions Schemes (Disclosure of Information) (Amendment) Regulations 1986 (SI 1986 No. 1717) - to which reference is made in this note.

1.3 These guidelines relate primarily to defined benefit schemes where the ultimate costs are initially unknown but the guidelines should also be followed as far as possible for other types of schemes.

1.4 The guidelines have been prepared with United Kingdom requirements and conditions in mind. Where a member is practising outside the United Kingdom and the Council of the Institute or the Faculty (as the case may be) has agreed, the guidelines may be replaced by guidance given by an actuarial body of the country in which the actuary practises.

2. PURPOSE OF THE GUIDELINES

2.1 The purpose of the guidelines is to ensure that the reports contain sufficient information to enable the expected future course of a scheme's contribution rate and funding level to be appreciated. (See Regulation 8(1)(a)). It is not intended to restrict the actuary's freedom of judgement in choosing the method of valuation and the underlying assumptions.

2.2 Although any report will be addressed to the actuary's client, normally the employer or the trustees, the actuary needs to bear in mind that his advice may be made available to third parties who can reasonably be expected to rely on it. In connection with the actuarial reports required under the Regulations, these specify in paragraphs 8(10)-(12) the third parties to whom the trustees must make reports available.

3. THE REPORT

3.1 The items in the following list are normally to be regarded as essential components of any report. Other information may often be desirable and suitable explanations of some features may be very important, for example the effect on the funding level of an improvement in benefits with retroactive effect.

Basic Information

3.1.1 An opening statement showing to whom the report is addressed, the purpose for which the valuation is made and the dates as at which the current valuation and, if applicable, the immediately preceding valuation were conducted.

3.1.2 A statement of benefits which have been valued (for example, by a summary of the terms of the scheme or by reference to appropriate documents). Reference should be made to the extent to which allowance has been made for discretionary increases in benefit especially where there has been a recent practice of granting such increases.

3.1.3 A brief summary of the data on which the investigation is based including a description of the assets. If the actuary has any reservations as to the reliability of the data, such explanation or qualification as is appropriate should be given.

Inter-valuation Period

3.1.4 A statement of the rates of contribution payable during the intervaluation period: and a commentary on any material developments during such period and on any significant variations in experience from the assumptions made at the previous valuation.

Funding Objectives

3.1.5 An explanation of the funding objectives and the method being employed to achieve those objectives. The implications in terms of stability of contribution rates and of future funding levels should also be explained.

Valuation Assumptions and Method

3.1.6 A statement of the assumptions made in valuing both the liabilities and the assets of the method employed in deriving the contribution rate in 3.1.8 below. Attention should be directed particularly to those assumptions to which the contribution is sensitive.

3.1.7 Comments on the compatibility of the basis of valuing the assets with that of valuing the liabilities. The actuary should also comment if it is considered that the investment policy is inappropriate to the form and incidence of the liabilities.

Contribution Rate

3.1.8 The contribution rate recommended to achieve the funding objectives. If such objectives imply a changing contribution rate (as a percentage of the relevant earnings), an indication as to the extent and timing of such change should be given.

Current Funding Levels

3.1.9 A statement as to whether or not, in the actuary's opinion, the assets would have been sufficient at the valuation date to cover liabilities arising (including any dependants' contingent benefits) in respect of pensions in payment, preserved benefits for members whose pensionable service has ceased and accrued benefits for members in pensionable service which will normally be related to pensionable service to, and pensionable earnings at, the date of valuation including revaluation on the statutory basis (or on such higher basis which has been promised). If there is any shortfall in the coverage, an indication of the degree of shortfall should be given having regard to the priorities attaching to various categories of benefits on winding up.

3.1.10 A statement as to the ongoing funding position if this is not otherwise conveyed by the comments on the funding objectives and the contribution rate.

General

3.1.11 A statement as to whether the valuation has been prepared in accordance with GN9 current at the date of signature of the valuation report (Regulation 8(1)(b)). Regulation 8(1)(c) states that any material departures from GN9 should be indicated. The actuary is however expected to comply with GN9 unless in exceptional circumstances he is convinced that full compliance would be inappropriate in which case he should give a complete explanation.

4. THE ACTUARIAL STATEMENT

4.1 This section relates to the Actuarial Statement required under Regulation 8(7) and Schedule 4 to the Regulations.

4.1.1 For the purpose of Section 1 of the Statement it should be assumed that the scheme is not discontinuing. Regulation 8(8)(b) describes how accrued rights and liabilities are to be calculated and valued for this purpose and these are stated to be benefits to which the member would be entitled on leaving pensionable service. This statement may thus be less rigorous than the requirement in 3.1.9. If the actuary feels that there is likely to be misinterpretation of the expression 'liabilities' by members, he should feel free to include an explanation under Section 3 bearing in mind that the word 'liabilities' also appears in Section 2 in a rather different sense.

4.1.2 Section 2 of the Statement requires an opinion from the actuary on the adequacy of the resources of the scheme in the normal course of events. In interpreting this expression at the date of each statement the actuary should take a prudent view of the future without taking into account every conceivable unfavourable development.

The actuary should regard this as excluding the possibilities of events—including those external to the scheme—which he cannot reasonably be expected to have allowed for in a conservative approach to the matter. The certificate cannot say more than can be inferred from the actuarial valuation to which the statement relates. The actuary will not generally need to give a negative or qualified opinion provided that any statement under 3.1.10 does not indicate cause for concern. If a negative or qualified opinion is given, attention should be drawn to the relevant sections of the latest valuation report.

4.1.3 For the purpose of Section 3, use may be made of the specimen descriptions of commonly used valuation methods in a note entitled 'Pension Fund Terminology' issued by the Institute and Faculty in May 1986. The actuary should endeavour to express the summary in language which is likely to be understood by the members. It is sufficient to describe the key funding assumptions; these are not necessarily limited to the financial assumptions. Members may be referred to the latest valuation report for fuller details, although such reference of itself does not satisfy the Regulations.

4.2 Regulations 8(7) refers to the inter-valuation period. This is not designed to require the actuary to monitor the situation continuously; however, if he is made aware or becomes aware of developments which materially affect the continuing validity of the latest Statement, then a revised Statement should be prepared and issued under Regulation 8(7).

Appendix 33

Schedule 3—Disclosure Regulations
Contents of Accounts

1. An account of the financial additions to and withdrawals from the fund of the scheme during the scheme year to which the accounts relate.

2. A statement, as at the end of the scheme year to which the accounts relate, of the assets (which expression in this Schedule does not include insurance policies which are specifically allocated to the provision of benefits for, and which provide all the benefits payable under the scheme to, particular members or other persons in respect of particular members or both) at market value, or a trustees' estimate thereof where market value is not readily ascertainable, and liabilities of the scheme, other than liabilities to pay pensions and benefits after the end of that scheme year—

(a) giving, in the case of any assets which are stated at an estimate of their market value, the reasons why:

(b) showing the distribution of the investments of the scheme between each of the following categories (so, however, that where none of the investments falls within a particular category, that fact is not required to be stated), namely—

    (i) insurance policies;
    (ii) public sector fixed interest investments;
    (iii) other fixed interest investments;
    (iv) index-linked securities;
    (v) equities (including convertible shares);
    (vi) properties (which in this paragraph means any right or interest in freehold or leasehold land or buildings);
    (vii) unit trusts invested in property;
    (viii) other unit trusts;
    (ix) managed funds (other than unit trusts) invested in property;
    (x) other managed funds (not being unit trusts);
    (xi) loans (whether or not secured by mortgages);
    (xii) cash deposits and cash in hand;
    (xiii) investments not included in heads (i) to (xii) above; and

(c)   showing separately, in the case of investments in each category, investments in the United Kingdom and investments outside the United Kingdom, and in the case of investments mentioned in heads (vii) to (x) of sub-paragraph (b) investments where the company operating the unit trust or managed fund is, and investments where it is not, a company registered in the United Kingdom.

3.   A reconciliation of the account mentioned in paragraph 1 with the statement mentioned in paragraph 2.

4.   Where any assets or liabilities are denominated in currencies other than sterling, a translation of those assets into sterling and an explanation of the basis on which they have been translated.

5.   Particulars of any investment in which more than 5 per cent of the total value of the net assets of the scheme is invested and if any such investment is an insurance policy, a statement of its main characteristics.

6.   Particulars of any self-investment in excess of 5 per cent of the total value of the net assets of the scheme.

7.   In respect of every amount shown in the accounts, a statement of the corresponding amount for the scheme year previous to the one to which the accounts relate, except in a case where regulation 7 (i.e. requirement to produce audited accounts) is complied with by trustees of a scheme for the first time.

8.   The total amount of the purchases, and the total amount of the sales, of investments during the scheme year to which the accounts relate.

9.   A statement whether the accounts have been prepared in accordance with parts 2 and 4 of the Statement of Recommended Practice No. 1, the guidelines published by the Accounting Standards Committee, current at the end of the scheme year to which the accounts relate, and if not, an indication of where there are any material departures from those guidelines.

Appendix 34

Form of Actuary's Statement — Appendix 5 to JOM 84

Amendment No 1 (June 1990)   *Memorandum No 84*

APPENDIX 5
(paragraph 48)
FORM OF ACTUARY'S STATEMENT

reg 8   ACTUARIAL STATEMENT MADE FOR THE PURPOSES OF REGULATION 8 OF
Sch 4   THE OCCUPATIONAL PENSION SCHEMES (DISCLOSURE OF INFORMATION)
                   REGULATIONS 1986

Name of scheme ....

Effective date of valuation ....

1   **Security of accrued rights**

In my opinion, the scheme's assets existing on the effective date fully cover its liabilities as at that date with the following exceptions:

Description of liability   **Percentage covered**

....

....

The measure(s) to be taken to bring these to 100% and the date by which it is expected that this will be achieved are as follows:

....

....

....

....

2   **Security of prospective rights**

In my opinion, the resources of the scheme are likely in the normal course of events to meet in full the liabilities of the scheme as they fall due. In giving this opinion, I have assumed that the following amounts will be paid to the scheme:

Description of contributions

....

....

3   **Summary of methods and assumptions used**

Signature ....   Date ....

Name ....   Qualification ....

Address ....   Name of employer ....
                                                                                                                              (*if applicable*)

NOTES (*see overleaf*)

234

NOTES

(i)   Where the statement is a revised statement, the line "Effective date of valuation" may be deleted.

(ii) In paragraph 1

    (a)   where note (i) is applicable a specific date may be substituted for the words "the effective date";

    (b)   the words from "with the following exceptions" to the end may be omitted where, in the actuary's opinion, there are no exceptions;

    (c)   in relation to members whose pensionable service was continuing on the effective date, the accrued rights and liabilities referred to mean respectively the rights to, and liabilities to provide, benefits for each member and his survivors which would have been payable from normal pension age or from his death if his service in relevant employment had terminated on the effective date, and must be valued accordingly;

    (d)   liabilities which are not fully covered must be shown separately in the descending order of priority provided for on the scheme's winding-up.

(iii) In paragraph 2, if the statement is not in accordance with the actuary's opinion, he must substitute a negative or qualified opinion which gives his reasons.

(iv) In paragraph 3, the summary should be a brief description of the methods and key assumptions used by the actuary.

Appendix 35

Occupation Pension Scheme Registration

Registrar of Pension Schemes	Occupational Pension Scheme Registration	**PR1**

For the purpose of

providing information

under section 59K of the

Social Security

Pensions Act 1975 (as

introduced by the Social

Security Act 1990) and

corresponding Northern

Ireland legislation

Please **print** the information requested

About the registrable scheme (see note 1 on page 8)

1 Name of scheme
(a) Please give the current scheme name   (a)

(b) Please give any other names under which the scheme has been known together with the names of schemes which in whole or in part have merged with, or been replaced by, the scheme since 6th April 1975.   (b)

2 Address of scheme
Please give the place or, if more than one, the principal place in the United Kingdom at which the management of the scheme is conducted.

Postcode

3 Northern Ireland schemes
Is scheme established in Northern Ireland?
If yes enter 1, if no enter zero.

4 Scheme status at the date of signing the form
See note 2 on page 8.

Open scheme,   enter 1 in box
Paid up or frozen scheme,   enter 2 in box
Closed scheme.   enter 3 in box

5 Year scheme commenced   1 9

6 Number of active members of the scheme
Active members are members of a registrable scheme whose employment in the United Kingdom (see note 3 on page 8) qualifies them for benefits under the scheme (whether or not contributions are currently payable to the scheme by or in respect of them), other than only benefits payable on their death while in that employment. In the case of a scheme which has been established for not less than one scheme year, the number of active members should be counted at the end of the scheme year immediately preceding the period in respect of which the levy in question is payable. In any other case, the number of active members at the date at which the scheme was established.

7 Amount of levy payable
See note 4 on page 8.

£   p

8 Cheque number

9 Bank sort code

10 Inland Revenue Superannuation Funds Office (SFO) reference number
This number will be shown on any correspondence you receive from the SFO about the scheme.

FORM PR1 (90)   Page 1

236

11 Scheme administration

Self-administered,   enter 1 in box
Insured,   enter 2 in box

For insured schemes only

12 Name of life office

An insured scheme has the
benefits secured by one or more
policies of insurance or annuity
contracts and which is <u>managed</u>
by the insurance company which
issued the policy or contract.

13 Address of life office
        where the pensions
        department is located

Postcode

About the scheme trustees

14 Names of scheme trustees

Please give the full names of all
the trustees or corporate trustees.
Alternatively, in the case of a
scheme which is not set up under
a trust, or which is established
outside the United Kingdom, give
the full name of the person who is
treated as the administrator of the
scheme for the purposes of
Chapter I of Part XIV of the
Income and Corporation Taxes
Act 1988.

About the scheme administrator

15 Name of scheme administrator

Please give the full name of the
person in the United Kingdom
who is treated as having the
management of the scheme (to
whom the Registrar can direct
tracing enquiries) even if this is
the same name as box **14**

237

Appendix 35

About the principal employer (where relevant)

16 Principal employer's name

Please give the current name of the principal employer.

17 Principal employer's address

Please give the current address, or head office if there is more than one address.

Postcode

Please give any other names and addresses under which the current principal employer and the names and addresses of any former principal employers have been known since 6th April 1975.

Employer's name

Employer's address

Postcode

Employer's name

Employer's address

Postcode

Employer's name

Employer's address

If necessary please continue on the continuation sheet on page 6.

Postcode

238

About current employers associated with the scheme

Please give the current names and addresses or head offices, if there is more than one address, of all employers currently associated with the scheme or any related schemes eg schemes which have merged with, or been replaced by, the scheme.

18 **Employer's name**

19 **Employer's address**

Postcode

Please give any other names and addresses under which the employers currently associated with the scheme, or any related schemes, have been known since 6th April 1975.

Employer's name

Employer's address

Postcode

Employer's name

Employer's address

Postcode

Employer's name

Employer's address

If necessary please continue on the continuation sheet on page 6.

Postcode

239

Appendix 35

Please give all the names and addresses, or head offices if there is more than one address, of any other employers who have previously been associated with the scheme or any related schemes since 6th April 1975.

20 Employer's name

21 Employer's address

Postcode

Employer's name

Employer's address

Postcode

Employer's name

Employer's address

Postcode

Employer's name

Employer's address

If necessary please continue on the continuation sheet on page 6.

Postcode

22 Continuation sheets

Please state the number of continuation sheets completed including page 6. If none, enter zero.

If any of this information is not available at the time of registration you should inform the Registrar of the reason why it cannot be provided. But you should supply as much information as is practicable within the time limit laid down, and pay the levy.

Page 5

240

**Continuation sheet
(please indicate relevant
box numbers)**

If there is not enough room
on this page for the entries you
have, please photocopy the page
as required.

Any photocopied pages should
be enclosed with this form.

Employer's name

Employer's address

Postcode

Employer's name

Employer's address

Postcode

Employer's name

Employer's address

Postcode

Employer's name

Employer's address

Postcode

241

Appendix 35

---

1. Please supply, in the box below, the name, address and telephone number of the person(s) to whom any enquiries about this form should be sent.

Tel:

2. Please make sure the form is completed correctly.

3. Please send the form and cheque covering the levy to the address shown at the bottom of this page. The crossed cheque for the appropriate amount should be endorsed "not negotiable" and made payable to the "Department of Social Security"

Signature ....

NAME ....
(Please use capitals)

STATUS ....
(A scheme trustee or a person authorised to act on the trustees' behalf)

Date ....

For official use only

Send this form to

Registrar of Pension Schemes
Occupational Pensions Board
PO Box 1NN, Newcastle upon Tyne NE99 1NN

Telephone 091-22-56393/4

Page 7

242

Additional information

1. A registrable scheme means an occupational pension scheme which is established in the United Kingdom or which has a place at which its management is conducted in the United Kingdom and has a representative appointed to carry out the functions of a trustee or manager in the United Kingdom and in respect of which a person has applied for or received the approval of Inland Revenue for the purposes of sections 590 and 591 (excluding section 591 (2) (g)) of Chapter I of Part XIV of the Income and Corporation Taxes Act 1988 and is not a scheme which has less than 2 active members or only provides benefits on the death of a member while in employment.

2. An open scheme is one which has active members and to which new members may be admitted. Such schemes are required to provide scheme information and to pay the levy

   A paid up or frozen scheme is one under which benefits continue to be payable to existing members, but to which no new members may be admitted and no further contributions are payable by or in respect of existing members and no further benefits accrue to existing members, although benefits which have already accrued to them may be increased. Such schemes are required to provide scheme information, but not to pay the levy.

   A closed scheme is one to which no new members may be admitted, but to which contributions are payable by or in respect of, and benefits accrue to, existing members. Such schemes are required to provide scheme information and to pay the levy.

3. Employment in the United Kingdom means the employment of members in the United Kingdom or the employment of members elsewhere in circumstances where they are liable to make primary Class 1 contributions within the meaning of section 1(2) of the Social Security Act 1975, or section 1(2) of the Social Security (Northern Ireland) Act 1975, or would be so liable but for the fact that their income falls below the lower earnings limit within the meaning of section 4 of the Social Security Act 1975, or as the case may be, section 4 of the Social Security (Northern Ireland) Act 1975.

4. Under the terms of section 60ZA of the Social Security Pensions Act 1975 (as introduced by paragraph 12 of Schedule 4 to the Social Security Act 1990 and the corresponding Northern Ireland legislation), a levy is payable to the Secretary of State for Social Security or the Secretary of State for Health and Social Services for Northern Ireland by the scheme trustees. For administrative convenience it is being collected by the Registrar of Pension Schemes.

   The basis on which the levy is calculated is shown on the enclosed information sheet.

5. The Registrar will need to know if there are any changes to the details you have given on this form, except the number of active members. You should report the changes as quickly as possible, and no later than 6 months from when the change occurred.

   You will be contacted periodically to renew your registration of scheme information. (The Registrar will write to the address of the scheme shown at box **2**)

6. If you require confirmation that your scheme details have been recorded in the register, you should enclose a stamped envelope addressed to the scheme address recorded at box **2** Please also show the SFO number on the back of the envelope.

Appendix 36

Social Security Press Release:
New Measures to Protect Occupational Pensions

89/477   7 November 1989

NEW MEASURES TO PROTECT OCCUPATIONAL PENSIONS

Tony Newton, Secretary of State for Social Security, today
announced that there would be greater protection for members of
pension schemes whose companies are involved in takeovers
or mergers. He also announced that he would be setting up a
Pensions Ombudsman.

Mr Newton also announced:

* a tracing service based on a register of pension schemes to
help people track down pensions held with their previous
employers; and

* increased help and advice for members of occupational
and personal pension schemes by a strengthening of the
voluntary Occupational Pension Advisory Service.

These measures will improve both the value and security of
pension benefits.

Speaking to the Society of Pension Consultants tonight Mr Newton
said that the Ombudsman for the pensions industry would have
power to settle individuals' grievances. There would be a
statutory requirement that the pensions industry abide by the
Ombudsman's decisions.

Turning to the Occupational Pensions Advisory Service, Mr Newton
said, "We must put its finances on a sound basis so that its
future is guaranteed.

                            - MORE -

"What is more,at present it is only able effectively to help pensioners of occupational schemes. It would surely be a great advance if it could help all members of all types of schemes, including personal pensions.OPAS has certainly indicated that it would like to do so."

To improve benefit security for present and future pensioners Mr Newton proposed four measures.

"First,we will strengthen the protection for early leavers from occupational pension schemes which we introduced in 1985 by requiring schemes to revalue all future early leavers' preserved pension rights. Pension rights which go beyond the Guaranteed Minimum Pension will have to be revalued in line with prices,up to a maximum of 5 per cent a year.

"Second, where a pension scheme winds up, the same revaluation requirement will also apply to future pensions and to pensions in payment.

"Third,again on wind-up,any deficiency in a scheme's assets to meet scheme liabilities,including these new liabilities,will become a debt on the employer.

"Fourth,we shall introduce a new ceiling on self-investment for pension schemes which will allow them to hold no more than 5 per cent of their assets in the employer's business."

NOTE TO EDITORS

The Occupational Pensions Board report,"Protecting Pensions : Safeguarding Benefits in a Changing Environment",was published on 1 February 1989.The then Secretary of State, John Moore, launched a consultation exercise on that day.Today's announcement takes into account the views expressed by respondents.

- ENDS -

245

Appendix 37

Social Security Press Release:
Small Self-Administered Pension Schemes
Exempted from 5% Self-Investment Limit

89/568   20 December 1989

SMALL SELF-ADMINISTERED PENSION SCHEMES EXEMPTED FROM FIVE PER
CENT SELF-INVESTMENT LIMIT

Small Self-Administered Pension Schemes (SSAPs) will be exempt
from the proposal to limit self-investment to five per cent,
where all members of the SSAP are controlling directors, Tony
Newton, Secretary of State for Social Security, announced today.

In answer to a Parliamentary Question from Colin Shepherd MP
(Hereford), Mr Newton said:

"In the case of pension schemes covering employees, the proposal
to restrict to five per cent investment by the scheme in the
company to which it relates has been generally well received.
It is widely agreed that it must be right to avoid the risk of
'double jeopardy' to both jobs and pensions if a company should
get into difficulties.

"We have however received numerous strong representations that
different considerations apply to Small Self-Administered
Pension Schemes (SSAPs), which cater mainly and often
exclusively for shareholding directors, who are themselves
normally the trustees, and whose investment decisions therefore
can only create that double risk for their own jobs and pension
prospects rather than those of other people.

"We accept the force of this argument, and have therefore
decided that the proposed restrictions will not apply to SSAPs
in cases where all members are trustees, each member is a '20
per cent director' as defined for Inland Revenue purposes, and
trustee decisions require a 'nem con' vote.

"Restrictions on SSAP's investments for tax purposes will of
course continue."

Issued by: DSS, Richmond House, 79 Whitehall, London SW1A 2NS **Telephone 01-210 5968**

NOTES TO EDITORS

1 Self-investment is investment in a scheme's sponsoring
employer, or investment closely connected with that employer (ie
a loan for buying or investment in a property occupied by him).

2 The Government proposal is to limit self-investment to five
per cent for all schemes, with the exception of Small
Self-Administered Pension Schemes. They will be exempted from
the self-investment proposals, where all the members of the
SSAP are controlling directors. These schemes, restricted to
12 members, have generally between one and four members who are
usually the directors and major shareholders of small companies.
The schemes offer greater flexibility in the range of investment
permitted and allow the pension fund to make a tax-free loan to
the company on an unsecured basis. Under current tax law, such
a loan can be up to 50 per cent of the fund.

-end-

Appendix 38

Extract from Lord Henley's (DSS) Letter to Local MP . . . .

'The principal of restricting self-investment has been widely supported, but its practical effects have brought a number of representations from interested parties. They argued that Small Self-Administered Pension Schemes (SSAPs) are different from others as the risks of self-investment are usually limited to the trustees themselves. We accepted that argument, and announced that the proposed restrictions would not apply to SSAPs which meet certain conditions of exemption.

Further representations have been made by employers whose pension schemes are not covered by this exemption, outlining the possible effects on their business and pension schemes. At the same time a recent survey for 1989 seems to show an increase in the number of schemes which are self-investing.

As the position appears more serious than was originally thought when we framed our proposals, we intend to have a survey carried out to provide up to date information on the extent of self-investment, where it is concentrated and what the particular problems will be in restricting it. This report will guide us as to the appropriate limits, and timescale we should adopt in regulations which we will then introduce. It remains the Government's intention to reduce the practice of self-investment'.

Appendix 39

Social Security Press Release:
Investment of Resources by Pension Schemes

91/75   3 May 1991

INVESTMENT OF RESOURCES BY PENSION SCHEMES

Tony Newton, Secretary of State for Social Security, today
announced proposals to restrict self-investment by pension
funds. In answer to a written Parliamentary Question from Mrs
Teresa Gorman MP (Billericay) Mr Newton said:

"Because of the possible double jeopardy to job and pension that
can be caused by a pension scheme investing in a related
employer, broad powers were taken in the Social Security Act
1990 to restrict the practice. Messrs Ernst and Young were
asked to report on the overall extent of self-investment and
any implications there might be in imposing restrictions. A
copy of their report*, "Study of Self Investment by Pension
Funds", is being published and I have arranged for a copy to be
placed in the Library of the House.

"Draft regulations have been referred for consideration by the
Occupational Pensions Board. We propose that the overall
proportion of a scheme's resources that may be self-invested
should be limited to 5 per cent. Schemes that are currently
above the limit will be required to take steps to reduce their
level of self-investment, but only in respect of certain types
of investments. A period of two years will be allowed for loans
and equities listed on the Stock Exchange, and five years for
equities traded on the Unlisted Securities Market.

"Most small Self-Administered schemes and individual insured
schemes will be exempted from the regulations where written
agreement by all the members is provided to each act of
self-investment. Where schemes currently have holdings of
property or equity in private companies, they will not be
required to take action to disinvest. In such circumstances no
further self-investment may be made."

* "Study of Self - Investment by Pension Funds" ISBN
0-11-761784-9 Price £5.80 available from HMSO or booksellers.

ENDS

Issued by: DSS, Richmond House, 79 Whitehall, London SW1A 2NS **Telephone 071-210 5968**

Appendix 40

Summary of Main Changes Introduced by SI 1991 No 1614

1. SSAS approved by 5 August 1991.

Rule Amendments	— in line with Model Rules to be executed by 5 August 1994 (see 3.20).
Borrowings	— may be undertaken from 5 August 1991 in line with new criteria (see 7.44–7.45).
Non-income producing assets	— acquisition banned from 5 August 1991 except for choses in action (see 7.30–7.32). If acquired before 15 July 1991 may be retained if acceptable under SFO's previous discretionary practice (see 2.16).
Residential property	— acquisition banned from 5 August 1991 with only 2 exceptions (see 6.28). If acquired before 15 July 1991 may be retained if acceptable under SFO's previous discretionary practice (see 2.16).
Unquoted shares	— acquired from 5 August 1991 limited to 30% of issued share capital (see 7.15). If in the employer or connected company amount limited to 25% of value of fund unless SSAS established for more than 2 years, otherwise 50% of value of fund (see 5.8–5.9). 25% and 50% limits include value of any loans (see 5.7–5.8).

Loans (made from 5 August 1991)	—	terms must conform to provisions of Regulations (see 5.32–5.33).
	—	amount limited to 25% of value of fund unless SSAS established for more than 2 years, otherwise 50% of value of fund may be lent (see 5.8–5.9). 25% and 50% limits include value of any shares in the employer or connected company (see 5.7–5.8).
Trustee/member transactions	—	banned from 5 August 1991, but if investment made before 15 July 1991 and acceptable under SFO's previous discretionary practice may be sold later to scheme members at open market value (see 2.16).
Pensioneer Trustee	—	provisions as to resignation and appointment of successor from 5 August 1991 (see 2.26).
Reporting requirements	—	transactions from 5 August 1991 that include purchase and sale of property, loans to employers, purchase and sale of unquoted shares, borrowings and purchase from or sale to employer or connected company of any asset other than property to be reported within 90 days (see 5.34, 6.50, 7.16, 7.33 and 7.48).

2. SSAS not approved by 5 August 1991, but established before that date.

Rule amendments	—	in line with Model Rules to be executed before approval will be granted (see 3.20).
Borrowings	—	may be undertaken from 5 August 1991 in line with new criteria (see 7.44–7.45).
Non-income producing assets	—	acquisition banned from 15 July 1991 except for choses in action (see 7.30–

7.32). If acquired before 15 July 1991 may be retained if acceptable under SFO's previous discretionary practice (see 2.17).

Residential property — acquisition banned from 15 July 1991 with only two exceptions (see 6.28). If acquired before 15 July 1991 may be retained if acceptable under SFO's previous discretionary practice (see 2.17).

Unquoted shares — acquired from 15 July 1991 limited to 30% of issued share capital (see 7.15). If in the employer or connected company amount limited to 25% of value of fund unless SSAS established for more than 2 years, otherwise 50% of value of fund (see 5.8–5.9). 25% and 50% limits include value of any loans (see 5.7–5.8).

Loans (made from 5 August 1991) — terms must conform to provisions of Regulations (see 5.32–5.33).

— amount limited to 25% of value of fund unless SSAS established for more than 2 years, otherwise 50% of value of fund may be lent (see 5.8–5.9). 25% and 50% limits include value of any shares in the employer or connected company (see 5.7–5.8).

Trustee/member transactions — banned from 5 August 1991 (see 2.17). If investment made before 15 July 1991 and acceptable under SFO's previous discretionary practice may be sold later to scheme members at open market value (see 2.17).

Pensioneer Trustee — provisions as to resignation and appointment of successor from 5 August 1991 (see 2.26).

Reporting requirements — transactions from 15 July 1991 that include purchase and sale of property, loans to employers, purchase and sale of unquoted shares, and purchase from and sale to employer or connected company of any asset other than property to be reported within 90 days (see 5.34, 6.50, 7.16 and 7.33).

— borrowings from 5 August 1991 to be reported within 90 days (see 7.48).

3. SSAS established from 5 August 1991 et seq.

Rule amendments — in line with model rules to be executed before approval will be granted (see 3.20).

Borrowings — to be undertaken in accordance with Regulations (see 7.44–7.45).

Non-income producing — acquisition banned except for choses assets in action (see 7.30–7.32).

Residential property — acquisition banned with only two exceptions (see 6.28).

Unquoted shares — limited to 30% of issued share capital (see 7.15). If in the employer or connected company amount limited to 25% of value of fund for first two years of SSAS, then 50% of value of fund (see 5.8–5.9). 25% and 50% limits include value of any loans (see 5.7–5.8).

Loans — terms must conform to provisions of Regulations (see 5.32–5.33).

— limited to 25% of value of fund for first two years of SSAS then 50% of value of fund may be lent (see 5.8–5.9). 25% and 50% limits include value of any shares in the employer or connected company (see 5.7–5.8).

253

Trustee/member transactions	—	banned (see 2.17).
Pensioneer Trustee	—	provisions as to appointment, resignation and appointment of successor (see 2.26).
Reporting requirements	—	transactions that include purchase and sale of property, loans to employers, purchase and sale of unquoted shares, borrowings and purchase from or sale to employer or connected company of any asset other than property to be reported within 90 days (see 5.34, 6.50, 7.16, 7.33 and 7.48).

Index

255